'SECRETS OF ENOCH'
INSIGHTS
FROM THE 2ND BOOK OF ENOCH

S.N.Strutt

© S.N.Strutt 2024

Published by S.N.Strutt

The rights of S.N.Strutt to be identified as the author of this work have been asserted by him in accordance with the Copyright, Designs and Patents Act of 1988.

All rights reserved; no part of this publication may be reproduced, stored in a retrieval system, or transmitted in any form or by any means, electronic, mechanical, photocopying, recording or otherwise without the prior written consent of the publisher or a licence permitting copying in the UK issued by the Copyright Licensing Agency Ltd. www.cla.co.uk

ISBN 978-1-78792-056-9

Book design, layout and production management by Into Print

www.intoprint.net

+44 (0)1604 832149

CREDITS: Secrets of Enoch also known as 2nd Enoch was translated from Slavonic by:

W.K Morfill M.A

Edited and improved by

R.H Charles M.A in 1896 -Oxford, Clarendon

Artwork: front cover by Susanne Strutt

www.suzannestruttartist/instagram.com

www. suzannestruttartist/facebook.com

PREFACE

My book "Secrets of Enoch' 'Insights" contains the entire book of 'The Second Book of Enoch, also known as the Slavonic Enoch or 2 Enoch. This study book is full of cross-referenced Bible verses, and extensive comments, which explain or make plain the wording in this ancient book of the 'Secrets of Enoch' or the '2nd Book of Enoch'. The original book of 2nd Enoch is known to have originally been written in ancient Hebrew.

It is traditionally told that Secrets of Enoch was written by Enoch, who was taken up to heaven and shown divine revelations according to Hebrews 11 in the Bible.

The book exists in various versions, with the most well-known being the Slavonic manuscript preserved in the Russian National Library.

The Second Book of Enoch is composed of 4 sections - In the first section (chapters 1–22), Enoch, at the age of 365, is taken by two angels through the ten heavens, one by one. In the second section (chapters 23–37), Enoch, now guided by Gabriel, speaks with God in the tenth heaven face to face. The third section (chapters 38–68) is a list of doctrinal and ethical instructions given by Enoch to his sons. The fourth section (Exaltation of Melchizedek) outlines the priestly succession of Enoch.

In the beginning of the book, we see Enoch's ascent through the heavens, guided by 2 very tall angels with massive wings upon which Enoch sits and flies away into the heavens. There he encounters heavenly mysteries and is given insights into the workings of the universe. Much of the text involves descriptions of heavenly realms and the levels of angels, as well as Enoch's conversations with these angelic beings. The book also delves into themes such as Pre-Creation, the creation of the physical world, and the nature of the universe. Enoch is also shown the destinies of both the righteous and the wicked.

This 2nd Book of Enoch brings out God's final judgment on the wicked, the fate of the fallen angels, and the eventual establishment of God's kingdom on Earth. Evil is eventually destroyed and Good prevails.

The Second Book of Enoch offers readers a unique insight and it blends with the 1st Book of Enoch. Its combination of celestial journeys, angelic hierarchies, and End-time events as mentioned in the Bible in the Book of Daniel and Revelation makes it very exciting and well worth the read.

CONTENTS LIST

CREDITS	2
PREFACE	3
THE FORMAT OF THIS BOOK	7
INTRODUCTION	8
CHAPTERS & APPENDIX	11
CHAPTER 1 ENOCH THE WISEMAN	12
CHAPTER 2 VANITY OF VANITIES	18
CHAPTER 3 ENOCH'S ASCENSION	21
CHAPTER 4 200 ANGEL STAR RULERS	23
CHAPTER 5 TERRIBLE STOREHOUSES	25
CHAPTER 6 DEW OF HEAVEN	26
CHAPTER 7 ASCENSION OF ENOCH 2ND HEAVEN	28
CHAPTER 8 ASCENSION OF ENOCH TO 3RD HEAVEN	31
CHAPTER 9 PLACE OF ETERNAL INHERITANCE	34
CHAPTER 10 TERRIBLE PLACE AND VARIOUS TORTURES	35
CHAPTER 11 4TH HEAVEN: COURSES OF THE SUN AND MOON	43
CHAPTER 12 PHOENIXES AND CHALKYDRI	46
CHAPTER 13 ENOCH AT THE SUN'S GATES	48
CHAPTER 14 ENOCH TAKEN TO THE WEST	50
CHAPTER 15 PHOENIXES AND CHALKYDRI	52
CHAPTER 16 COURSE OF THE MOON	54
CHAPTER 17 SINGING OF ANGELS	57
CHAPTER 18 5TH HEAVEN -THE GRIGORI	59
CHAPTER 19 6TH HEAVEN	64
CHAPTER 20 7TH HEAVEN	66
CHAPTER 21 CHERUBIM AND SERAPHIM	70
CHAPTER 22 10TH HEAVEN -THE THRONE OF GOD	72
CHAPTER 23 PRAVUIL OR THE HOLY SPIRIT?	76
CHAPTER 24 GREAT SECRETS OF GOD	82
CHAPTER 25 PRE-CREATION -THE LIGHT	84
CHAPTER 26 PRE-CREATION -THE DARKNESS	98
CHAPTER 27 CREATION OF WATER, LIGHT AND 7 ISLANDS	111
CHAPTER 28 HEAVENLY CIRCLE	118
CHAPTER 29 THE FIERY ESSENCE	123
CHAPTER 30 PARADISE	128

CHAPTER 31 ANGELS SONG OF VISTORY	133
CHAPTER 32 2ND COMING OF CHRIST	143
CHAPTER 33 7000 YEARS OF WORLD HISTORY	145
CHAPTER 34 'WICKEDNESS TOO DISGUSTING TO RELATE'	149
CHAPTER 35 DEMONS TAKE OVER	154
CHAPTER 36 30 DAY WARNING	162
CHAPTER 37 MENACING ANGELS	163
CHAPTER 38 METHUSALAH AWAITS ENOCHS RETURN	164
CHAPTER 39 7000 YEARS OF HISTORY TO ETERNITY	165
CHAPTER 40 ENOCH WROTE 366 BOOKS	166
CHAPTER 41 ENOCH LAMENTS ADAM'S SIN	169
CHAPTER 42 KEY HOLDERS OF HELL	170
CHAPTER 43 GOD'S JUDGEMENT	181
CHAPTER 44 REFRAIN FROM ANGER	182
CHAPTER 45 BURNT OFFERINGS	183
CHAPTER 46 ABOMINATIONS	184
CHAPTER 47 MARK MY WORDS	185
CHAPTER 48 7 HEAVENLY CIRCLES	187
CHAPTER 49 DON'T SWEAR	191
CHAPTER 50 HIDDEN OR REVEALED?	193
CHAPTER 51 GIVE ALMS TO THE POOR	195
CHAPTER 52 PRAISE	197
CHAPTER 53 ALONE BEFORE GOD	199
CHAPTER 54 366 HANDED DOWN	200
CHAPTER 55 ENOCH WARNS HE WILL SOON ASCEND TO HEAVEN	202
CHAPTER 56 ENOCH'S LAST MEAL	203
CHAPTER 57 METHUSALAH SUMMONS ENOCH	204
CHAPTER 58 ADMONITIONS	205
CHAPTER 59 BEASTS	207
CHAPTER 60 SOW AND REAP	210
CHAPTER 61 REFRAIN FROM INJUSTICE	215
CHAPTER 62 GIFT OF FAITH	216
CHAPTER 63 ENOCH DIES SAME DAY HE WAS BORN	217
CHAPTER 64 LAST EMBRACE	218
CHAPTER 65 ENOCH'S INSTRUCTIONS TO HIS SONS	219

CHAPTER 66 IDOLS	222
CHAPTER 67 ENOCH IS TRANSLATED	230
CHAPTER 68 BIG FEAST ON ENOCH'S DEATH	231
APPENDIX I BACKGROUND HISTORY OF ENOCH	232
APPENDIX II EVIDENCE OF AUTHENTICITY	233
APPENDIX III SON OF MAN	235
APPENDIX IV WHY NOT IN THE BIBLE?	237
APPENDIX V WHY NOT CANONISED?	238
APPENDIX VI TRANSLATION OF ENOCH	239
APPENDIX VII SEPTUAGINT	240
APPENDIX VIII PRISCA SAPIENTIA	245
APPENDIX IX TIME CHARTS	247
APPENDIX X ABOUT THE AUTHOR	251

Contact E-mail: stephen.strutt@btinternet.com
NEW WEBSITE: www.insightspublication.com

THE FORMAT OF THIS BOOK

i) I have typed a chapter of the Book of 'Secrets of Enoch' or also known as 2nd "Enoch, and included in each chapter my commentaries, which are just that: my opinions, speculations and theories, which are gleaned from much study of the subject matter. Most, if not all of which, could prove to be true, and are written with the express intention to motivate the reader to do a more thorough investigation for him or herself, to prove whether correct or not, as I am sure that some of the ideas, speculations and conjecture will be quite far out there, to some people.

ii) I have also put cross-references to the Bible, and other Apocryphal books where appropriate.

iii) **Details:**

The first '**comment**' in each chapter, will be noted as being '**Comment 1**' & then **C.2, C.3**, etc. The original Text from the 2nd Book of Enoch is in slightly larger text than either the 'comments' or 'Bible verses'. Three different types of writing are used. One for the original text, and another type of writing for my comments, and yet another for the bible verses.

iv) There are more commentaries and conclusions in the '**APPENDICES**'

v) All Bible references are from the King James Version.

vi) I have done extensive background research, in order to put my 'Insights books' together, which do have an exceptional amount of information and revelations in them.

vii) This book of the 'Secrets of Enoch Insights' is a sequel to my 1st book 'Enoch Insights'.

INTRODUCTION

The ancient Hebrew Books of the Books of Enoch 1 & 2 are mentioned in the Hebrew book of 'Testaments of the Twelve Patriarchs' from around 3700 years ago. See my book with the same name 'Testaments of the Twelve Patriarchs' 'Insights'.

The 12 Patriarchs were the 12 sons of Jacob (Israel), who laid the foundation to Israel. These manuscripts were originally in Hebrew, and then translated into Greek around 300-100 BC at the Library of Alexandria. A copy was then left there at Alexandria for the prestige of the whole Grecian empire. The Apocryphal books were copied from original ancient Hebrew manuscripts as proven by the findings of the Dead Sea Scrolls in 1947. Manuscripts of leather, papyrus, and copper on the northwestern shore of the Dead Sea.

Some facts about the Books of Enoch: (Excerpt from my book Enoch Insights Book 1, which was based on the 1st Book of Enoch). It is possibly also true about the 2nd Book of Enoch.

The 1st Book of Enoch was found in Abyssinia (Ethiopia) in 1773 after being lost for about 1600 years. It was translated into English in 1821.

The Books of Enoch was readily accepted by the early church fathers.

For the first three centuries A.D. they were accepted as scripture by the early church. They were eventually dismissed from the Scriptures at the Council of Laodicea in 365 AD.

Fragments were also found along with the Dead Sea Scrolls. Enoch was an amazing person, who was totally dedicated to God Himself, and visited God's Throne. He received countless revelations directly from God and His angels, so why the lack of mentioning Enoch in the Bible, *when the early Christians were all believing in the Book of Enoch, and set it as one of their foundation stones?*

It was read by the Jewish people in the two centuries before Christ & by the early Christians, including those who were willing to be martyrs for Jesus. The fact is, that the early Christians all referred to the "Book of Enoch" and the "Septuagint" version of the Old Testament, which was originally written in Greek. The Septuagint version of the Old Testament is more revealing, and has more details of the events, than even the King James version of the Bible.

The Book of Enoch was not included in the cannon of the Bible, because the *council of Laodicea,* which was responsible for which books would be part of the original Canon in 365 AD, *decided to exclude any books deemed too radical or supernatural in content.*

Enoch himself, is mentioned in the Bible in both the Old Testament in

Genesis 5.18-24, & in the New Testament in Hebrews chapter 11.5

The Book of Enoch itself is mentioned in Jude verses 14-16. The big question is why was not much more said about Enoch in the Bible, when he was instrumental in passing on most of God's Word and instructions from before the FLOOD, which was taken on the ark by Noah, for the sake of future generations. Why no mention of this big event in the Bible? It doesn't make any sense!

In the Book of Jude there is a reference made to a man named Enoch.

Jude 1:15-16 " And Enoch also, the seventh from Adam, prophesied of these, saying, Behold, the Lord cometh with ten thousands of his saints, To execute judgment upon all, and to convince all that are ungodly among them of all their ungodly deeds which they have ungodly committed, and of all their hard speeches which ungodly sinners have spoken against him."

Obviously, someone back there in 365 AD at the council of Laodicea, *did not like the radical and supernatural ways of true Christianity, and the teachings of Creation,* and wanted to water down & compromise the message, probably in an attempt to become more accepted by the majority of the people of those Roman times, with their idol worshipping.

In this book you see how many books have been deliberately 'hidden' from the view of the public for different reasons over the centuries. It is easy to prove that the apocryphal books had ancient Hebrew origins.

Later in time, many books have been labelled as pseudepigraphic - which just means that someone other than the name given was the author. I challenge that assertion in this book, as many of the things described by Enoch could not have been known around 2000 years ago.

There are simply too many details about Creation and Pre-Creation times as well as mention of the Fallen angels and what happens to them in great detail. Not to mention a myriad of other happenings. I believe that you will find this book very informative and revealing.

'SECRETS OF ENOCH' - 'INSIGHTS' by S.N.Strutt 2024

(Based Upon the Apocryphal 'Secrets Of Enoch' Or The '2nd Book Of Enoch' - From The Slavonic Language Translated Into English In 1896) -

[W.K Morfill M.A

Edited and improved by

R.H Charles M.A in 1896 -Oxford, Clarendon]

CHAPTER 1

> 1 THERE was a wise man (Enoch), a great artificer*, and the Lord 'conceived love for him' and received him, that he should behold the *uppermost dwellings and be an eye-witness of the wise and great and inconceivable and *immutable realm of God Almighty, of the very wonderful and glorious and bright and *many-eyed station of the Lord's servants, and of the inaccessible throne of the Lord, and of the degrees and manifestations of the incorporeal hosts, and of the ineffable ministry of the multitude of the elements, and of the various apparitions and inexpressible singing of the host of *Cherubim, and of the boundless light.

C.1 Definitions
* **great artificer** = a skilled craftsman or inventor.
* **conceived love for him'** = this is a 'feminine expression' meaning conception or pregnant or receiving or born
* **uppermost dwellings** = highest levels of Heaven
* **immutable realm** = unchangeable realm =permanent
* **many-eyed station** of the Lord's servants», are celestial beings of a high angelic order, residing in the Seventh heaven.
* **Cherubim** =a winged angelic being described in biblical tradition as attending on God, represented in ancient Middle Eastern art as a lion or bull with eagles' wings and a human face and regarded in traditional Christian angelology as an angel of the second highest order of the ninefold celestial hierarchy.
C.2 The Cherubim are stated as being 'full of eyes' in Revelation 4 and in Ezekiel 1 and 10 - thus the many-eyed station of the Lord's servants.

Revelation Chapter 4

And the **four beasts** had each of them six wings about *him*; and *they were* **full of eyes** within: and they rest not day and night, saying, Holy, holy, holy, Lord God Almighty, which was, and is, and is to come.

Ezekiel Ch 1

As for their rings, they were so high that they were dreadful; and their rings *were* **full of eyes** round about them four.

C.3 1st verse: I would summarize verse 1 like this: There was a great man of God, or one totally dedicated to God. God found Enoch to be unique and took him up to heaven to reveal the different levels of heaven or dimensions. He saw that God's realm was unchangeable and eternal. Enoch saw the angels and the 4 Beasts as described in Revelation 4 and Ezekiel 1 & 10, as well as the hosts of angels.

C.4 I would like to mention that in my opinion this very first verse no 1, which is supposed to the Introduction to the Book of 2nd Enoch, is far too complicated, and difficult to understand. It has been altered to fit intellectual and religious preference - using words to describe a 'self-made' man instead of a man of God's grace. It talks in the 3rd person and is not Enoch directly talking. It just states who Enoch was. However, God's genuine people live by 'faith' and 'trust' in God and operate through the 'Grace of God' and the inspiration of God's Holy Spirit and are certainly not 'self-made' people.

Titus 3.5 For by grace are ye saved through faith and that not of yourselves it is the gift of God, <u>not of works</u> lest any man should boast.

C.5 First of all, Enoch himself, would never state that he was a great artificer or a 'skilled craftsman or inventor'. Perhaps the words used in this first verse has something to do with Orthodox Christianity in that the manuscript was translated from Slavonic to English and perhaps some of their expressions for different things are expressed with different words than what we would use in English?

C.6 We know that Enoch was chosen by God and was an anointed vessel for God's service. He was both a prophet and visionary.

C.7 Self-Works religions always try to make God's people into 'self-made' people instead of 'empowered by the Holy Spirit of God'. They try to explain away the supernatural in physical terms when that is often not possible to do. All of God's truly 'great men and women' have had a special anointing from God. It was never their own talents and works that made them great. It is the supernatural that makes all the difference and not the dead works of man.

Hebrews 11.5-6 By faith Enoch was translated that he should not see death; and was not found, because God had translated him: for before his translation he had this testimony that he pleased God. But without faith it is impossible to please Him: for he that cometh to God must believe that he is and that he is a rewarder of them that diligently seek him.

C.8 'conceived love for him' – this sounds like a feminine expression for love. Why does it state it in this way? What if we have God the Father and God the Holy Spirit Mother and God the Son? Then the above expression would make a lot more sense. There are many people today who believe that the Holy Spirit is female. A Brief History of the Holy Spirit as Mother - The Mother God Experiment

C.9 Ancient Hebrew references to the Holy Spirit were always using a feminine pronoun - *ruach*.

See Chapter 25 of this book, where I wrote a lot more about the Holy Spirit being female, and how that fact totally alters our perception of Creation in a very good way.

The fruits of the Spirit are known to be feminine values and sound much like the virtues-

Galatians 5.22-23 For the fruit of the spirit is love joy peace longsuffering, gentleness goodness faith, meekness temperance, against such there is no law.

> 2 At that time, he said, when my 165th year was completed, I begat my son Mathusal.

C.10 Mathusal - Known in the KJV of the Bible as - Methuselah

C.11 Immediately, we can see that by the above text stating that Enoch was 165 years old when he begat Methuselah that this text is from the Greek version or like the Septuagint version of the Old Testament. The KJV states that Enoch was 65 years old when he begat Methuselah. Why is this very important to know?

C.12 [See my video on Alexandria with greatest library in the world and how they obtained their books: See my books: Jubilees 'Insights & Enoch Insights Books' By S N Strutt: Alexandrian Library, The Septuagint & The Apocrypha Books: (606) 'INSIGHTS BOOKS' by S N Strutt: ALEXANDRIAN LIBRARY, THE SEPTUAGUINT & THE APOCRYPHA BOOKS - YouTube]

C.13 Why is there a conflict between the KJV and the Septuagint versions concerning the actual age of Enoch. Was he 65 when he begat Methuselah as stated in the KJV of the Bible or was he 165, as stated in the Septuagint? Apparently, those who put the Septuagint together were 72 Jewish scholars down in Alexandria in the times of the Greek empire at its heyday.

C.14 Ptolemy, the Pharoah at that time apparently wanted to take credit for building the ancient Pyramids, when in fact they had been built in pre-flood times, so since he had already paid the 72 scholars a lot of money for making a copy of the book of the Septuagint, Pharaoh required one little favour of the 72 scribes, and that was to change the timeline of the Patriarchs so that 100 years was added to all from Adam down to the first 5 Patriarchs after the Great Flood. The result was that the Septuagint tells us that the age of the earth is 5500 from Creation to Christ or 1500 years older than the KJV of the Bible which states that there was 4000 years from Creation to Christ. [See my Insights book 'Jubilees Insights', which talks about this in detail and mentions the evidence of all this – for more on this - See the Appendix of this book].

C.15 Other important information from my video about the Library at Alexandria: Many of the very old manuscripts were taken to the world-famous Library in Alexandria in Northern Egypt between 300 to 100 BC, during the times of the Greek empire to the greatest library in the world. Good money was paid for such original documents, in order to make copies of them for the Alexandria Library, and the originals given back to the bearers. This explains why we are told that so many books were written much later than the originals by some *pseudepigraphic writer such as the Apocryphal books and ancient Hebrew books such as Enoch, Jasher, Jubilees and the Lost Books of Adam and Eve. (See also my book Eden Insights) [*Pseudepigraphic writer means a writer other than the person named has having written the book]

C.16 According to my research, these books were not written by some so-called pseudepigraphic writer or anonymous scribe at a later date, as is often taught, but they were in fact original documents written by the original writers such as Enoch in ancient times. Often old manuscripts were first written in Hebrew, then translated into Greek, then into Latin and then finally into English. The intermediate scribes involved were not the originators of the manuscripts. This is what my repeated research has shown.

C.17 For example, I believe that the Books of Enoch 1 & 2 were originally written by Enoch in the times before the Great Flood. They were then passed on down to future generations through Noah. There is a lot of evidence for this.

C.18 The Apocryphal book of the Testaments of the Twelve Patriarchs mentions these Books of Enoch, which books I have traced back to the ancient Patriarchs themselves or the sons of Jacob known as Israel. Jacob lived around 3800 years ago or circa or 500 years after the Great Flood. These manuscripts were originally in Hebrew and then translated into Greek around 300-100 BC and a copy was left in the Library at Alexandria for the prestige of the whole Grecian empire.

C.19 Books placed at the Alexandrian Library were read by all the great teachers and philosophers of the ancient Grecian empire, and no longer just read by a few people in ancient Israel.

> 3 After this too I lived two hundred years and completed of all the years of my life three hundred and sixty-five years.
>
> 4 On the first day of the first month I was in my house alone and was resting on my couch and slept.
>
> 5 And when I was asleep, great distress came up into my heart, and I was weeping with my eyes in sleep, and I could not understand what this distress was, or what would happen to me.
>
> 6 And there appeared to me two men, exceeding big, so that I never saw such on earth; their faces were shining like the sun, their eyes too *were* like a burning light, and from their lips was fire coming forth with clothing and singing of various kinds in appearance purple, their wings *were* brighter than gold, their hands whiter than snow.

C.20 Here is a definition of a Seraphim or the highest level of God's angels:

The origin of the word **Seraphim** comes from the Hebrew word seraph, meaning «to burn» or «fiery». In that sense, a Seraph could mean «The One who burns», or «The One who Shines». Because of this, the alternative name of the Seraphim is Fire Spirits. They are beings of pure light, Angels of love and fire. They irradiate Pure Divine Light. Look at the following description of Jesus at his transfiguration:

C.21 Here is a description of Jesus:

Matthew 17.2 "And was transfigured before them: and his face did shine as the sun, and his raiment was white as the light."

Revelation 1:14-16

14 His head and his hairs were white like wool, as white as snow; and his eyes were as a flame of fire.

15 And his feet like unto fine brass, as if they burned in a furnace; and his voice as the sound of many waters. 16 And he had in his right hand seven stars: and out of his mouth went a sharp two-edged sword: and his countenance *was* as the sun shineth in his strength.

C.22 How tall were these two angels who appeared to Enoch 'exceeding big', like he had never seen on earth before? This suggests that he had seen other angels, whilst on earth, but that these two were much taller.? In fact, this book states that Enoch climbed up on their wings so the angels much have been huge. Angels can apparently appear as any size depending on the occasion. What is their real height? It would seem that from the testimony of many that angels are normally around 7 feet tall.

> 7 They were standing at the head of my **couch** and began to call me by my name.
>
> 8 And I arose from my sleep and saw clearly those two men standing in front of me.
>
> 9 And I saluted them and was seized with fear and the appearance of my face was changed from terror, and those men said to me:
>
> 10 'Have courage, Enoch, do not fear; the eternal God sent us to thee, and lo! thou shalt to-day ascend with us into heaven, and thou shalt tell thy sons and all thy household all that they shall do without thee on earth in thy house, and let no one seek thee till the Lord return thee to them'.

Proverbs 14.26 In the fear of the Lord is strong confidence: and his children shall have a place of refuge.

C.23 Is Enoch being translated to heaven permanently here or is just going on one of his many spirit trips? It would appear that in the following example it is just a trip as he comes back and instructs his family.

> 11 And I made haste to obey them and went out from my house, and

> made to the doors, as it was ordered me, and summoned my sons Mathusal and Regim and Gaidad and made known to them all the marvels those *men* had told me.

C.24 These names Mathusal and Regim and Gaidad are the Slavonic names since this version of 2nd Enoch was found in the Slavic language.

C.25 Slavonic = relating to or denoting the Slavic language family.

CHAPTER 2

> LISTEN to me, my children, I know not whither I go, or what will befall me; now therefore, my children, I tell you: turn not from God before the face of the vain, who made not Heaven and earth, for these shall perish and those who worship them, and may the Lord make confident your hearts in the fear of him. And now, my children, let no one think to seek me, until the Lord return me to you.

C.1 *'turn not from God before the face of the vain who made not Heaven and earth, for these shall perish and those who worship them'* - Who is Enoch talking about here? He is talking about those who are vain.

Vain - definition: without meaning, shallow - or that anything goes.

C.2 Vanity of Vanity for all is vanity

Ecclesiastes 1.2 'Vanity of vanities, saith the Preacher, vanity of vanities; all is vanity- Solomon.:

C.3 Those who rule this present world, and I mean the demonic forces behind the physical rulers - believe that there are no Absolutes, no God, no Jesus, no love, no meaning to life, and therefore there is no consequence to ones actions, so just do anything that you want to do, which is in itself idol worship of devils and demons, because that is exactly what they do and how they behave. They distract most people by getting them to lust after and to eventually worship Mammon or money and riches and popularity and fame come next. They get mankind to constantly strive for vain things which cannot satisfy, and then get them addicted to money and things and pleasures which have no lasting value or eternal value.

C.4 The 'vain' entities know that 'The Judgment' is coming, in spite of them pretending to be blind to reality, but they try to forget about it as brought out with the demons talking to Jesus:

Matthew 8.29 Behold, they cried out, saying, 'What have we to do with thee, Jesus, thou Son of God? 'Art thou come hither to torment us before the time?'

C.5 These demons along with the devils and Satan himself will all get locked up in the Bottomless Pit for the 1000 Years of the Golden Age when Jesus Christ the King of Kings shall reign on earth. After the 1000 years will come the Great White Throne Judgement when finally, the devils and demons are all thrown into the Lake of Fire. So, the 'Vain' will come to an end. 'Vain' also means 'shallow' and 'without purpose' and no point to what they are doing!

C.6 Notice in the above verse it mentions *'the vain who made not Heaven and earth, for these shall perish and those who worship them'*

C.7 The 'vain' wicked did not even repent after the plagues dealt out upon them in Revelation 9, during the Great Tribulation and therefore were more than worthy of the Wrath of God which came in chapter 16 of the Book of Revelation.

Revelation 9.20-21 And the rest of the men which were not killed by these plagues yet repented not of the works of their hands, that they should not **worship devils**, and **idols** of **gold**, and silver, and brass, and stone, and of wood: which neither can see, nor hear, nor walk. **Neither repented they of their murders, nor of their sorceries, nor of their fornication, nor of their thefts.**

C.8 This is exactly what these devils and demons are trying to do today. Satanic values are taking over - they destroy all absolute values and bring in the worship of anything but the true God. It could even be A.I. and soon the 'Mark of the Beast' implant system of Revelation 13. However, eventually all destructive and mischievous behaviour will come to a final end and be totally destroyed.

Revelation 20.1-3 And I saw an angel come down from heaven, having the key of the bottomless pit and a great chain in his hand. And he laid hold on the dragon, that old serpent, which is the Devil, and Satan, and bound him a thousand years. And cast him into the bottomless pit, and shut him up, and set a seal upon him, that he should deceive the nations no more, till the thousand years should be fulfilled: and after that he must be loosed a little season.

Revelation 20.10 And the devil that deceived them was cast into the lake of fire and brimstone, where the beast and the false prophet are, and shall be tormented day and night for ever and ever.

Revelation 20.14-15 And death and hell were cast into the lake of fire. This is the second death. And whosoever was not found written in the book of life was cast into the lake of fire.

C.9 Just today, I read that the British medical association no longer accepts the word 'mother'. Why get rid of basic words? In a few words: 'To sow confusion'. The Motto of the Elite is 'Out of Chaos we rule'. 'They are fast destroying all 'real meaning' to life. Soon there will be no 'fathers' or 'mothers' or 'babies' or 'children' as the plan is to replace the 'family unit' and eventually replace mankind altogether with machines. What utter madness to their demonic plans. Erasing women: British General Medical Council (GMC) scrubs "mother" from all internal policies – only gender-neutral "parent" references allowed – NaturalNews.com

C.10 All that Satan can do is destroy, as he is a monster according to Revelation 12, and in fact he is represented by a 7-headed red dragon.

The 7 heads denote the 7 major governments of man since the Great Flood:
1) Egypt
2) Assyria
3) Babylon
4) Medio-Persia
5) Greece
6) Rome
7) Antichrist

Notice how it mentions the word devour in the next Bible verse when talking about Satan as the red dragon:

Revelation 12.3-4 "And there appeared another wonder in heaven; and behold a great **red dragon**, having seven heads and ten horns, and seven crowns upon his heads." And his tail drew the third part of the stars of heaven, and did cast them to the earth: and the **dragon** stood before the woman which was ready to be delivered, for to **devour** her child as soon as it was born.

C.11 Another good description of Satan is found in Job 41 which is also talking about a massive monster dragon called Leviathan which lives in the sea.

JOB 41.34 He beholds all high things: he is a king over all the children of pride.

C.12 We need rules, we need the absolute, and we certainly need our creator - God. What we don't need is chaos!

C.13 Our current world is being turned upside down as all good values and morals are being eroded.

C.14 The essence of Bible scripture is for us to be humble before God and learn not to be like Satan or proud. God lifts up the humble but not the proud and arrogant who always act as if they always know better.

1 Peter 5.6 Humble yourselves therefore under the mighty hand of God, that he may exalt you in due time:

C.15 Just like George Orwell predicted they would 'change' the meaning of 'words' in order to confuse people in his famous book 1984. That is now rampant upon the scene of this world and is fast pulling the world down to hell and destruction.

C.16 Enoch's conclusion for this chapter in his talk with his children is: 'turn not from God'.

1Timothy 4.15 "Meditate upon these things; give thyself wholly to them; that thy profiting may appear to all."

CHAPTER 3

> It came to pass, when Enoch had told his sons, that the angels took him on to their wings and bore him up on to the first heaven and placed him on the clouds. And there I looked, and again I looked higher, and saw the **ether**, and they placed me on the first heaven and showed me a very great sea, **greater** than the **earthly sea.**

C.1 What is the ether? Def. -The clear sky -the upper regions of the air above the clouds.

C.2 There is only one verse in this chapter, but it is telling us a lot.

1) The angels took Enoch on their wings, so these angels must have been very tall angels.

2) They took him up to the 1st Heaven and placed him on the clouds. How could Enoch sit on a cloud, if he was still physical, unless his body had been altered for a higher dimension. How is that done instantly? Well, only God knows the answer to that question.

3) He looked higher or above where he had been placed on the clouds and saw the ether or the clear sky - the upper regions of the air above the clouds.

4) 'Showed me a very great sea, greater than the earthly sea'. A sea greater than the sea on the earth? Wow! If we look to Revelation 21-22 in the KJV of the Bible, we read about a crystal blue sea. We also read about the Heavenly City being 1500 high, long, and wide. The heavenly city looks like giant crystal pyramid. The pyramid is encased in a giant globe which it fits inside exactly. This globe could fit right inside the moon with a space of 40 miles below the surface all the way around the moon.

Revelation 4.6: "And before the throne there was a **sea of glass** like unto **crystal**: and in the midst of the throne, and round about the throne, were four beasts full of eyes before and behind."

Revelation 15:2: "And I saw as it were a **sea of glass** mingled **with fire**: and them that had gotten the victory over the beast, and over his image, and over his mark, and over the number of his name, stand on the **sea of glass**, having the harps of God."

5) How deep is the blue crystal sea and what is the total volume of water in those seas?

6) Consider our planet earth which only has its highest mountain as about 6 miles high. The heavenly city is 1500 miles high. A globe containing the seas all around the Heavenly City would contain a lot more water than our oceans just by the definition of the size of the Heavenly City.

7) This is staggering that Enoch could see some of the exact same things that John saw in the Book of Revelation some 3000+ Years earlier in time as he saw the Crystal Sea.

8) This information is also mentioned in the Apocryphal books of the Lost Books of Adam and Eve. See my book 'Eden Insights' to know much more.

CHAPTER 4

> THEY brought before my face the elders and rulers of the stellar orders, and showed me two hundred angels, who rule the stars and *their* services to the heavens and fly with their wings and come round all those who sail.

C.1 It states that Enoch met the Elders. Who are the Elders? I will make an educated guess from knowing the Bible. There are 24 Elders mentioned in the Book of Revelation Chapter 4.

Revelation 4.4 "And round about the throne *were* four and twenty seats: and upon the seats I saw four and twenty elders sitting, clothed in white raiment; and they had on their heads crowns of gold."

C.2 It would appear that the most important Elders are the greatest of the righteous leaders in Biblical History such as Adam, Enoch, Methuselah, Noah, Abraham, Jacob, Joseph, Moses, David, Isaiah, Jeremiah, Ezekiel, Daniel, John the disciple of Christ -who wrote the Book of Revelation - along with Peter and Paul the apostles of Christ. Well that only makes 16 so far. Who were the other 8 Elders? The other 8 were probably the rest of the minor prophets of God as mentioned in the Bible or kings who served God so faithfully ever since the times of Daniel the prophet some 2500 years ago. Maybe even a few modern prophets such as the last 2 prophets, as mentioned in Revelation 11.

Revelation 11.3-6 And I will give power unto my two witnessed, and they shall prophesy a thousand two hundred days, clothed I sackcloth. These are the two olive trees, and the two candlesticks standing before the God of the earth. And if any man will hurt them, fire proceeds out of their mouth, and devours their enemies: and if any man will hurt them, he must in this manner be killed. These have power to shut heaven, that it rain not in the days of their prophecy: and have power over waters to turn them to blood, and to smite the earth with all plagues, as often as they will.

C.3 The elders mentioned in this chapter however, are 'the elders and rulers of the stellar orders or orders of the stars. That is to be exact 200 hundred angels, who rule the stars and *their* services to the heavens.' We are not exactly sure who they are, except that according to the only verse in this chapter, they are powerful angels of God in charge of taking care of the stars and 'of all who sail' - whatever that means? Sail where, and in what vessels?

C.4 'Two hundred angels who rule the stars'. This clearly shows that there are many angels who take care all of God's Creation.

C.5 It also states that 'and fly with their wings and come round all those who sail.' It would appear that these angels who take care of the stars are also in charge of those who sail on the sea, but which sea? Is it talking about some heavenly sea where people sail?

C.6 What Sea is this talking about? The seas of the earth, or the crystal seas just mentioned in heaven?

CHAPTER 5

> AND here I looked down and saw the treasure-houses of the snow, and the angels who keep their **terrible storehouses**, and the clouds whence they come out and into which they go.

Deuteronomy 32.34 Is it not laid up in store with Me,
Sealed up in **My treasuries**?

Job 38.22 KJV: Have thou entered the treasuries (storehouses) of the snow, or have thou seen the treasures of the hail. "Have you entered the storehouses of the snow, or have you seen the **storehouses** of the hail,

Jer.10.13 When He utters His voice, there is a tumult of waters in the heavens,
And He causes the clouds to ascend from the **end of the earth**;
He makes lightning for the rain,
And brings out the wind from His **storehouses**.

Jeremiah 51.16 When He utters His voice, there is a tumult of waters in the heavens,
And He causes the clouds to ascend from the **end of the earth**;
He makes lightning for the rain
And brings forth the **wind from His storehouses**.

Psalm 135.7 He causes the vapours to ascend from **the ends of the earth**;
Who makes lightnings for the rain,
Who brings forth the wind from His **treasuries**.

C.1 It is mentioned in many places in the Bible including the Psalms and the Books of Enoch and 2nd Esdras about the 'Treasures of the snow and ice' being reserved for the day of judgement. What judgment is it talking about? The Wrath of God?

C.2 It stated that there were angels in charge of 'terrible storehouses' of snow. What could this be talking about? There are many verses about this topic.

Psalm 148.8 Fire and hail, snow and clouds.
Stormy wind, fulfilling His word.

CHAPTER 6

> THEY showed me the treasure-house of the dew, like oil of the olive, and the appearance of its form, as of all the flowers of the earth; further many angels guarding the treasure-houses of these *things, and* how they are made to shut and open.

Genesis 27.28 Therefore God give thee of the dew of heaven, and the fatness of the earth, and plenty of corn and wine.

C.1 'Why is the dew of the earth compared with oil of the olive? 'treasure-house of the dew', 'like oil of the olive'. It is stating how important and precious is the dew as it feeds all the flowers of the earth.

C.2 Another major point is that the earth was very different back then in Pre-Flood times. In modern times, the dew could not be described as the above verse, as we don't have the same universal climate that the world used to have. Today there are very hot areas of the planet and deserts and today only 3% of the planet is actually inhabitable, and many areas are without water or 'dew.' The planet is a far cry from how God made it originally and is but a shell of its former pre-Flood glory, which will eventually be totally restored.

C.3 What was so different back then about the world's climate in Pre-Flood times? Apparently there used to be a canopy of water of ice surrounding the earth around 100 miles above the earth which acted as a barrier to protect the earth from the sun's harmful rays, and which also made the earth like a greenhouse effect with uniform temperature all around the world. Back then only 1/7 of the earth was seas. There were no deserts and there was 'dew' everywhere first thing every morning to water the plants as apparently it did not actually rain in those days before the Great Flood. When one studies a greenhouse, you will notice drops of water on the inside glass and this is how the dew was formed.

C.4 In Pre-Flood times the 'canopy' around the earth caused the planet to be like a hyperbaric Oxygen chamber where the atmosphere was under more pressure or atmospheres as we say today. The content of the Oxygen was much higher in the atmosphere. CO_2 levels were also much higher which caused the vegetation to grow much bigger.

C.5 '*Further - many angels guarding the treasure-houses of these things', and 'how they are made to shut and open.*' These angels were probably removed at the time of the Great Flood or reassigned, as after the Great Flood the whole topography of the entire planet was changed, and the climate became much rougher and 'rains' replaced the 'dews'.

C.6 Now it is telling us that originally in Pre-Flood times the climate was very different than it is today. There were many angels in Pre-Flood times to take care of all the nature to make sure that there was enough water on the planet to cause the flowers on earth to blossom not to mention all the plants and trees. Very interesting as according to the Bible it did not rain until the floods came at the time of the Great Flood.

C.7 This is ground-breaking information as this one verse of this chapter 6 is revealing so much.

1) It is talking about a different time than modern times and mentioning the exact conditions as were before the Great Flood.

2) The writer certainly sounds as if he personally was accustomed to a world where it did not 'rain', but that the ground was watered by the 'dew'

3) This would to give credence to the fact that it was in fact Enoch himself writing about these things in the Pre-Flood times and not a pseudepigraphic writer, writing much later in time.

Genesis 2:5–6 Now no shrub of the field was yet in the earth, and no plant of the field had yet sprouted, for the Lord God had not sent rain upon the earth; and there was no man to cultivate the ground. But a **mist** used to rise from the earth and water the whole surface of the ground.

CANOPY THEORY - In Pre-Flood times the earth was protected: Canopy theory and fault lines - Kent Hovind: (837) Canopy theory and fault lines - Kent Hovind - YouTube

CHAPTER 7

> AND those men took me and led me up on to the second heaven, and showed me darkness, greater than earthly darkness, and there I saw prisoners hanging, watched, awaiting the great and boundless judgement, and these angels were dark-looking, more than earthly darkness, and incessantly making weeping through all hours.

C.1 Officially, and according to many Christians, there are only 3 heavens: 1) The sky 2) Outer Space 3) Where God lives.

C.2 I have read that the spiritual warfare apart from going on all around us in another dimensions, that it is also going on in the 2nd heaven or physically speaking outer space.

C.3 Many strange things have been spotted as going on in outer space including what look like 'light' battles between good and evil angels, which does make a lot of sense. A battle between UFO's or between light and darkness.

C.4 The angels are always on missions to earth from the higher realms of the spirit world, which are on many levels, then they have to materialize into our dimension.

C.5 Sometimes the angels, as well as those who travel into the spiritual world and back again, encounter the spiritual opposition of the Fallen Angels and their agents. [See the book Journey to Tricon by Alan Trenholm about spiritual warfare in the form of UFOs]

C.6 The Fallen angels however are no match for God's angels, not to mention the demons are no match for the angels of God. There is a constant warfare going on in the spirit world, which is sometimes manifest in the physical realm, and people say that they have seen UFOs.

C.7 Look at the spiritual warfare between good and evil angels as mentioned very clearly in the Book of Daniel chapter 10. It took this angel 21 days to battle though from the spiritual realm to get to speak to Daniel. He only succeeded when he called one of the chief archangels - Michael to assist him, then the angel got through with a powerful message about the future of the Endtimes.

Daniel 10.12-14 Then said he unto me, Fear not, Daniel: for from the first day that thou didst set thine heart to understand, and to chasten thyself before thy God, thy words were heard, and I am come for thy words. But the **prince of the kingdom of Persia** withstood me one and twenty days: but, lo, **Michael, one of the chief princes**, came to help me; and I remained there with the kings of Persia. Now I am come to make thee understand what shall befall thy people in the latter days: for yet the vision is for many days.

C.8 Observation from those who have visited the spirt world: In the spirit world there are many levels going both up and down: See the Book by Alan

Trenholm 'Journey to Gragau', which is available at Amazon.

C.9 There are apparently a lot more than just 3 levels as mentioned in Christian literature. 1) The sky 2) Outer Space 3) Where God lives.

C.10 Where is the 2nd heaven located?: **What is Second Heaven in the Bible? (thomastaylorministries.org)**

QUOTE: The 2nd heaven is the unseen realm just above the earth where Satan and his fallen angels dwell - Spiritual Wickedness in High Places Eph 6.12

C.11 This realm is all around us, including above us in the 2nd heaven and also below us in the underworld and in millions of cases within people such as the demon-possessed.

C.12 Of course God's own children are possessed by His Spirit, and Jesus the Word of God from a much higher heaven - like the 7th Heaven.

Job 1.6-7 Now there was a day when the sons of God came to present themselves before the Lord, and **Satan** came also among them. And the Lord said unto Satan, 'Whence came thou?' Then Satan answered the Lord, and said, 'From going **to and fro in the earth,** and from **walking up and down in it**'.

> 2 And I said to the men who were with me: 'Wherefore are these incessantly tortured?' They answered me: 'These are God's apostates, who obeyed not God's commands, but took counsel with their own will, and turned away with their prince, who also is fastened on the fifth heaven.'

C.13 It has been mentioned in the above verse that Satan is bound on the 5th level.

Unfortunately for Satan, according to the Book of Isaiah chapter 14**,** Satan is to be made an end of and probably all the ruling spiritual powers that exist today and who rule the world through their puppets on the earth, insane demon-possessed leaders and controllers of the earth in finance and politics. [See chapter 29 of this my book for a lot more details on this topic]

3 And I felt great pity for them, and they saluted me, and said to me: 'Man of God, pray for us to the Lord'; and I answered to them: 'Who am I, a mortal man, that I should pray for angels? Who knows whither I go, or what will befall me? or who will pray for me?'

C.14 The truth be known, God is not some sort of a walk-over or push over that the Fallen angels are suddenly going to be forgiven just because they are weeping. They are tortured for all of their crimes and iniquities and then done away with in the Lake of Fire. The only reason that they are weeping is because they are no longer the powers and rulers over mankind, and they are no longer able to lord it over mankind and abuse them in every way possible. They along with Satan are never sorry for their crimes, as they are always trying to wangle their way out of being punished as there are totally reprobate, they will have no place in God's future loving, creative, peaceful eternal world.

C.15 The Bible states: 'What, know ye not that ye shall judge angels'?

1 Corinthians 6.3 Know ye not that we shall judge angels? How much more things that pertain to this life?

If every one of us must give account before God for every idle word that we speak, then how much more all the evil deeds that the Fallen angels have committed over thousands of years will they yet have to account for? They can't even get saved because they are not human. The fallen angels had already rejected Jesus in heaven before the Creation of the earth.

Matthew 12.36 But I say unto you, 'That every idle word that men shall speak, they shall give account thereof in the day of judgment.'

CHAPTER 8

> AND those men took me thence, and led me up on to the third heaven, and placed me there; and I looked downwards, and saw the produce of these places, such as has never been known for goodness.

C.1 Where is the third heaven?

2 Cor 12.2 I knew a man in Christ above fourteen years ago, (whether in the body, I cannot tell; or whether out of the body, I cannot tell: God knows) such an one caught up to the third heaven.

> 2 And I saw all the sweet-flowering trees and beheld their fruits, which were sweet-smelling, and all the foods borne *by them* bubbling with fragrant exhalation.

Exodus 30.34-38 Then the Lord said to Moses, "Take for yourself spices, stacte and onycha and galbanum, spices with pure frankincense; there shall be an equal part of each. With it you shall make incense, a perfume, the work of a perfumer, salted, pure, and holy. You shall beat some of it very fine and put part of it before the testimony in the tent of meeting where I will meet with you; it shall be most holy to you.

> 3 And in the midst of the Tree of life, in that place where the Lord rests, when he goes up into paradise; and this tree is of ineffable goodness and fragrance, and adorned more than every existing thing; and on all sides *it is* in form gold-looking and vermilion and fire-like and covers all, and it has produce from all fruits.

1ˢᵗ Enoch 25.4 As for this fragrant tree no mortal is able to touch it until the Great Judgement, when He shall take vengeance on all and bring everything to its consummation for ever. It shall then be given to the righteous.

[See my book Enoch Insights book 1 chapters 24-25 about the throne of God and the Tree of Life]

C.2 a) Ineffable -def = too great or extreme to be expressed or described in words:

"the ineffable mysteries of the soul" b) Vermilion -def (sometimes vermillion) is a **colour family** and **pigment** most often used between antiquity and the **19th century** from the powdered mineral cinnabar (a form of mercury sulfide). It is synonymous with red orange,

> 4 Its root is in the garden at the **earth's end.**

Book of 1 Enoch 1.5-7

All the ends of the earth will be shaken, and trembling and great fear will seize them (the Watchers) unto the **Ends of the earth**. The high mountains will be shaken and fall and break apart, and the high hills will be made low and melt like wax before the fire. The earth will be wholly rent asunder, and everything on earth will perish.

Book of 1 Enoch 23.1 From thence I went to another place at the West of the **Ends of the Earth** and I saw a burning fire, which ran without resting.

Book of 1 Enoch 33.1-2 And from thence I went to the **Ends of the earth** and saw there great beasts and each differed from the other…And to the East of those beast, I saw the Ends of the earth whereon the heaven rests and the **Portals of Heaven** open

> 5 And paradise is between **corruptibility** and **incorruptibility**.

C.3 *'Paradise, which is another name for the Garden of Eden is between corruptibility and incorruptibility'.* This is a big statement.

C.4 See my book 'Eden Insights' that explains this last verse very well. What this verse is stating, is that the Garden of Eden was between dimensions.
- The Heavenly spiritual dimension and the earthly dimension of flesh and blood.

C.5 When Adam and Eve fell, they had to leave the eternal world and enter the physical world as they lived in a dimension in 'between' dimensions whilst they were still in The Garden of Eden.

C.6 Here is a quote from my book Eden Insights which came on in 2021:

Chapter 2. 3 'I would propose that the Garden of Eden was created as an 'in' between world' or a higher dimension than the earth - part spiritual and part physical in order to prepare Adam and Eve for the much harsher existence, that they would soon have to endure once they left the Garden of Eden.'

BIBLE -1 Cor 15.50-57 Now this I say, brethren, that flesh and blood cannot inherit the kingdom of God; neither doth **corruption** inherit **incorruption**.

[51] Behold, I shew you a mystery; we shall not all sleep, but we shall all be changed,

[52] In a moment, in the twinkling of an eye, at the last trump: for the trumpet shall sound, and the dead shall be raised incorruptible, and we shall be changed.

[53] For this corruptible must put on incorruption, and this mortal must put on **immortality**.

[54] So when this corruptible shall have put on incorruption, and this mortal shall have put on immortality, then shall be brought to pass the saying that is written, death is swallowed up in victory.

[55] O death, where is thy sting? o grave, where is thy victory?

[56] The sting of death is sin; and the strength of sin is the law.

[57] But thanks be to God, which giveth us the victory through our lord Jesus Christ.

> 6 And two springs come out which send forth honey and milk, and their springs send forth oil and wine, and they separate into four parts, and go round with quiet course, and go down into the Paradise of Eden, **between** corruptibility and incorruptibility.

C.7 a) 'Honey and milk': Is this literal or does it have some other meaning? – Here is an excellent explanation: b) Oil and Wine: this is a definition of great wealth as shown in the Books of Revelation where it describes the situation of the disparity of wealth with great poverty and death alongside great wealth or great financial imbalance. (Land Flowing with Milk and Honey - Bible Verse Explained (biblestudytools.com),

Revelation 6.5-6 And when he had opened the third seal, I heard the third beast say, Come and see. And I beheld, and lo a black horse; and he that sat on him had a pair of **balances** in his hand.

And I heard a voice in the midst of the four beasts say, A **measure of wheat for a penny**, and three measures of barley for a penny; and *see* thou **hurt not the oil and the wine**.

C.8 Selling a 'measure of wheat for a penny' is selling a bag of flour in today's terms for a whole day's wages.

A 'measure of wheat' baked one loaf of bread. A penny was a whole day's wages in the time of the Romans and the times of Jesus. Imagine having to work all day just to make enough money for only one loaf of bread!

C.9 Eden is in a higher dimension - See my book 'Eden Insights'. My book explains about -1) Throne of God 2) Waters of life proceeding from the Throne 3) Rivers of life 4) Tree of Life 5) Ocean of Life 6) Eternal Life]

C.10 The Creator -The Word of God - Jesus talks frequently to Adam and Eve once they left the Garden of Eden and tells them that they are not allowed to come back into the Garden of Eden right then. Jeus tells them that one day He himself would come to earth and pay the price for our sins and then we would be allowed back into the Garden of Eden.

7 And thence they go forth along the earth and have a revolution to their circle even as other elements.

8 And here there is no unfruitful tree, and every place is blessed.

9 And *there are* three hundred angels very bright, who keep the garden, and with incessant sweet singing and never-silent voices serve the Lord throughout all days and hours.

10 And I said: 'How very sweet is this place,' and those men said to me:

CHAPTER 9

The showing to Enoch of the place of the righteous and compassionate.

> THIS place, O Enoch, is prepared for the righteous, who endure all manner of offence from those that exasperate their souls, who avert their eyes from iniquity, and make righteous judgement, and give bread to the hungering, and cover the naked with clothing, and raise up the fallen, and help injured orphans, and who walk without fault before the face of the Lord, and serve him alone, and for them is prepared this place for eternal inheritance.

Matthew 5.7-12 Blessed are the merciful: for they shall obtain mercy. Blessed are the pure in heart: for they shall see God. Blessed are the peacemakers: for they shall be called the children of God. Blessed are ye, when men shall revile you, and persecute you, and shall say all manner of evil against you falsely, for my sake. Rejoice and be exceeding glad: for great is your reward in heaven: For so persecuted they the prophets which were before you.

1ST **ENOCH 25.1,4-6** And as for this fragrant tree, no mortal is permitted to touch it till the great judgement, when He shall take vengeance on all and bring everything to its consummation for ever. It shall then be given to the righteous and holy.

5 Its fruit shall be for food to the elect. It shall be transplanted to the holy place, to the temple of the Lord, the Eternal King.

6 Then shall they rejoice with joy and be glad, and into the holy place shall they enter. Its fragrance shall be in their bones; and they shall live a long life on the earth, such as their fathers lived. In their days shall no sorrow or plague of torment or calamity touch them.

CHAPTER 10

> AND those two men (angels) led me upon to the Northern side, and showed me there a very terrible place, and *there were* all manner of tortures in that place: cruel darkness and unillumined gloom, and there is no light there, but murky fire constantly flames aloft, and *there is* a fiery river coming forth, and that whole place is everywhere fire, and everywhere *there is* frost and ice, thirst and shivering, while the bonds are very cruel, and the angels fearful and merciless, bearing angry weapons, merciless torture, and I said:

C.1 This sounds like the Lake of Fire which Jesus said is reserved for the Devil and his angels.

Matthew 25.41 Then shall he say also unto them on the left hand, 'Depart from me, ye cursed, into everlasting fire, prepared for the devil and his angels.'

Revelation 20.10.13-15 And the Devil which deceived them was cast into a lake burning with fire and brimstone where the beast and the false prophet are also; and they will be tormented day and night forever and ever. And the sea gave up the dead which were in it, and death and Hades gave up the dead which were in them; and they were judged, every one of them according to their deeds. Then death and Hades were thrown into the lake of fire. This is the second death, the lake of fire. And if anyone's name was not found written in the book of life, he was thrown into the lake of fire.

> 2 'Woe, woe, how very terrible is this place.'

1ST ENOCH 21.4-8 And from thence I went to another place, which was still more horrible than the former, and I saw a horrible thing. A great fire which burnt and blazed, and the place was cleft as far as the abyss, being full of great descending columns of fire, neither its extent or magnitude could I see, nor could I conjecture. 5 Then I said, "How fearful is the place and how terrible to look upon!" 6 Then Uriel answered me, one of the holy angels who was with me, and said unto me, "Enoch, why hast thou such fear and affright? 7 And I answered, "Because of this fearful place, and because of the spectacle of the pain." 8 And he said unto me, "This place is the prison of the angels, and here they will be imprisoned for ever."

> 3 And those men (angels) said to me: This place, O Enoch, is prepared for those who dishonour God, who on earth practise sin against nature, which is child-corruption after the sodomite fashion, magic-making, enchantments and devilish witchcrafts, and who boast of their wicked deeds, stealing, lies, calumnies*, envy, rancour, fornication, murder, and who, accursed, steal the souls of men, who, seeing the poor take away their goods and themselves wax rich, injuring them for other men's

> goods; who being able to satisfy the empty, made the hungering to die; being able to clothe, stripped the naked; and who knew not their creator, and bowed down to soulless (sc. lifeless) gods, who cannot see nor hear, vain gods, who also built hewn images and bow down to unclean handiwork, for all these is prepared this place amongst these, for eternal inheritance.

C.2 Here it describes the very sick child abuse linked with devilish witchcraft and murder. Things have not changed much since Pre-Flood times but are only getting worse by the day.

*Calumnies = the making of false and defamatory statements about someone in order to damage their reputation; slander: "a bitter struggle marked by calumny and litigation"

Romans 1.18-20

18. For the wrath of God is revealed from heaven against all ungodliness and unrighteousness of men, who hold the truth in unrighteousness;

19 Because that which may be known of God is manifest in them; for God hath shewed *it* unto them.

20 For the invisible things of him from the creation of the world are clearly seen, being understood by the things that are made, *even* his eternal power and Godhead; so that they are without excuse:

21 Because that, when they knew God, they glorified *him* not as God, neither were thankful; but became vain in their imaginations, and their foolish heart was darkened.

22 Professing themselves to be wise, they became fools,

23 And changed the glory of the uncorruptible God into an image made like to corruptible man, and to birds, and four-footed beasts, and creeping things.

24 Wherefore God also gave them up to uncleanness through the lusts of their own hearts, to dishonour their own bodies between themselves:

25 Who changed the truth of God into a lie, and worshipped and served the creature more than the Creator, who is blessed for ever. Amen.

26 For this cause God gave them up unto vile affections: for even their women did change the natural use into that which is against nature:

27 And likewise also the men, leaving the natural use of the woman, burned in their lust one toward another; men with men working that which is unseemly, and receiving in themselves that recompence of their error which was meet.

28 And even as they did not like to retain God in *their* knowledge, God gave them over to a reprobate mind, to do those things which are not convenient;

29 Being filled with all unrighteousness, fornication, wickedness, covetousness, maliciousness; full of envy, murder, debate, deceit. Malignity; whisperers,

30 Backbiters, haters of God, despiteful, proud, boasters, inventors of evil things, disobedient to parents,

31 Without understanding, covenant breakers, without natural affection, implacable, unmerciful:

32 Who knowing the judgment of God, that they which commit such things are worthy of death, not only do the same, but have pleasure in them that do them.

C.3 According to the 1st Book of Enoch it will be the Fallen angels who end up torturing and killing their own offspring and descendants and abominable creations and half-human creatures and chimeras which God has not created.

C.4 In general, anything that God did not create will have to be destroyed. God will use the Fallen angels to carry this out before they themselves then go into the Lake of Fire unless both they and Satan repent before the Great Judgement. Thus, will be fulfilled the simple rule 'Whatsoever man sows he shall also reap.'

1 Enoch 56.1-2 And I saw the angels of punishment going and they held scourges and chains of iron and bronze, and I asked the angels of peace who went with me, saying, 'to whom are these who hold the scourges going?

And he said unto me: "To their elect and beloved ones that they may be cast into the chasm of the abyss of the valley; and them that valley shall be filled with 'their elect and beloved", and the days of their lives shall be at an end, and the days of their leading astray shall not thence forward be reckoned.

Galatians 6.7 Be not deceived; God is not mocked: for whatsoever a man soweth, that shall he also reap.

1 Enoch 62. 6 And the kings and the mighty and exalted and those who rule the earth shall fall down before Him on their faces and worship and set their hope upon this Son of Man, and petition Him and supplicate for mercy at this hands; nevertheless that Lord of Spirits will so press them that they shall hastily go forth from His presence and their faces shall be filled with shame, and the darkness grow deeper on their faces and he will deliver them to the angels of punishment to execute vengeance on them because they have oppressed His children and His elect.

1 Enoch 67.4-5 And He will imprison those angels, who have shown unrighteousness, in that burning valley which my grandfather Enoch had formerly shown to me in the West among the mountains of gold and silver and iron and soft metal and tin. The 'valley of the angels' who had led astray mankind beneath that land.

1 Enoch 68.4 And it came to pass when he stood before the Lord of Spirits, Michael said thus to Raphael, "I will not take their part under the eye of the Lord; for the Lord of Spirits has been angry with them, because they do as if they were the Lord.

Therefore, all that is hidden shall come upon them forever and ever; for neither angel nor man shall have his portion, but alone they have received their judgement for eve and ever."

1 Enoch 58.3 For the Darkness shall first have been destroyed and light established before the Lord of Spirits. And uprightness established forever before the Lord of Spirits.

C.5 It is stated that what a man sows that he shall reap. The rich elite think that there is no consequence to their evil actions. I sometimes wonder if certain evil people die and go to another dimension where they are the victims to all the crimes that they have committed, as there is no forgiveness without Christ. Like down in Hell. I do not envy the very wicked as they will get away with nothing at all. After all, the Bible tells us that every man shall give account of every idle word that he spake whilst on the earth. It is also stated that no man will be able to utter a lie in the presence of God. This means that those who rule the world and are very evil are already in big trouble. There is no forgiveness without Christ. So, for them it will be Hell and then the Lake of Fire.

Psalm 9.17 'The wicked shall be turned into hell and all the nations that forget God'.

Revelation 20.15 'For whosoever was not found in the Book of Life was cast into the Lake of Fire'.

Revelation 11.18 'God shall arise to destroy those who destroy the earth'.

C.6 In conclusion for these recent chapters, in line with this Book of 2nd Enoch it would appear that humans eventually will be restored to perfection as in the Pre-Creation, but all the evil spirits will have been eliminated. Those responsible for having created the evil beings in the first place – that is the Fallen angels according to Genesis 6 will be thrown into the Lake of first and will end up looking like the angels described in chapter 18 of this book. These same fallen angels will be given the job to destroy all of their progeny or aberrations such as the Giants or demons or chimeras and monsters.

C.7 ORIGIN OF EVIL:

Revelation 12:12 Therefore rejoice, ye heavens, and ye that dwell in them. Woe to the inhabitants of the earth and of the sea! For the devil is come down unto you, having great wrath, because he knows that he hath but a short time." Great Wrath. Wrath: is defined as anger, fury, rage, also, not to be confused with divine chastisement. Peter warns us that:

1 Peter 5:8 "Your adversary the devil, as a roaring lion, walketh about, seeking whom he may devour".

What have we, mankind, done to incur such hatred and anger from Satan.

C.8 Is it only irrational insanity of wanting to destroy God's creation, "except those days should be shortened, there should no flesh be saved" or is there an underlying reason behind this hatred.

C.9 To begin we want to examine the definition "image" followed by some scriptures concerning images and idols.

From: The King James Bible Page "A representation or similitude of any person or thing, formed of a material substance; as an image wrought out of stone, wood or wax.

An idol: the representation of any person or thing, that is an object of worship. The second commandment forbids the worship of images."

Revelation 9:20 "And the rest of the men which were not killed by these plagues yet repented not of the works of their hands, that they should not worship devils, and idols of gold, and silver, and brass, and stone, and of wood: which neither can see, nor hear, nor walk."

C.10 One of the best-known stories of idol worship or maybe it would be better to say the refusal of idol worship is the well-known story in Daniel 3 about the fiery furnace.

Daniel 3:1-7,16,18 "In his eighteenth year Nabuchodonosor the king made a golden image, its height was sixty cubits, its breadth six cubits: and he set it up in the plain of Deira, in the province of Babylon. And he sent forth to gather the governors, and the captains, and the heads of provinces, chiefs, and princes, and those who were in authority, and all the rulers of districts, to come to the dedication of the image. So the heads of provinces, the governors, the captains, the chiefs, the great princes, those who were in authority, and all the rulers of districts, were gathered to the dedication of the image which king Nabuchodonosor had set up; and they stood before the image. Then a herald cried aloud, To you it is commanded, ye peoples, tribes, and languages, at what hour ye shall hear the sound of the trumpet, and pipe, and harp, and sackbut, and psaltery, and every kind of music, ye shall fall down and worship the golden image which king Nabuchodonosor has set up. And whosoever shall not fall down and worship, in the same hour he shall be cast into the burning fiery furnace. And it came to pass when the nations heard the sound of the trumpet, and pipe, and harp, and sackbut, and psaltery, and all kinds of music, all the nations, tribes, and languages, fell down and worshipped the golden image which king Nabuchodonosor had set up. Then answered Shadrach, Meshach and Abdenago and said to king Nabuchodonosor...be it known to thee, O king, that we will not serve thy gods, nor worship the image which thou hast set up."

C.11 There are many such stories and examples in the Bible of idol worship. One such idol was "Dagon". "Dagon was the chief deity of the Philistines, and the worship of this pagan god dates to the third millennium BC. According to ancient mythology, Dagon was the father of Baal". One account of Dagon can be found in 1 Samuel chapter five. Of course, the world today is absolutely filled with images and idols. So, images and/or idols are something to be worshipped. We usually think of them in a negative light but are there any instances where images could be viewed in a positive light? There is. An exemplary example of this is found in 2 Corinthians 4:4 where Paul refers to Jesus "who is the image of God". We as Christians do worship an image, Jesus, who is the image of God!

Colossians 1:15 "Who hath delivered us from the power of darkness, and hath translated [us] into the kingdom of his dear Son: In whom we have redemption through his blood, [even] the forgiveness of sins: Who is the image of the invisible God, the firstborn of every creature."

C.12 Let's examine a few other interesting verses.

Genesis 1:26-27 "And God said, Let us make man according to our image and likeness, and let them have dominion over the fish of the sea, and over the flying creatures of heaven, and over the cattle and all the earth, and over all the reptiles that creep on the earth. And God made man, according to the image of God he made him, male and female he made them."

Genesis 9:6 "He that sheds man's blood, instead of that blood shall his own be shed, for in the image of God I made man."

1 Corinthians 11:7 "For a man indeed ought not to cover [his] head, forasmuch as he is the image and glory of God."

Psalm 8:5 For thou hast made him a little lower than the angels, and hast crowned him with glory and honour."

C.13 It is interesting to note that several versions of the Bible do not use the word angels but instead use the word "God". Other versions use the term "heavenly beings, a little less than divine, a little lower than yourself, and Young's Literal Translation uses the phrase "lack a little of Godhead". As is self evident we, mankind, were also created in the image of God.

C.14 How does all this figure in with the hatred Satan has towards us. We are now going to look at the book mentioned above called the 'Life of Adam and Eve'. Life of Adam and Eve, also known, in its Greek version, as the Apocalypse of Moses. It recounts the lives of Adam and Eve from after their expulsion from the Garden of Eden to their deaths. It provides more detail about the Fall of Man, including Eve's version of the story.

C.15 Satan explains that he rebelled when God commanded him to bow down to Adam. After Adam dies, he and all his descendants are promised a resurrection. The ancient versions of the Life of Adam and Eve are: the Greek Apocalypse of Moses, the Latin Life of Adam and Eve, the Slavonic Life of Adam and Eve, the Armenian Penitence of Adam, the Georgian Book of Adam, and one or two fragmentary Coptic versions.

Life of Adam and Eve –Adam talking to Satan: ' What evil have we done to you'?

11.2 For it is because of your calumnies that we went out from paradise. Is it because we have caused you to be expelled that you are angry against us?

11.3 Or is it because of us that you were despoiled of your glory? Or is it, in some way, by our action that you are in such deficiency? Or are we the only creatures of God that you fight against us alone? Satan reminds the human couple of events that transpired before, which they have no memory of (from the Armenian version):

12.1 Satan also wept loudly and said to Adam. "All my arrogance and sorrow came to pass because of you; for, because of you I went forth from my dwelling; and because of you I was alienated from the throne of the cherubs who, having spread out a shelter, used to enclose me; because of you my feet have trodden the earth."

12.2 Adam replied and said to him,

12.3 "What are our sins against you, that you did all this to us?"

13.1 Satan replied and said, "You did nothing to me, but I came to this measure because of you, on the day on which you were created, for I went forth on that day.

13.2 When God breathed his spirit into you, you received the likeness of his image. Thereupon, Michael came and made you bow down before God. God said to Michael, 'Behold I have made Adam in the likeness of my image.'

14.1 Then Michael summoned all the angels. and God said to them,'Come, bow down to god whom I made.'

14.2 Michael bowed first. He called me and said. 'You too, bow down to Adam.'

14.3 I said, 'Go away, Michael! I shall not bow down to him who is posterior to me, for I am former. Why is it proper for me to bow down to him?'

15.1 The other angels, too, who were with me, heard this, and my words seemed pleasing to them and they did not prostrate themselves to you, Adam.

16.1 Thereupon, God became angry with me and commanded to expel us from our dwelling and to cast me and my angels, who were in agreement with me, to the earth; and you were at the same time in the Garden.

16.2 When I realized that because of you I had gone forth from the dwelling of light and was in sorrows and pains,

16.3 then I prepared a trap for you, so that I might alienate you from your happiness just as I, too, had been alienated because of you."

17.1 When Adam heard this, he said to the Lord, 'Lord, my soul is in your hand. Make this enemy of mine distant from me, who desires to lead me astray, I who am searching for the light that I have lost."

17.2 At that time Satan passed away from him.

17.3 Adam stood from then on in the waters of repentance, and Eve remained fallen upon the ground for three days, like one dead. Then, after three days, she arose from the earth.

C.16 Solomon in the book of Ecclesiastes chapter one said: "What is that which has been? the very thing which shall be: and what is that which has been done? the very thing which shall be done: and there is no new thing under the sun."

It has also been said of the Devil he has no original ideas, all his ideas come from something God has said, or done.

C.17 If the account of his fall in The Life of Adam and Eve is correct Satan refused to bow before the image of God. And if this account is true it would give understanding to the hatred Satan has towards us. Could his refusal to obey God's command because of his pride also have provoked him to say:

Isaiah 14:13-14 "I will go up to heaven, I will set my throne above the stars of heaven: I will sit on a lofty mount, on the lofty mountains toward the north: I will go up above the clouds: I will be like the Most High."

C.18 If the above account is correct, it is understandable that his ultimate goal in the book of Revelation, chapter thirteen, is to get man to bow and worship before his image of the antichrist the Satanically possessed world leader of the End Time.

What a reversal of truth!

Revelation 13:14-15 "And deceives them that dwell on the earth by the means of those miracles which he had power to do in the sight of the beast; saying to them that dwell on the earth, that they should make an image to the beast, which had the wound by a sword, and did live. And he had power to give life unto the image of the beast, that the image of the beast should both speak, and cause that as many as would not worship the image of the beast should be killed."

1 Corinthians 15:45 "And so it is written, The first man Adam was made a living soul; the last Adam was made a quickening spirit."

John 10:34 "Jesus answered them, Is it not written in your law, I said, Ye are gods?"

CHAPTER 11

> *Here they took Enoch up on to the **fourth** heaven where is the course of sun and moon.*

C.1 Could it be that each heaven affects different areas of Creation in God's universe? 4 is the number of Creation as we live in the 3rd dimension + 1 or the 4th dimension = 4th dimension of Time.

> THOSE men took me, and led me up on to the fourth heaven, and showed me all the successive goings, and all the rays of the light of sun and moon.

Talk about time involving the rotation of the stars the sun and the moon.

> 2 And I measured their goings and compared their light and saw that the sun's light is greater than the moon's.
>
> 3 Its circle and the **wheels** on which it goes always, like a wind going past with very marvellous speed, and day and night it has no rest. **[See Eastern pictures of art with sun and moon in chariots.]**

C.2 Described here like the inner workings of a giant mechanism with the precision of an old-fashioned grandfather clock. The Book of 1st Enoch also mentions this same thing. It is as though Enoch can see the inner mechanisms behind our physical dimension or the inner workings of the spirit world.
See: 1 Book of Enoch – The Luminaries – chapters 72-82

> 4 Its passage and return *are accompanied by* four great stars, and each star has under it a thousand stars, to the right of the sun›s wheel, *and by* four to the left, each having under it a thousand stars, altogether eight thousand, issuing with the sun continually.

C.3 The sun's wheel – Again a mechanism which controls the sun and moon and the stars, which we cannot currently see with our physical eyes. It is obvious that something holds the universe together in perfect harmony. The scientists cannot fathom it or understand it, and it makes the diviners mad, as scripture tells us. It reminds me of what the famous physicist Milliken stated 'I believe in God because just as in my watch there is such intricate precision. So, also behind this complex universe there has to be a mechanism and a designer.

Isaiah 44.24-25 Thus saith the LORD, thy redeemer, and he that formed thee from the womb, I am the LORD that maketh all things; that stretches forth the heavens alone; that spreads abroad the earth by myself; That frustrates the tokens of the liars, and maketh diviners mad; that turns wise men backward, and maketh their knowledge foolish.

C.4 'Wheels' are some spiritual mechanisms mentioned in the Bible in Ezekiel chapter 1 & 10. They are found around the Throne of God.

> 5 And by day fifteen **myriads** of angels attend it, and by night a thousand.
>
> 6 And **six-winged one's** issue with the angels before the sun's wheel into the **fiery flames,** and a hundred angels **kindle the sun and set it alight.**

C.5 How The Scientists Altered Time: From Rotations Of The Earth And Sun To An Atomic Clock, Related To Radiation Instead, By 1967!

In ancient times before Christ, there used to be what is referred to today as the prophetic year containing only 360 days in the year as quoted in both the prophetic books of Daniel and Revelations. Why did God through His prophets refer to the year as having 360 days unless it was true?

C.6 In both the Book of Enoch and the Book of Jubilees it states that there are 364 days to the year, but is it just possible that the number of the days have been deliberately tampered with in both the books of Enoch and Jubilees? In reading the Book of Enoch repeatedly you will see that Enoch also describes the year as having 12 months of 30 days, which is 'The Prophetic Year' equal to 360 days. So why one announcement in the Book of Enoch as to 364 days? It is inconsistent with most of the text. Again, in this Book of Jubilees it states also 364 days. My opinion: I think the numbers have indeed been tampered with. Why? As I have stated in 'Enoch Insights' and 'Jasher Insights' as well as this book of Jubilees Insights, the exact dates of historical events differ slightly between these books upon occasion. Most times and dates are very similar but occasionally one time or day seems out of place. Why is that you may ask? Probably at some time in the past the books, or around 150 years ago when modern science was really starting to take off with Evolution many books were slightly tampered with by those who didn't want the books to remain canonized – in other words discourage most people from reading the books. The original books of Enoch, Jasher and Jubilees have incredibly revealing information for those who take the time to study them thoroughly and repeatedly.

C.7 Example: Consider an object rotating around another in a perfect circle. How can we describe this action other than stating the object rotates in a perfect circle of 360 degrees? If one was to therefore put any given number of days in the year, it would be logical to put exactly 360 days to the year which is what used to be called an Absolute number.

C.8 If people were to think that there were 360 days in the year it might get them to thinking:

I) That sounds like the number of the degrees in a circle.

II) 360 is divisible by 12. Like 12 months in the year.

III) 360 is also related to the number of minutes and seconds. 60 x 6. Wow 360 is a very special number so maybe there is a God of the absolutes a person may deduce. So, science as so often guided by Satan or evil spirits decided they had to corrupt the concept of Time itself!

C.9 Why would Science deliberately want to alter the number of days in the year, you might ask? Simple: because if the number is 360 it proves the existence of God as it is not a random number and it also it proves total order and shows a reliable constant. However, the scientists in their desire to disprove the existence of God tried to alter the days to 365 ¼, but we now have the messy add-on of the leap year. This means that we add on a missing day every 4 years. I am sure that is not how God originally created the Time-Sequence.

CHAPTER 12

Of the very marvellous elements of the sun.

> AND I looked and saw other flying elements of the sun, whose names *are* **Phoenixes** and **Chalkydri**, marvellous and wonderful, with feet and tails in the form of a lion, and a **crocodile's head**, their appearance *is* empurpled, like the rainbow; their size *is* **nine hundred measures**, their **wings** *are* **like those of angels**, each *has* **twelve**, and they attend and accompany the sun, bearing heat and dew, as it is ordered them from God.

C.1 See my book 'OUT OF THE BOTTOMLESS PIT 2' CHAPTER 35 about the phoenix and a vision of a dragon and phoenix over Iceland on 22/02/2019. Was that vision in the sky prophetic? Strangely some 6 months later the world saw massive worldwide devastation with a pandemic and a worldwide clampdown by the governments of the world. Millions have died including many young and athletic people from that pandemic and from the treatments given.

> 2 Thus *the* **sun revolves** and goes, and rises under the heaven, and its course goes **under the earth** with the light of its rays incessantly.

C.2 Modern science tells us that the earth revolves around the sun but apparently that is not the truth. The earth is apparently the centre of the universe, and all celestial bodies revolve around it as brought out by the Geo-Centric earth scientific theory. Helio-centric is the sun being stationary and the earth revolving around it. If the earth is stationary, does it spin on its axis in order to give night and day?

C.3 LIES IN SCIENCE: They deliberately lie about ancient wisdom and knowledge as though it was ridiculous. They try to ridicule the old wisdom and the old knowledge as though it were all false & mere superstition, and in fact according to them (the modern scientists) they are the only ones that really know anything of value, and furthermore they've only found it out lately and are revealing these marvellous truths to you for the first time! The truth is that man has forgotten so much of the ancient science and mathematics which was much more advanced than the sciences of today. As mentioned by Sir Issac Newton, who was the discoverer of gravity in the 17th century. Author: Better said 'he re-discovered gravity. Modern man is not as smart as he thinks he is. [SEE ASTRONOMICAL FAKERY: http://www.peopleofthekeys.com/news/docs/library/Astronomical+Fakery%21] 363

C.4 I know science tells us that the rotation of the earth is slowing down, but is that true? Isn't the whole universe created perfectly and governed by absolute Maths, of which the so-called Ancients were aware of.

C.5 Stating that orbits are decaying or that the spinning of the earth is slowing could be just a method of 'controlling the facts'. After all, most people don't understand science that well! We know from scriptures that there used to be 360 days to the year, which were 12 x 30-day months, and not like modern times with the random length of the months being 31, 30 or 28 days or even 29 as in the case of February in a Leap Year. Man has really 'messed up the days and times and seasons. It used to be very simple with 360 days to the year; 12 months of exactly 30 days each. 24 hours to each day.

C.6 So how did the 'Powers that be' manage to alter the length of the year? The 'Powers that be' added the minutes and seconds and set the exact length of the second and minute to fit their 'Altered Calendar', to become the confusion mentioned above of 365 ¼ days to the year etc. However, in their desire to prove that 'time is random' they still left traces of their errors. The fact that every 4 years they still must add on exactly one day to the calendar.

C.7 Did you know that according to Solomon, who was the wisest man to have lived on earth, with the exception of Jesus the Messiah, stated that 'No man can know the workings of Creation under the sun. Even if he thinks he knows he cannot find it! Why? Such knowledge is hidden from mankind'. Enoch however could see the inner workings of the universe and all the intricate control systems behind this physical universe.

CHAPTER 13

> THOSE men bore me away to the east, and placed me at the sun's gates, where the sun goes forth according to the regulation of the seasons and the circuit of the months of the whole year, and the number of the hours, day and night,

C.1 How is it even possible that there exist gates or portals through which the sun emerges and that the sun is travelling in a circuit? If so, what is the sun revolving around? I thought that the earth was supposed to be revolving around the sun according to modern science. Something does not add up in this picture. Enoch has it right with the sun revolving around the earth, which means science has got it wrong. We have a Geo-central earth and not a Helio-central earth.

C.2 What everyone needs to know about, is that that what education, science, and history teach are mostly deliberate false narratives put in place by the ruling controllers.

C.3 It is the conquerors who write or 'right' the history books, as in the novel 1984 by George Orwell.

C.4 Today according to the elite 'controllers' or the rulers and merchants 'The truth is whatever they say it is'.

C.5 I predict that very soon there will be a modern 'book banning' including the Bible and like the movie '451 Fahrenheit' from 1966. As is said by the Elite controllers in modern times 'Knowledge is power' – so take away knowledge and wisdom from the masses by force. Take away the books that don't agree with satanic dogma like Hitler's Nazism, Communism, Fascism and now Globalism. Hitler did this. Stalin did this, Mao did this. The New World Order is already doing this through AI censoring of the internet. Communist started in 2023 to rewrite the Bible to conform with communist dogma or satanic dogma - which is that no mercy is to be shown. In the story where Jesus forgave the woman who committed adultery, the narrative has been altered - to now show Jesus stoning the poor woman to death.

C.6 Amazing how the knowledge of the sun the moon and the stars was revealed to Enoch some 5000 years ago. Yet modern man gets it all wrong! Why? Because He is not connected with God and therefore knows nothing of real value. Without God there is no wisdom.

C.7 God told Enoch that the earth is stationary, whilst the sun moon and stars revolve around the earth. This has been borne out by many honest scientists. Many of the modern scientists and historians and intellectuals are just like their paying masters -arrogant in their positions of their so-called knowledge and understanding, when often they simply do not have the truth of the subject matter that they are studying and passing on to their students.

C.8 People who take an arrogant stance are just acting like Satan himself.

C.9 Solomon, the wisest man who ever lived, stated that man cannot find out the secrets of Creation as they are hidden from the eyes of unbelievers. He also stated that there is nothing new under the sun. That which is has already been. That which is past you shall see again in the future. Man is not progressing and evolving as Evolution would falsely teach you. He is going backwards and becoming more reprobate with every passing day, as this world is fast descending into 'chaos by design' of the satanic Merchants of this world.

Ecclesiastes 1.9-10 The thing that hath been, it is that which shall be;and that which is done is that which shall be done: and there is no new thing under the sun. Is there anything whereof it may be said, See, this is new? it hath been already of old time, which was before.

> 2 And I saw six gates open, each gate having sixty-one stadia and a quarter of one stadium, and I measured *them* truly, and understood their size *to be* so much, through which the sun goes forth, and goes to the west, and is made even, and rises throughout all the months, and turns back again from the six gates according to the succession of the seasons; thus *the period* of the whole year is finished after the returns of the four seasons,

C.10 'And I saw six gates open' - What are these 6 gates supposed to be? How is it even possible to measure the sun and the invisible gates that it passes through? This could not be measured in a human measurement system.

Stadia -definition: a surveying method for determination of distances and differences of elevation by means of a telescopic instrument having two horizontal lines through which the marks on a graduated rod are observed.

Stadia – The old distance of the length of a Roman stadium.

C.11 Obviously, the sun is a lot bigger than the measurements given in the above verse, so why the very small measurements? Now that is a mystery. I have noticed in studying the Apocrypha and ancient Hebrew books such as Jasher, Jubilees that when it comes to dates, times and measurements that the books don't always agree. Maybe the reason is that God Himself does not consider those exact details to be very important for us to know at this particular time. Many things of God are shrouded in mystery. I guess we will find out many more details when we get to heaven.

Daniel 2.22 It is He who reveals the profound and hidden things; He knows what is in the darkness. And the light dwells with Him.

CHAPTER 14

> 1. And again those men led me away to the western parts, and showed me six great gates open corresponding to the Eastern gates, opposite to where the sun sets, according to the number of the days *three hundred and sixty-five and a quarter.

C.1 *This number I believe has been added later, or in modern times. * *three hundred and sixty-five and a quarter.*

C.2 All the ancient nations used to say that there were 360 days in the year like the number of degrees in a circle, which would make a lot more sense. Enoch stated in the 1st Book of Enoch that there are 364 days or 360 + 4 intercalary days.

C.3 Six great gates in the West and six great gates in the East. What are they? Are these time portals for the sun? God has a complicated 'behind the scenes' of the physical realm machinery or 'behind the face of the big clock' of the sun and the physical world 'intricate machinery', which keeps our physical world moving and time ticking away and so perfectly synchronized.

C.4 The first Book of Enoch states that the year is 360 days plus 4 intercalatory days for a total of 364 days. See my book Jubilees Insights that explains how science has changed the time and the number of the days of the year. Modern science does not measure time according to rotations of the earth but by an atomic clock that has nothing to do with the real time. Science started doing this in circa1954.

> 2 Thus again it goes down to the western gates, *and* draws away its light, the greatness of its brightness, under the earth; for since the crown of its shining is in heaven with the Lord, and guarded [by four hundred angels, while the sun goes round on wheel under the earth, and stands seven great hours in night, and spends half *its course* under the earth, when it comes to the eastern approach in the eighth hour of the night, it brings its lights, and the crown of shining, and the sun flames forth more than fire.

C.5 Clearly this verse is stating that the sun rotates around earth and not the earth around the sun. This is stating that our solar system is in fact Geocentric and not Heliocentric. Scientists tell us that whether the earth revolves around the sun or the sun around the earth - from an observation point on the earth it would look the same.

C.6 It would appear that Enoch is seeing the inner workings in higher dimensions which control all that goes on in this physical universe. This is also mentioned in 1 Enoch in the Book of the Luminaries: 1 Enoch 72.1 The Book of the courses of the Luminaries of heaven, the relations of each, according to their courses, their dominion and their seasons, according to their names and places and origin, and according to their months, which Uriel (archangel) the holy angel who was with me, who is their guide, showed me; and he showed me all of their laws exactly as they are, and how it is with regard to all the years of the world and unto eternity, till the New Creation (The New Heaven and New Earth as described in Revelation 21-22) is accomplished which endures unto eternity

CHAPTER 15

> 1. Then the elements of the sun, called Phoenixes and Chalkydri break into song, therefore every bird flutters with its wings, rejoicing at the giver of light, and they broke into song at the command of the Lord.

CHALKYDRI Definition: **Chalkydri** (Ancient Greek: χαλκύδραι *khalkýdrai*, compound of χαλκός *khalkós* «brass, copper» + ὕδρα *hýdra* "hydra", "water-serpent" — lit. "brazen hydras", "copper serpents") are mythical creatures mentioned in the apocryphal Second Book of Enoch from the 1st century CE, often seen as an angelic species.[1][2] In the narrative, chalkydri and phoenixes dwell near the Sun and ran its course around the Earth with it bringing heat and dew to the Earth. The chalkydri are described as having the head of a crocodile and the feet and tail like that of a lion, each having twelve wings, and are the colour purple like the rainbow.[3] At sunrise, all the chalkydri break into song with their counterparts, alerting the birds of the world for a new day to rejoice.[4]

The name has been interpreted as a translation of Nehushtan, the bronze serpent constructed by Moses to protect the Israelites from attacks by fiery flying serpents, and destroyed by King Hezekiah as idolatrous,[5] from Hebrew into Greek. Source: Chalkydri - Wikipedia

C.1 How can a creature be both a snake and a crocodile and have lion's feet and tail and how could it also be a melodic colourful bird? The phoenix of ancient mythology was a melodic and very colourful bird. There seems to be some confusion in the description of these creatures known as the Chalkydri and Phoenixes. They sound like some sort of an exotic chimera. That is a very interesting topic.

C.2 Wasn't it the Fallen angels who created the different chimeras and not God? What about the 4 Beasts around the Throne of God in Revelation 4? They are also a type of chimera. It would seem that God does have some sort of spiritual chimera beings. In the case of the spiritual chimeras, perhaps they are not limited in their form and can change shape at will as the angels of God and indeed Fallen angels can according to the **1st Book of Enoch**.

C.3 CROCODILE GOD OF THE EGYPTIANS: Sobek is the Egyptian crocodile god of strength and of pharaonic power.

In the divine Egyptian pantheon, the strength of this enormous crocodile quickly led him to the position of head of the Egyptian armies, making him the protector of the divine Egyptian pharaoh Osiris and the Egyptian people.

Some Egyptian legends said that Sobek was born at the very creation of the world, at the same time as the Sun god Ra, to whom he served as a relentless bodyguard when Ra tried to create human life.

Sobek was represented as either a giant crocodile or as a man with a muscular human body and a crocodile head. Sobek often wears a crown that Ra gave him after he had achieved many military feats.

This crown, called the "**Crown of Hemhem**" consists of a **Sun** disk decorated with feathers of Benu (the Egyptian **phoenix** bird) resting on a base of ram's horns. The ram horns are themselves decorated with the symbols of the cobra uraeus (the cobra that is always present on the headdresses of the gods of Egypt). SOURCE: Sobek, the Crocodile God | Egyptian History (egyptian-history.com)

> 2 The giver of light comes to give brightness to the whole world, and the morning guard takes shape, which is the rays of the sun, and the sun of the earth goes out, and receives its brightness to light up the whole face of the earth, and they showed me this calculation of the sun's going.
>
> 3 And the gates which it enters, these are the great gates of the **computation** of the hours of the year; for this reason the sun is a great creation, whose circuit lasts twenty-eight years, and begins again from the beginning.

C.4 [computation = modern word. This word seems out of place I the text]

CHAPTER 16

> THOSE men showed me the other course, that of the moon, twelve great gates, crowned from west to east, by which the moon goes in and out of the customary times.

C.1 'Twelve great gates crowned from East to West' – This would appear to be talking about the 12 Constellations which pass around the earth every year, and which give rise to the Zodiac. In the Book of Genesis, it states that God created the stars for 'signs and seasons'.

Genesis 1.14 And God said, 'Let there be lights in the firmament of the heaven to divide the day from the night; and let them be for **signs**, and for **seasons**, and for **days**, and **years**'.

C.2 It would appear that there is a lot of truth in the science of Astrology, which used to be part of Astronomy until recent modern times. Why was Astronomy separated from Astrology? Simply put, because modern man does not want to believe in God, and so anything that proves that God exists has been taken away from science such as the Zodiac of Star Signs - which show clearly that God created each person with a sun sign at birth and with the rising of the moon and the influence of the constellations.

C.3 The stars influence what type of a person the individual will be and determined by the location and exact time of birth. This way God has an automatic system of planets and stars as well as the sun and the moon and the earth itself that all work together like the great workings of a gigantic mechanism or clock which tells us the 'times and season' as mentioned clearly in the Book of Genesis.

C.4 It is so clear that some people are born under each of the 12 Star signs and that the characteristics assigned to that star sign in the Zodiac books of Astrology are correct with the basics. I myself am a Leo, and I act like one. My wife is a Pisces, and she also is like her star sign describes her. All our children are largely like the star signs under which they were born.

C.5 God's Creation with the constellations and stars and sun and moon are a very amazing way of giving lots of variety to humans. Humans are not some random mistake of evolution as taught by science (falsely called -1 Timothy 6.20)

C.6 It would appear that God Himself is stressing to Enoch the importance of the stars and their influences and that they have 'guardian angels' to look after them to make sure nothing goes wrong with their orbits and that everything stays constant.

C.7 In spite of the hateful and vengeful Satan and his fallen angels he has not been able to destroy the earth and the moon and the sun and the stars and constellations during the 6000 years of physical Creation. Why? Because powerful beings are watching over all of God's Creation. Powerful archangels and other creatures as mentioned in this 2nd Book of Enoch chapter 12.

> 2 It goes in at the first gate to the western places of the sun, by the first gates with thirty-one days exactly, by the second gates with *thirty*-one *days* exactly, by the third with thirty days exactly, by the fourth with thirty days exactly, by the fifth with thirty-one days exactly, by the sixth with thirty-one days exactly, by the seventh with thirty days exactly, by the eighth with thirty-one days perfectly, by the ninth with thirty-one days exactly, by the tenth with thirty days perfectly, by the eleventh with thirty-one days exactly, by the twelfth with twenty-eight days exactly.

C.8 Have the days been altered to suit modern science by altering time sequence of the number of the days in the year. Where did we get such an odd number of 365 1/4 days in the year. The ancients always taught that there were 360 days in the year like the number of degrees in a circle which would make a lot more sense. The number 360 is an absolute constant which shows up in creation a lot of the time along with π and the number 7 or God's number.

C.9 Modern science, in order to prove that God does not exist (just because one cannot see Him) had to get rid of any science that proves the absolute in all topics.

C.10 The joke is on the lies of science falsely so called, because even if science claims that the years is 365 ¼ days in the year. It is still a constant even though we have to add one day to the year on every leap year. It still shows a constant number of days even if they have altered the original number of days just to cause random chaos.

C.11 There is clearly so many miracles in the whole Creation all around us that the Bible states that only a fool does not believe in God, as His presence is made known to all.

Romans 1.20 For the invisible things of him from the creation of the world are clearly seen, being understood by the things that are made, *even* his eternal power and Godhead; so that they are without excuse:

> 3 And it goes through the western gates in the order and number of the eastern and accomplishes the three hundred and sixty-five and a quarter days of the solar year while the lunar year has three hundred and fifty-four, and there are wanting *to it* twelve days of the solar circle, which are the lunar epacts of the whole year.
>
> 4 [Thus, too, the great circle contains five hundred and thirty-two years.]
>
> 5 The quarter *of a day* is omitted for three years, the fourth fulfils *it* exactly.

> 6 Therefore they are taken outside of heaven for three years and are not added to the number of days, because they change the time of the years to two new months towards completion, to two others towards diminution.
>
> 7 And when the western gates are finished, it returns and goes to the eastern to the lights, and goes thus day and night about the heavenly circles, lower than all circles, swifter than the heavenly winds, and spirits and elements and angels flying; each angel has six wings.
>
> 8 It has a sevenfold course in nineteen years.

C.12 I would sate that there is a lot that we simply do not understand in the Books of both 1st and 2nd Enoch, as some things are just so mysterious. I think that Enoch was obviously taken up to a higher plain by the power of God's Spirit to see the inner workings of this dimension. Enoch was shown the sun and the moon and their movements or what makes our whole universe tick and I assure you that it is not just gravity.

C.13 There are apparently angels according to the Books of Enoch in charge of all the work and creatures that take care of the sun, moon and stars. I think that it is incredible that the whole universe still functions so well, when you have reprobate Fallen angels on the loose trying to destroy God's Creation.

C.14 I think that the Fallen angels used to have more freedom to do strange things out in the Solar system and perhaps on other star systems like Orion' Belt and other places. Satan and his fallen angels are being more and more confined in their abilities and that is why they are here on the earth causing us a lot of trouble right now, as they are now mostly confined to the 2nd heaven or the earth's atmosphere and the inner earth world as well as the lower dimensions contained within it.

C.15 The Fallen angels can masquerade as aliens with UFO's as much as they want, and pretend that they are a superior species from far away, who have come to lord it over mankind, and solve his pressing problems, but the truth be known they are soon to get locked up in the Bottomless Pit according of Revelation chapter 20 - for being a bunch or arrogant and murderous liars.

Revelation 20.1-3

2 And I saw an angel come down from heaven having the key of the Bottomless Pit and a great chain in his hand. And he laid hold on the dragon, that old serpent, which is the Devil, and Satan, and bound him a thousand years. And cast him into the bottomless pit, and shut him up, and set a seal upon him, that he should deceive the nations no more, till the thousand years should be fulfilled: and after that he must be loosed a little season.

CHAPTER 17

> IN the midst of the heavens I saw armed soldiers, serving the Lord, with tympana and organs, with incessant voice, with sweet voice, with sweet and incessant voice and various singing, which it is impossible to describe, and which astonishes every mind, so wonderful and marvellous is the singing of those angels, and I was delighted listening to it.

Luke 2:13-14 13 And suddenly there was with the angel a multitude of the heavenly host praising God, and saying, 14 Glory to God in the highest, and on earth peace, good will toward men.

Job 38.7 When the morning stars sang together, and all the sons of God shouted for joy?

Zephaniah 3.17 "The LORD thy God in the midst of thee *is* mighty; he will save, he will rejoice over thee with joy; he will rest in his love, he will joy over thee with singing."

Revelation 5.13 And every creature which is in heaven, and on the earth, and under the earth, and such as are in the sea, and all that are in them, heard I say, Blessing, and honour, and glory, and power, *be* unto him that sits upon the throne, and unto the Lamb for ever and ever.

C.1 Songs of praise drive away evil spirits. If the angels are singing incessantly in a certain location, then the evil spirits such as devils and demons would not be able to get close to the areas where the angels are singing, whether it be near the sun or the moon or other locations in the universe.

C.2 A new detail which someone just sent me was explaining how starting with the Nazi's, musical sounds were altered in frequency of Hertz. All of nature is tuned into 432 Hertz. This frequency is biological sound to the human brain and in fact to all of Creation.

The satanists decided to change sounds to 440 Hertz starting with the note A . Apparently, the fruit of this change has brought disharmony and disease, discord and confusion, causing people to no longer be in tune with God's Creation.

Sounds on 432 Hz AND 528 Hz have a healing effect on the human brain and in fact the whole body.

It would seem that we need to re-tune all of our instruments to the frequency that has a healing effect on the human brain. See: 432 Hz(A just above middle C) and 528 Hz (equals C - one octave above middle C)

Explained: The Most Powerful Frequencies in The Universe: 432 Hz and 528 Hz Explained: The Most Powerful Frequencies in The Universe (youtube.com)

C.3 It is amazing how so many things in nature have been deliberately altered during the past 100 years to suit a diabolic agenda of Nazis, Communists, Globalists and their ilk. Like Satan they hate mankind, God and Creation are now well on their way to trying to destroy mankind.

C.4 Look how today the media talk about WWIII inevitably coming etc. The main media are full of satanic poison and constant fear mongering. They all leave God out of the picture and one of these days they will have to reckon with God Himself and that will be their total downfall according to the Book of Revelation.

CHAPTER 18

> THE men took me on to the fifth heaven and placed me, and there I saw many and countless soldiers, called Grigori, of human appearance, and their size was greater than that of great giants and their faces withered, and the silence of their mouths perpetual, and there was no service on the fifth heaven, and I said to the men who were with me:

C.1 This is very interesting, as I often wondered why the Fallen angels begat great giants when mating with normal sized human women. The angels are shape-shifters according to 1 Enoch, and some people have seen angels of very great height. Perhaps they appeared to women on earth as around 7 feet tall, but that was not the full extent of their potential height. However, when they mated with human woman this height characteristic came from the angel's genes and was thus manifested in the physical realm in the form of their progeny with human women being massive giants.

C.2 In this chapter we are told that these angels now looked human but of very great stature. It would seem that these former Fallen angels and even Satan himself have been reduced to being human looking but in giant form and that their wings have been clipped. Maybe it all means that they are now on probation until they prove themselves as they have clearly lost all of their supernatural powers and are just a shadow of their former glory and power.

C.3 By this stage in time or after the 'Lake of Fire' Judgement as mentioned in Revelation 20, all evil has been destroyed and the choice to do evil is no longer available as there is no evil anymore.

> 2 Wherefore are these very withered and their faces melancholy, and their mouths silent, and *wherefore* is there no service on this heaven? [heaven = dimension]

Psalm 102.6 I am like a mournful vulture of the wilderness; I am like a desolate owl of the wasteland.

Psalm 102.14 For Your servants find [**melancholy**] pleasure in the stones [of her ruins] And feel pity for her dust. [Talking about the ruin of Zion]

> 3 And they said to me: These are the Grigori, who with their prince Satanail (Satan) rejected the Lord of light, and after them are those who are held in great darkness on the second heaven, and ***three** of them went down on to earth from the Lord's throne, to the place Ermon, and broke through their vows on the shoulder of the hill Ermon (Hermon) and saw the daughters of men how good they are, and took to themselves wives, and befouled the earth with their deeds, who in all times

> of their age made lawlessness and mixing, and giants are born and marvellous big men and great enmity.

C.4 Maybe the mention of 3 angels departing from the presence of God really means 1/3 of the angels of God fell as shown in the book of Revelation chapter 12.

C.5 Ermon = Hermon which just north of the Tribe of Dan's territory in Old Testament times.

Revelation 12.3-5 - And there appeared another wonder in heaven; and behold a great **red dragon (Satan)**, having seven heads and ten horns, and seven crowns upon his heads. And his tail drew the **third part of the stars of heaven**, and did cast them to the earth: and the **dragon** stood before the woman which was ready to be delivered, for to **devour her child** as soon as it was born. And she brought forth a man child, who was to rule all nations with a rod of iron: and her child was caught up unto God, and to his throne. .

C.6 According to the 1st Book of Enoch initially or in the early days after Creation only 200 angels fell from grace around the year 500 AC, or from the Presence of God, in the days of Jared the father of Enoch. They were bound in the earth later in time, and well before the Great Flood circa 1000 AC or in the early days of Noah.

C.7 Between 500 AC (Years After Creation) and the Great Flood in 1658 AC millions of angels fell away from God and His light or mostly in the 500 years leading up to the Great Flood.

C.8 This really messed up the earth as these angels did Lucifer's bidding by following his rotten example, as set by Satan's escapades in the Garden of Eden.

C.9 Many believe that Satan did much more than just tempt Eve with an apple. Thus, the Fallen angels also lusted after the human women on the earth some hundreds of years later and many angels fell from heaven.

C.10 The big question is 'Who was tempting who? Were the women tempting the angels with their beauty or was it the beauty and strength of the angels tempting the women to abandon their human husbands and run off - to cohabitate with the fallen angels and thus they became known as the sirens according to the 1st Book of Enoch. The resultant progeny of the women and angels became the infamous giants of old. [**SEE MY BOOK ENOCH INSIGHTS**]

C.11 Who is the Lord of light but Jesus the Creator of this physical universe being the Word of God

John 1.1-3 In the beginning was the Word and the Word was with God and the Word was God. All things were made by Him and without Him was not anything made that was made. The same was in the beginning with God. In Him was life and the life was the light of the world.

C.12 WHO ARE THE GRIGORI? Second Book of Enoch

For the masculine given name, see Grigory.

The Jewish pseudepigraphon Second Book of Enoch (*Slavonic Enoch*) refers to the *Grigori*, who are the same as the Watchers of 1 Enoch. The Slavic word *Grigori* used in the book is a transcription of the Greek word ἐγρήγοροι *egrḗgoroi*, meaning "wakeful". The Hebrew equivalent is עירם, meaning "waking", "awake".

C.13 The Jewish pseudepigraphon Second Book of Enoch: All this word 'pseudepigraphal' means is that another writer took an old manuscript of the Book of "2nd Enoch and had it re-written or translated into Greek from the original Hebrew around 100-300 BC because the Library in Alexandria, which was the most prestigious library of the Grecian Empire at the time, and the largest library in the world would pay lots of money for copies of old documents and in act the older the document the more money was paid out.

SEE MY VIDEO ON THE LIBRARY AT ALEXANDRIA: (702) 'INSIGHTS BOOKS' by S N Strutt: ALEXANDRIAN LIBRARY, THE SEPTUAGUINT & THE APOCRYPHA BOOKS - YouTube

C.14 Modern ungodly education tries to explain away amazing visions and prophecies by amazing writers like Enoch and Ezra by saying that the books of Enoch and Ezra and others were written by someone else at a later date or a pseudepigraphic writer as they call them. It is odd that they can't even name who the so-called pseudepigraphic writers are?

Modern education also like to make up fancy words that the average person does not understand like 'The Jewish 'pseudepigraphon'.

When investigating this topic of 'pseudepigraphic' writers one finds that this is simply not the case.

The ancient books of old time were indeed written by the ancients and not by a modern sceptical writer, who does not have God's wisdom anyway. Why is it that modern science denies the Bible and the prophets and is always trying to re-write it to fit their narrative of Evolution. Why? Satan has always been trying to stamp out the truth of the word of God.

Communist China is presently re-writing the Bible. It's like the dystopian narrative of the Book 1984 by George Orwell.

C.15: 2 ENOCH Chapter 18 presents the Grigori as countless soldiers of human appearance, "their size being greater than that of great giants". They are located in the fifth heaven and identified as "the Grigori, who with their prince Satanail rejected the Lord of light". One version of 2 Enoch adds that their number was 200 myriads (2 million). Furthermore, some «went down on to earth from the Lord›s throne» and there married women and «befouled the earth with their deeds", resulting in confinement underground. The number of those who descended to earth is generally put at three, but Andrei A. Orlov, while quoting the text as saying three, remarks in a footnote that some manuscripts put them at 200 or even 200 myriads.

C.16 2 ENOCH Chapter 29 is referring to the second day of creation, before the creation of human beings, and it states that "one from out the order of angels" or, according to other versions of 2 Enoch, "one of the order of archangels" or "one of the ranks of the archangels" "conceived an impossible thought, to place his throne higher than the clouds above the earth, that he might become equal in rank to [the Lord's] power. And [the Lord] threw him out from the height with his angels, and he was flying in the air continuously above the bottomless." Although in this chapter the name "Satanail" is mentioned only in a heading added in one manuscript, this chapter too is often understood to refer to Satanail and his angels, the Grigori.

The *Mercer Dictionary of the Bible* makes a distinction between the Grigori and the fallen angels by stating that in fifth heaven, Enoch sees «the giants whose brothers were the fallen angels.»[30]

The longer recension of 2 Enoch 18:3 identifies the prisoners of second heaven as the angels of Satanail.[31]

SOURCE: Watcher (angel) - Wikipedia

C.17 "the giants whose brothers were the fallen angels." This is an inaccurate statement. The Fallen angels were the fathers, the human women the mothers who became known as the sirens, and their sons the giants. The giants had some of the angelic characteristics of their fathers but only some of those qualities. They were not eternal beings like the angels as God had not created them.

C.18 It is very interesting that in this 18th chapter of the 2nd Book of Enoch that the Fallen angels described are all moth-eaten or not what they were and have lost their powers and melancholy and somehow diminished, and yet it states that they are now looking like giant humans who are bigger that the old Giants were. Well, that is what they look like after their punishment of having been in the Lake of Fire. That is easy to explain as they were the original fathers and creators of the Pre-Flood giants.

> 4 And therefore God judged them with great judgement, and they weep for their brethren and they will be punished on the Lord's great day.
>
> 5 And I said to the Grigori: 'I saw your brethren and their works, and their great torments, and I prayed for them, but the Lord has **condemned them *to be* under earth** till heaven and earth shall end for ever.'
>
> 6 And I said: 'Wherefore do you wait, brethren, and do not serve before the Lord's face, and have not put your services before the Lord's face, lest you anger your Lord utterly?'
>
> 7 And they listened to my admonition, and spoke to the four ranks in heaven, and lo! as I stood with those two men four trumpets trumpeted together with great voice, and the Grigori broke into song with one voice, and their voice went up before the Lord pitifully and affectingly.

C.19 The only way back to God for Satan and the Fallen angels was to praise Him, like all the rest of His Creation does. Wow! It sure took these evil entities a very long time to learn their lesson – more than 7000 years. The good news is that one day all evil things will no longer come to mind. All the Evil that has gone on before the eternal Age is ushered in by God Himself will have vanished and be no more. Just wonderful and something to look forward to.

C.20 Unfortunately for Satan, according to the **Book of Isaiah chapter 14,** Satan is to be made an end of or he is to be completely destroyed and probably all the ruling spiritual powers that exist today and who rule the world through their puppets on the earth insane demon-possessed leaders and controllers of the earth in finance and politics. [See chapter 29 of this my book for a lot more details on this topic]

Isaiah 14.19 All they that know thee among the people shall be astonished at thee: thou shalt be a **terror**, and **never** *shalt* thou *be* **any more.**

C.21 God's fallen Creation will finally be restored to perfection once more in the Eternal Age.

C.22 What will people be doing in the Eternal Age? The way it should have been at the time of Creation but unfortunately collapsed into chaos due to evil. Therefore, for the Eternal age there will be no more evil or even the choice to do evil.

C.23 I think that the peoples of the world will be learning to create like their Creator and using all the talents that He has given them to the full as many people in this life at present are prevented from fully realizing their talents, gifts and abilities for many reasons. God is our Father, and we are His children, and we will all be very happy together in the far future. There are many Bible verses on this topic. Good will triumph in the End.

Isaiah 65. For behold I create a new heavens and a new earth and the former shall not be remembered nor come to mind.

Isaiah 2.4 And he shall judge among the nations, and shall rebuke many people: and they shall beat their swords into plowshares, and their spears into pruninghooks: nation shall not lift up sword against nation, neither shall they learn war any more.

Hosea 2.18 And in that day will I make a covenant for them with the beasts of the field, and with the fowls of heaven, and *with* the creeping things of the ground: and I will break the bow and the sword and the battle (war) out of the earth, and will make them to lie down safely.

See Universal Reconciliation Audio On My Youtube Channel About This Chapter 18 Of The 2nd Book Of Enoch: UNIVERSAL RECONCILIATION: 2 ENOCH CH 18: THE FALLEN ANGELS FINALLY REPENT AFTER THE LAKE OF FIRE! - YouTube

***** SEE ALSO MY BOOKS 'ENOCH INSIGHTS' AND 'EDEN INSIGHTS' ON MY WEBSITE: www.insightspublication.com**

CHAPTER 19

> AND thence those men took me and bore me up on to the sixth heaven, and there I saw seven bands of angels, very bright and very glorious, and their faces shining more than the sun's shining, glistening, and there is no difference in their faces, or behaviour, or manner of dress; and these make the orders, and learn the goings of the stars, and the alteration of the moon, or revolution of the sun, and the good government of the world.

C.1 These angels seem to be 'in charge of' the moon and the sun and stars. This could explain why Satan and his fallen angels have not been able to destroy God's larger Creation since the beginning of time. Why? Because there are powerful angels of God who take care of the entire universe. So, this random idea of Evolution of modern science is absolute nonsense. The truth is that everything is under God's perfect control and in the control of His faithful and loyal angels and creatures as mentioned earlier the Chalkydri and Phoenixes mentioned in Chapter 15. They apparently have something to do with the sun itself.

> 2 And when they see evil doing they make commandments and instruction, and sweet and loud singing, and all *songs* of praise.

> 3 These are the archangels who are above angels, measure all life in heaven and on earth, and the angels who are *appointed* over seasons and years, the angels who are over rivers and sea, and who are over the fruits of the earth, and the angels who are over every grass, giving food to all, to every living thing, and the angels who write all the souls of men, and all their deeds, and their lives before the Lord›s face; in their midst are six Phoenixes and six Cherubim and six six-winged ones continually with one voice singing one voice, and it is not possible to describe their singing, and they rejoice before the Lord at his footstool.

C.2 Have you ever wondered why God created all of his wonderful creatures and so many different types? It is because God is Love and he loves each one of us very much and He has created all things for His pleasure the Bible states, and the least we can all do as His creatures is to love and worship Him in return out of thankfulness and appreciation for His Love and for us His Creation. This is why these amazing creatures mentioned here in this chapter are singing with great joy unto their Creator. They are joyous to exist and so should we be. Singing and praising the Lord is the best way to stay victorious in spirit. Or, as has been said, 'Singing is the highest form of praise unto God':-

Psalms 150:1 - Praise ye the LORD. Praise God in his sanctuary: praise him in the firmament of his power.

Psalms 95:1-11 - O come, let us sing unto the LORD: let us make a joyful noise to the rock of our salvation.

James 5:13 - Is any among you afflicted? Let him pray. Is any merry? let him sing psalms.

Psalms 115:1 - Not unto us, O LORD, not unto us, but unto thy name give glory, for thy mercy, and for thy truth›s sake.

Psalms 24:8 - Who is this King of glory? The LORD strong and mighty, the LORD mighty in battle.

Deuteronomy 28:1 - And it shall come to pass, if thou shalt hearken diligently unto the voice of the LORD thy God, to observe and to do all his commandments which I command thee this day, that the LORD thy God will set thee on high above all nations of the earth.

Psalm 22.3 But thou art holy, O thou that inhabits the praises of Israel.

Psalms 144:1 - Blessed be the LORD my strength, which teaches my hands to war, and my fingers to fight:

CHAPTER 20

> AND those two men lifted me up thence on to the seventh Heaven, and I saw there a very great light, and fiery troops of great archangels, incorporeal forces, and dominions, orders and governments, cherubim and seraphim, thrones and many-eyed ones, nine regiments, the Ioanit stations of light, and I became afraid, and began to tremble with great terror, and those men took me, and led me after them, and said to me:

C.1 Seventh Heaven – officially according to scriptures the 7th Heaven is where the Lord dwells, but in this 2nd Book of Enoch it makes out as it there are 10 heavens or levels in the spirit world.

C.2 Very great light – Is this talking about God the Father or God the Son which is all on the 10th level and Enoch can see above him three levels higher up than where he was on the 7th level? Now that is a very good question. Sometimes in scripture it is difficult to know which of these two it is talking about. Scriptures also tell us that these three God the Father and God the Son and God the Holy Spirit Mother all agree in One. They are all creatures of intense light and love. God is Love – 1 John

C.3 Fiery troops of great archangels -The 1st Book of Enoch tells us that Enoch saw fiery angels and that they were dancing of fire. This 2nd Book of Enoch tells us in the early chapters that God created the angels out of fire. Not physical fire but some kind of spiritual fire.

C.4 Incorporeal forces -This means forces or armies, but they have no definite form, or they are ghost - like in appearance.

C.5 Dominions - Those who rule over others forces below them in rank – A very high rank which is above the governments.

C.6 Orders or Powers – The spirit or angels behind a particular country on earth (in modern terms).

C.7 Governments – The spirit behind the existing government of a particular country in particular.

C.8 Many-eyed ones - nine regiments of angels

C.9 Ioanit stations of light - The "Ioanit stations" - from Greek - would then be "the stations of God's favored."

C.10 According to Christian Angelology, Angels are divided into three types and nine orders –

First Sphere: Seraphim (Burning), Cherubim (Streams of Wisdom), and Thrones.

Second Sphere: **Dominions** (Lordships), **Virtues** (Strongholds), and **Powers** (Authorities)

Virtues: These angels are responsible for maintaining the natural order and harmony in the universe. They are the fifth ranking order of angels. The

Virtues are a type of angels that rule over miracles, blessings, grace, valour, and encouragement. Known as Brilliant or Shining Ones, they mainly help people struggling with their faith.

Third Sphere: Principalities, Archangels, and Guardian Angels.

1. Angels: These celestial beings serve as messengers and intermediaries between God and humans.

2. Archangels: They hold a higher rank than regular angels and are often associated with significant divine messages or events.

3. Powers: They have authority over evil forces and protect against spiritual threats.

4. Principalities: Principalities oversee nations, cities, and other large groups, ensuring divine guidance.

5. Dominations: These angels regulate the duties of lower angels and maintain cosmic order.

6. Thrones: Thrones represent God's justice and authority, serving as His divine chariots. They are the third-ranking order of angels that reside over the cosmos, especially where the material starts to take form Often called the Many-Eyed Ones, they are portrayed as colossal wheels comprising many eyes and sparkle with the color of burnished brass. They are also correlated with the Cherubim Angels.

7. Cherubim: Cherubim guard sacred spaces and symbolize wisdom and knowledge. – They also are known as the Many-Eyed Ones

8. Seraphim: The highest order, Seraphim are closest to God, embodying intense love and devotion.

Isaiah 6.1-2 "In the year that king Uzziah died I saw also the LORD sitting upon a throne, high and lifted up, and his train filled the temple. Above it stood the seraphim: each one had six wings; with twain, he covered his face, and with twain, he covered his feet, and with twain, he did fly."

> 2 'Have courage, Enoch, do not fear,' and showed me the Lord from afar, sitting on His very high throne. For what is there on the <u>tenth heaven</u>, since the Lord dwells here?
>
> 3 On the tenth heaven is God, in the Hebrew tongue he is called Aravat.

C.9 Aravat (or Avarat) - meaning – **"Father of Creation"**; mentioned once in 2 Enoch, «On the tenth heaven is God, in the Hebrew tongue he is called Aravat". –'Our Father, Our King'.

> 4 And all the heavenly troops would come and stand on the ten steps according to their rank, and would bow down to the Lord, and would again go to their places in joy and felicity, singing songs in the boundless light with small and tender voices, gloriously serving him.

C.10 There are apparently 10 steps before the Lord's Throne where the different levels of angels, incorporate beings, and powers stand before God and worship Him. Then God fills them with the power of His Holy Spirit and blessings of joy and happiness. It sounds like the Holy Spirit Mother is there also pouring out her blessings upon the angels.

C.11 From my own experience, research and investigation, I would have to testify that the Virtues that I have seen and heard about, were female beings, and they bring the fruits of Holy Spirit Mother with them. I don't know if they are all female and that remains to be identified.. See my videos on YOUTUBE: @stephenstrutt 'HOLY SPIRIT MOTHER' FROM ''SECRETS OF ENOCH' - INSIGHTS'' TO BE PUBLISHED SOON - by S N Strutt (youtube.com)

Proverbs 9.3 "She hath sent forth her maidens: she cries upon the highest places of the city,"

Galatians 5.22-23 But the fruit of the Spirit is love, joy, peace, longsuffering, gentleness, goodness, faith, meekness, temperance: against such there is no law.

HOLY SPIRIT MOTHER, THE WIFE OF GOD THE FATHER: The following verses from Proverbs, chapter three, helps to bring this point forward. The Holy Spirit Mother is also known as **WISDOM** in Hebrew:-

Proverbs 3:15-19 - "She is more precious than rubies: and all the things thou canst desire are not to be compared unto her. Length of days is in her right hand; and in her left hand riches and honour. Her ways are ways of pleasantness, and all her paths are peace. She is a tree of life to them that lay hold upon her: and happy is every one that retains her. The Lord by Wisdom hath founded the earth; by understanding hath he established the heavens."

Since it is written that God created man in His image, male and female, one might ask is there a possibility that the Holy Ghost, the third person of the Trinity is Wisdom. You can decide and see what you think. Below are more verses on Wisdom. Wisdom cries without; she utters her voice in the streets: She cries in the chief place of concourse, in the openings of the gates: in the city she utters her words.

Proverbs 1:20-21 So that thou incline thine ear unto wisdom, and apply thine heart to understanding; Yea, if thou cry after knowledge, and lift up thy voice for understanding; If thou seek her as silver, and search for her as for hid treasures,

Proverbs 2:2-4 Get wisdom, get understanding: forget it not; neither decline from the words of my mouth. Forsake her not, and she shall preserve thee: love her, and she shall keep thee. Wisdom is the principal thing; therefore, get wisdom: and with all thy getting get understanding. Exalt her, and she shall promote thee: she shall bring thee to honour, when thou dost embrace her. She shall give to thine head an ornament of grace: a crown of glory shall she deliver to thee.

Proverbs 4:5-9 Say unto Wisdom, 'Thou art my sister'; and call understanding thy kinswoman:

Proverbs 7:4 Doth not wisdom cry? and understanding put forth her voice? She stands in the top of high places, by the way in the places of the paths. She cries at the gates, at the entry of the city, at the coming in at the doors.

Proverbs 8:1-3 Before the mountains were settled, before the hills was I brought forth: While as yet he had not made the earth, nor the fields, nor the highest part of the dust of the world. When he prepared the heavens, I was there: when he set a compass upon the face of the depth: When he established the clouds above: when he strengthened the fountains of the deep: When he gave to the sea his decree, that the waters should not pass his commandment: when he appointed the foundations of the earth: Then I was by him, as one brought up with him: and I was daily his delight, rejoicing always before him.

Proverbs 8:25-30 Wisdom hath built her house, she hath hewn out her seven pillars: She hath killed her beasts; she hath mingled her wine; she hath also furnished her table. She hath sent forth her maidens: she cries upon the highest places of the city.

C.12 As God the Father is masculine and His wife the Holy Spirit Mother is feminine it is very obvious that all of creation is both masculine and feminine in nature. This means that of course there are female angels. The spirit world is a balance between male and female beings.

C.13 I have reported to others before that I personally have seen a female angel on 4 different occasion and believe her to be a guardian angel. See my video about this on YOUTUBE:

CHAPTER 21

> AND the **cherubim** and **seraphim** standing about the throne, the six-winged and '**many-eyed ones**' do not depart, standing before the Lord's face doing his will, and cover his whole throne, singing with gentle voice before the Lord's face: **'Holy, holy, holy**, Lord Ruler *of* Sabaoth, heavens and earth are full of Thy glory.›

C.1 'MANY-EYED ONES'?

Revelation 4.6-8 And before the throne *there was* a sea of glass like unto crystal: and in the midst of the throne, and round about the throne, *were* four beasts **full of eyes** before and behind.

And the first beast *was* like a lion, and the second beast like a calf, and the third beast had a face as a man, and the fourth beast *was* like a flying eagle.

And the four living creatures **(Cherubim)**, each one of them having six wings, are full of eyes around and within; and day and night they do not cease to say, "**Holy, holy, holy** is the Lord God, the Almighty, who was and who is and who is to come."

CHERUBIM

1 Samuel 4.4 So the people sent to Shiloh, and from there they carried the ark of the covenant of the Lord of hosts who sits above the **cherubim**; and the two sons of Eli, Hophni and Phinehas, were there with the ark of the covenant of God.

2 Samuel 6:2

And David arose and went with all the people who were with him to Baale-Judah, to bring up from there the ark of God which is called by the Name, the very name of the Lord of hosts who is enthroned above the **cherubim**.

Isaiah 37:16

"O Lord of hosts, the God of Israel, who is enthroned above the **cherubim**, You are the God, You alone, of all the kingdoms of the earth. You have made heaven and earth".

Psalm 80:1 For the choir director set to El Shoshannin, Eduth. A psalm of Asaph. 'Oh give ear O shepherd of Israel. You who lead Joseph like a flock. You who are enthroned above the **Cherubim** shine forth.

Psalm 99:1 The Lord reigns. Let the peoples tremble. He is enthroned above the **Cherubim**, le the earth shake!

SERAPHIM

Isaiah 6.2 Seraphim stood above Him, each having six wings: with two he covered his face, and with two he covered his feet, and with two he flew. And one called out to another and said, **"Holy, Holy, Holy**, is the Lord of Hosts, The whole earth is full of His glory."

Isaiah 6.6-7 Then one of the **Seraphim** flew to me with a burning coal in his hand, which he had taken from the altar with tongs. He touched my mouth with it and said, "Behold, this has touched your lips; and your iniquity is taken away and your sin is forgiven."

2 When I saw all these things, those men (angels) said to me: 'Enoch, thus far is it commanded us to journey with thee,' and those men went away from me and thereupon I saw them not.

3 And I remained alone at the end of the seventh heaven and became afraid, and fell on my face and said to myself: 'Woe is me, what has befallen me?'

4 And the Lord sent one of his glorious ones, the archangel Gabriel, and *he* said to me: ‹Have courage, Enoch, do not fear, arise before the Lord›s face into eternity, arise, come with me.›

5 And I answered him, and said in myself: 'My Lord, my soul is departed from me, from terror and trembling, and I called to the men who led me up to this place, on them I relied, and *it is* with them I go before (thy) the Lord's face.'

6 And Gabriel caught me up, as a leaf caught up by the wind, and placed me before the Lord's face.

7 And I saw the eighth Heaven, which is called in the Hebrew tongue Muzaloth, changer of the seasons, of drought, and of wet, and of the twelve signs of the zodiac, which are above the seventh Heaven.

8 And I saw the ninth Heaven, which is called in **Hebrew Kuchavim**, where are the **heavenly homes** of the **twelve signs of the zodiac**.

CHAPTER 22

> ON the tenth Heaven, Aravoth, I saw the appearance of the Lord's face, like iron made to glow in fire, and brought out, emitting sparks, and it burns.

Revelation 1.13-16 And in the midst of the seven candlesticks *one* like unto the **Son of man**, clothed with a garment down to the foot, and girt about the paps with a golden girdle. His head and his hairs were white as snow; and his **eyes** were as a **flame of fire**: And his feet like unto fine brass, as if they burned in a furnace; and his voice as the sound of many waters. And he had in his right hand seven stars: and out of his mouth went a sharp two-edged sword: and his countenance *was* as the sun shineth in his strength.

C.1 What is the tenth heaven? Definition: **ARAVOTH** -The tenth and final heaven is where God's throne resides and God's face may be seen up close.

C.2 The seventh heaven, is the holiest of the seven heavens because it houses the Throne of God attended by the Seven Archangels and serves as the realm in which God dwells; underneath the throne itself lies the abode of all unborn human souls.

C.3 The eighth heaven is described as that above the first 7 heavens which leads to the Throne of God and the highest levels of Heaven.

C.4 The ninth heaven is the upper firmament in which are fixed the constellations and the changer of the seasons.

C.5 If there are the 8th, 9th, 10th levels when traditionally there are only supposed to be 7 levels. Then what are the last 3 levels for? Afterall if we already have God's Throne and the Cherubim and his 7 top archangels mentioned as being on the 7th level, what could be above the Throne of God? On the surface it would seem unlikely that anything could be above God's Throne. However, consider the following: There have been perhaps a total of 20 billion souls born on the earth throughout all time, so far. What does this text in 2nd Enoch say about the tenth level? - **ARAVOTH** -The tenth and final heaven is where God's throne resides, and God's face may be seen up close. I think that the tenth level is for those who want to see God 'face to face' and not have to visit Him on the more formal setting of the whole entourage of angels and the 4 Beasts but just to see and talk to God Himself face to face.

C.6 I am just theorizing here of course, but perhaps many people would feel out of place coming into the Throne of God and seeing all the magnificence of His entire heavenly entourage and might just want to be alone with God Himself or talk with Him and in many cases something even more important – get a personal message from God to take back for those on earth, like all the prophets of old.

I could imagine that since there have been so many souls created through time, that indeed, it might take some extra levels in heaven for God personally to sort out billions of problems and to reassure so many people in their myriad of situations back down on the earth. God is not limited by time or space.

There must be millions of people praying to God every day, so where does God have the time and space to deal with each individual when He also has to run the universe? Just a suggestion, that the very highest levels of heaven are for God's communications systems, where God's computers are, so that all prayers can be answered quickly and efficiently. Or at least the requests received, and recorded, until God decides to answer that particular prayer in His perfect time.

C.7 So, it could be possible that the highest levels of Heaven are communication levels and levels to record information about all peoples on the earth. God's communication and records departments. Afterall is it not written – 'of every idle word every man must give an account', so it must all be recorded somewhere.

C.8 So, someone is recording every idle word that a man shall speak, every attitude towards God good and bad. Perhaps a lot of that happens on the higher levels of heaven and is recorded on very advanced heavenly computers. God certainly has to have some levels of heaven to deal with an on-going multitude of possibly trillions of communications/day on a daily basis.

C.9 When people are asleep, they are often much more receptive to spiritual things and are likely to reach up to God and ask Him questions. I am convinced that sleep time is a spiritual time good and bad and also a time for deeper communications with heaven. You just don't remember it when you wake up!.

However, your dreams do affect your daily life. There are billions of people on the planet. Many communicate with God every day and even more communicate during their sleep. So where is all of those communications kept and recorded?

Believe it or not many people who say they are undecided in their belief in God do communicate with God in their sleep but just don't remember once they wake up.. Now, that is a whole topic in itself.

C.10 Doctors tell us that without our dreams we would die! Why is that? Are dreams an essential communication system with God Himself?

> 2 Thus I saw the Lord's face, but the Lord's face is ineffable, marvellous and very awful, and very, very terrible.

Psalm 66.3-5 Say unto God, 'How terrible art thou in thy works! through the greatness of thy power shall thine enemies submit themselves unto thee. All the earth shall worship thee and shall sing unto thee; they shall sing to thy name. Selah. Come and see the works of God: he is terrible in his doing toward the children of men.'

> 3 And who am I to tell of the Lord's unspeakable being, and of his very wonderful face? And I cannot tell the quantity of his many instructions, and various voices, the Lord's throne very great and not made

> with hands, nor the quantity of those standing round him, troops of cherubim and seraphim, nor their incessant singing, nor his immutable beauty, and who shall tell of the ineffable greatness of his glory?

Revelation 4.2-5 And immediately I was in the spirit: and behold, a throne was set in heaven, and one sat on the throne. And he that sat was to look upon like a jasper and a sardine stone: and there was a rainbow round about the throne, in sight like unto an emerald. And round about the throne were four and twenty seats: and upon the seats I saw four and twenty elders sitting, clothed in white raiment; and they had on their heads crowns of gold. And out of the throne proceeded lightnings and thunderings and voices: and there were seven lamps of fire burning before the throne, which are the seven Spirits of God.

> 4 And I fell prone and bowed down to the Lord, and the Lord with his lips said to me:
>
> 5 'Have courage, Enoch, do not fear, arise and stand before my face into eternity.'
>
> 6 And the archistratege Michael lifted me up and led me to before the Lord's face.

C.11 From a literal standpoint, "archistratege" appears to be the combination of two ancient Greek words: ἀρχι (archi), which means chief, first, or primary (as in archbishop or archangel); and στρατηγός (strategos) which means general or more literally, army leader. Thus, "archistratege" would mean "First General" or more euphemistically, "Supreme Commander." This title is consistent with Michael's role as leader of Heaven's armies.

DANIEL 12.1 "And at that time shall **Michael** stand up, the **great prince** which stands for the children of thy people: and there shall be a time of trouble, such as never was since there was a nation *even* to that same time: and at that time thy people shall be delivered, every one that shall be found written in the book."

Revelation 12:7-12 And there was war in heaven: **Michael** and his angels fought against the dragon; and the dragon fought and his angels. And prevailed not; neither was their place found any more in heaven.

> 7 And the Lord said to his servants tempting them: 'Let Enoch stand before my face into eternity,' and the glorious ones bowed down to the Lord, and said: 'Let Enoch go according to Thy word.'
>
> 8 And the Lord said to Michael: 'Go and take Enoch from out his earthly garments, and anoint him with my sweet ointment, and put

him into the garments of My glory.'

9 And Michael did thus, as the Lord told him. He anointed me, and dressed me, and the appearance of that ointment is more than the great light, and his ointment is like sweet dew, and its smell mild, shining like the sun's ray, and I looked at myself, and was like one of his glorious ones.

C.12 This is quite staggering as Enoch is being dressed like the Lord Himself. Why would this be? When we consider that we as humans are all eternal beings and those that love Jesus are part of His Bride then it does begin to make sense that Jesus will one day exalt his saints and we shall be close to His side. We were created to become the Bride of Christ.

10 And the Lord summoned one of his archangels by name Pravuil, whose knowledge was quicker in wisdom than the other archangels, who wrote all the deeds of the Lord; and the Lord said to Pravuil:

C.13 WHO IS THE ARCHANGEL PRAVUIL? I don't know how much of the following is accurate but it certain seems interesting:-

'**Pravuil** is an archangel mentioned in the 2nd Book of Enoch who is "quicker in **wisdom** than the other archangels" and writes all the deeds of the Lord.'

C.14 I am not saying that we know for certain who Pravuil is, but as it mentions that Pravuil is wiser than all the angels, it could be the **Holy Spirit Mother**.

In Proverbs it talks about Wisdom personified as a person or entity which is feminine and also as the Holy Spirit in the Old Testament - or the Holy Spirit Mother.

C.15 In the book, God commands Pravuil to get books and a reed of (for) quick-writing for Enoch. Pravuil then tells Enoch to "write all the souls of mankind, however many of them are born, and the places prepared for them to eternity".

11 'Bring out the books from my store-houses and a reed of quick-writing, and give *it* to Enoch, and deliver to him the choice and comforting books out of thy hand.'

CHAPTER 23

> AND he was telling me all the works of heaven, earth and sea, and all the elements, their passages and goings, and the thunderings of the thunders, the sun and moon, the goings and changes of the stars, the seasons, years, days, and hours, the risings of the wind, the numbers of the angels, and the formation of their songs, and all human things, the tongue of every human song and life, the commandments, instructions, and sweet-voiced singings, and all things that it is fitting to learn.
>
> 2 And Pravuil told me: 'All the things that I have told thee, we have written. Sit and write all the souls of mankind, however many of them are born, and the places prepared for them to eternity; for all souls are prepared to eternity, before the formation of the world.'

C.1 Others seem to think that Pravuil was an angel greater in wisdom than all the other archangels, but if that is true, why is Michael known as the chief of the archangels and also the leader of the hosts of heaven. There cannot be an archangel above Michael, so who is Pravuil?

C.2 It would seem that Pravuil is a power above Michael the archangel and the only candidate that would fit the bill is Wisdom herself or the Holy Spirit Mother.

C.3 The big question is if Pravuil was the Holy Spirit Mother, why didn't Enoch mention that Pravuil was female? Well, the answer to that is that since the 3rd to the 4th century AD there has been a big cover-up by the Catholic church of any beings that are feminine.

C.4 They covered up the facts about the Holy Spirit being female and Mother of God. They also covered up the fact that if there are male angels who could have mated with the human women, then there must also be female angels by deduction.

C.5 The Books of Enoch were banned at the council of Laodicea in 365 AD along with all books which stated that the Holy Spirit is female and Mother God.

C.6 Pravuil is an archangel mentioned in the Second Book of Enoch who is «quicker in wisdom than the other archangels» and writes all the deeds of the Lord.

In the book, God commands Pravuil to get books and a reed of (for) quick-writing for Enoch. Pravuil then tells Enoch to "write all the souls of mankind, however many of them are born, and the places prepared for them to enternity". Some scholars have associated Pravuil with the Holy Spirit. The Blessing God Gave Pravuil

We will discuss the promise God gave Pravuil the Holy Ghost SOURCE:

Pravuil (angel) definition and meaning | sensagent editor

C.7 The Catholic church also banned these Books of Enoch for 1000 years on the penalty of being burned at the stake. Why? What were they afraid of? It would seem that the female side of things physical and spiritual has been deliberately erased in the religious and intellectual circles of history.

C.8 Scholars in modern times are becoming aware that the truth has been hidden concerning the Holy Spirit being female. Marianne Widmalm and her book 'Our Mother The Holy Spirit' which came out in 2019 in the USA. Another scholar Ally Kateusz and her book 'Finding Holy Spirit Mother'. These are both excellent books and reveal a lot about the past and how the truth about thee matters was deliberately hidden. The Holy Spirit is also known as Wisdom or Sophia in ancient Greek

Enoch chapter 42.1 Wisdom found no place where she might dwell, then a dwelling place was assigned **her** in the heavens

C.9 Another very important question to ask oneself is: Has information been hidden from us in the history of the world by the historians and governments of this world? The answer is simple as the famous British historian Toynbee stated 'The ones who write history are the so-called victors' – the point being that the victors often change the story of what had happened in the past – so that there is a lot of material that is not 100% accurate. The only way to find the truth in any given topic is to do a lot of research and pray for the guidance of Jesus and the Holy Spirit Mother.

C.10 '**All souls are prepared to eternity** before the formation of the world'. This is clearly stating that people's souls cannot be destroyed, as they are all prepared for eternity.

C.11 Hell and the Lake of Fire. What about the many verses that Jesus spoke about people going to Hell and the Devil into the Lake of Fire with his Fallen angels along with all the wicked judged at the Great White Throne Judgement who are thrown into the Lake of Fire? The wicked shall be turned into Hell and the nations that forget God. 'If they will not obey, I will utterly pluck up and destroy that nation says the Lord.' Not to mention the whole Book of Revelation and the Wrath of God as mentioned in Revelation chapter 16?

C.12 I think that this verse in 2nd Enoch is trying to get the point over that certain of God's Creations are eternal – such as humans and angels. What can be destroyed completely are evil spirits such as devils and demons. Why? Because God did not create them. God does not invent evil. So how were the demons that influence mankind so strongly and in particular the rulers of our planet created ?

C.13 The demons were originally the 'disembodied spirits of the giants', which came back to torment mankind from the netherworld where they abode after the Great Flood according to the Book of Jubilees. The 1st Book of Enoch describes how it all started. The angels of God in heaven were told by God to provoke the giants to fight the one against the other until they were all made an end of. Why? Because there was nothing good in them at all they were 100% evil deceptive and destructive! [**1st Enoch 10.5; 16.1**]

ENOCH 10.5 And Gabriel said to the Lord 'Proceed against the bastards and reprobates, and against the children of fornication, and destroy the children of fornication, the children of the watchers from amongst men and cause them to go forth, 'Send them on against the other that they may destroy each other in battle. For length of days they shall not have.'

C.14 I think it more likely that Enoch 10.5 should read 'The Lord said to Gabriel 'Proceed against the bastards... Why? Because it is God that gives the orders and the angels that carry out His orders.

Enoch 16.1 From the days of the slaughter and destruction and death of the giants from the souls of whose flesh the spirits having gone forth shall destroy without incurring judgment; this they shall destroy until the day of the consummation, the great judgment in which the age shall be consummated over the Watchers and the godless yea , shall be wholly consummated.

C.15 Demons were created when the rebellious Fallen angels cohabitated with human women on the earth in the Pre-Flood times and great giants were born according to the 1st Book of Enoch and Genesis 6 as well as the books of Jasher Chapter 4, Jubilees Chapter 5 and the Lost Books of Adam and Eve. It is also mentioned in the Hebrew Book of The Testaments of the Twelve Patriarchs by many of the Patriarchs themselves.

C.16 After all the giants had killed each other in Pre-Flood times they then became the disembodied spirits of the giants which were bound in the underworld. They can get out of the underworld and onto the physical plane under certain circumstances including through the use of portals which are also mentioned in 1st Enoch or through demon-possession of both humans and animals or more easily through chimeras .

C.17 [SEE MY INSIGHTS BOOKS:- ENOCH INSIGHTS as well as **JASHER INSIGHTS, JUBILEES INSIGHTS, THE TESTAMENT OF THE TWELVE PATRIARCHS INSIGHTS AND EDEN INSIGHTS]**

> 3 And all double thirty days and thirty nights, and I wrote out all things exactly, and wrote three hundred and sixty-six books.

C.18 Wow! So, Enoch wrote a total of 366 Books! Now that is a lot of books. We only have a few of the Books of Enoch available to this day, which is not surprising when we consider that Enoch wrote the books around 5000+ years ago in Pre-Flood times! His books were taken on the Ark by Noah and passed on to his descendants as mentioned by the 12 Patriarchs who mentioned that they had read the Books of Enoch.

C.19 MOTHER GOD -THE FEMALE HOLY SPIRIT- DIVINE FEMININE

MAT.12:31 Wherefore I say unto you, 'All manner of sin and blasphemy shall be forgiven unto men: but the blasphemy against the Holy Ghost shall not be forgiven unto men.'

MAR.3:29-30 But he that shall blaspheme against the Holy Ghost hath never forgiveness, but is in danger of eternal damnation; because they said, He hath an unclean spirit.

LUK.12:10 And whosoever shall speak a word against the Son of man, it shall be forgiven him: but unto him that blasphemes against the Holy Ghost it shall not be forgiven.

C.20: Why did Jesus make a distinction between Himself and the Holy Spirit here? If God and Jesus and the Holy Spirit were all masculine, which is how they are portrayed by most modern churches, then perhaps Jesus would not have made this distinction!

Let me put in simple terms to understand. A man who has a beautiful wife, whom he both loves and adores, and also has a strong son. If perchance another man comes and gives a blow to his son, it is conceivable that the father will make light of it, and forgive the man. However, if the man hits his wife, I guarantee that he would neither forgive him or let him go unpunished. I do think that these above Bible verses prove one thing: The Holy Spirit has got to both feminine and God's wife. Nothing but wrath to those who would hurt and offend her!

THE FEMININE HOLY SPIRIT for more info:-

http://www.peopleofthekeys.com/news/docs/library/Dream+Queen

http://www.pistissophia.org/The_Holy_Spirit/the_holy_spirit.html

http://www.hts.org.za/index.php/HTS/article/view/3225/html

http://www.menorah.org/trinity1.html

https://www.saxo.com/dk/the-holy-spirit-the-feminine-nature-of-god-how-the-feminine-component-of-jehovah-god-was-erased-from-early-christian-and-jewish-belie_taylor-patricia-taylorpatricia-taylor_haeftet_9781440174841

'WISDOM' KNOWN AS 'THE HOLY SPIRIT' IN THE HEBREW OLD TESTAMENT.

Isaiah 34:16 "Seek ye out of the book of the LORD, and read: no one of these shall fail, none shall want her mate: for my mouth it hath commanded, and his spirit it hath gathered them." - None Shall Want Her Mate.

Most Bible scholars and teachers interpret the above verse to mean that no prophecy given in the Bible will go unfulfilled. Each prophecy will have its fulfilment, or mate.

C.21 Interestingly in checking nineteen different Bible translations of this verse, nine of the translations, including the King James version, use the **feminine** pronoun "her". Most of the remaining translations use the translation "its mate". If a prophecy, which the Bible states: "came not in old time by the will of man: but holy men of God spake as they were moved by the Holy Ghost", is referred to in the feminine then what or who would be the masculine fulfilment or "her mate".

Revelation 19:10 states: "the testimony of Jesus is the spirit of prophecy." Another clue may be the words "gathered them" in the above verse.

Matthew 24:31 says: "He (Jesus) shall send his angels with a great sound of a trumpet, and they shall gather together his elect from the four winds, from one end of heaven to the other."

C.22 Could it be the prophecy that is given by the Holy Ghost is given in the feminine and the fulfilment given in the masculine, Jesus? Is there really a possibility that this could be true?

The book of Genesis, chapter one, would seem to confirm this is a possibility. **Genesis 1:27** "God created man in his own image, in the image of God created he him; male and female created he them."

C.23 Every major Bible translation uses the words "male and female". When speaking of "her" there is a "her or she" that is very favourably spoken of in the Bible, especially in the book of **Proverbs**. The name given to 'her' in the Bible is 'Wisdom'. The following verses from Proverbs, chapter three, helps to bring this point forward.

Proverbs 3:15-19 "She is more precious than rubies: and all the things thou canst desire are not to be compared unto her. Length of days is in her right hand and in her left hand riches and honour. Her ways are ways of pleasantness, and all her paths are peace. She is a tree of life to them that lay hold upon her: and happy is everyone that retains her. The LORD by wisdom hath founded the earth; by understanding hath he established the heavens."

C.24 Since it is written that God created man in His image, male and female, one might ask is there a possibility the Holy Ghost, the third person of the Trinity is Wisdom. Below are more verses on Wisdom.

Proverbs 1:20-21 Wisdom cries without; she utters her voice in the streets: She cries in the chief place of concourse, in the openings of the gates: in the city she utters her words. So that thou incline thine ear unto wisdom, and apply thine heart to understanding; Yea, if thou cry after knowledge, and lift up thy voice for understanding; If thou seek her as silver, and search for her as for hid treasures,

Proverbs 2:2-4 Get wisdom, get understanding: forget it not; neither decline from the words of my mouth. Forsake her not, and she shall preserve thee: love her, and she shall keep thee. Wisdom is the principal thing; therefore, get wisdom: and with all thy getting get understanding. Exalt her, and she shall promote thee: she shall bring thee to honour, when thou dost embrace her. She shall give to thine head an ornament of grace: a crown of glory shall she deliver to thee.

Proverbs 4:5-9 Say unto wisdom, 'Thou art my sister; and call understanding thy kinswoman':

Proverbs 7:4 Doth not wisdom cry? and understanding put forth her voice? She stands in the top of high places, by the way in the places of the paths. She cries at the gates, at the entry of the city, at the coming in at the doors.

Proverbs 8:1-3 Before the mountains were settled, before the hills was I brought forth: While as yet he had not made the earth, nor the fields, nor the highest part of the dust of the world. When he prepared the heavens, I was there: when he set a compass upon the face of the depth: When he established the clouds above: when he strengthened the fountains of the deep: When he gave to the sea his decree, that the waters should not pass his commandment: when he appointed the foundations of the earth: Then I was by him, as one brought up with him: and I was daily his delight, rejoicing always before him.

Proverbs 8:25-30 Wisdom hath built her house, she hath hewn out her seven pillars: She hath killed her beasts; she hath mingled her wine; she hath also furnished her table. She hath sent forth her maidens: she cries upon the highest places of the city.

CHAPTER 24

> 1 AND the Lord summoned me, and said to me: 'Enoch, sit down on my left with Gabriel.'
>
> 2 And I bowed down to the Lord, and the Lord spoke to me: Enoch, **beloved,** all thou seest, all things that are standing finished I tell to thee even before the very beginning, all that I created from non-being, and visible things from invisible.
>
> 3 Hear, Enoch, and take in these my words, for not to My angels have I told my secret, and I have not told them their rise, nor my endless realm, nor have they understood my creating, which I tell thee to-day.
>
> 4 For before all things were visible, I alone used to go about in the invisible things, like the sun from east to west, and from west to east.
>
> 5 But even the sun has peace in itself, while I found no peace, because I was creating all things, and I conceived the thought of placing foundations, and of creating visible creation.

C.1 - ANCIENT HEBREW VISION OF THE CREATION OF HEAVEN AND HELL

Job 26:11 "The pillars of heaven are prostrate and astonished at his rebuke.

Ancient Hebrew Conception of the Universe.

Genesis 1:1-5 "In the beginning God created the heaven and the earth. And the earth was without form, and void; and darkness was upon the face of the deep. And the Spirit of God moved upon the face of the waters. And God said, Let there be light: and there was light. And God saw the light, that it was good: and God divided the light from the darkness. And God called the light Day, and the darkness he called Night. And the evening and the morning were the first day."

Genesis 1:14-19 "And God said, Let there be lights in the firmament of the heaven to divide the day from the night; and let them be for signs and for seasons, and for days, and years: and let them be for lights in the firmament of the heaven to give light upon the earth: and it was so. And God made two great lights; the greater light to rule the day, and the lesser light to rule the night: he made the stars also. And God set them in the firmament of the heaven to give light upon the earth, and to rule over the day and over the night, and to divide the light from the darkness: and God saw that it was good. And the evening and the morning were the fourth day."

1Chronicles 16:30 "Fear before him, all the earth: the world also shall be stable, that it be not moved."

Psalm 93:1 "The Lord reigns, he is clothed with majesty; the Lord is clothed with strength, wherewith he hath girded himself: the world also is stablished, that it cannot be moved."

Psalm 96:10 "Say among the heathen that the Lord reigns: the world also shall be established that it shall not be moved: he shall judge the people righteously

Psalm 104:5 "Who laid the foundations of the earth, that it should not be removed for ever. "

Deuteronomy 33:17 His glory is like the firstling of his bullock, and his horns are like the horns of unicorns: with them he shall push the people together to the ends of the earth: and they are the ten thousands of Ephraim, and they are the thousands of Manasseh.

1 Samuel 2:10 The adversaries of the LORD shall be broken to pieces; out of heaven shall he thunder upon them: the LORD shall judge the ends of the earth; and he shall give strength unto his king, and exalt the horn of his anointed.

Job 28:24 For he looks to the ends of the earth, and see under the whole heaven.

Job 37:3 He directs it under the whole heaven, and his lightning unto the ends of the earth.

Job 38:13 That it might take hold of the **ends of the earth**, that the wicked might be shaken out of it?

Psalms 48:10 According to thy name, O God, so is thy praise unto the ends of the earth: thy right hand is full of righteousness.

Psalms 59:13 Consume them in wrath, consume them, that they may not be: and let them know that God ruleth in Jacob unto the ends of the earth. Selah

CHAPTER 25

This Chapter Is About The Light And The Origins Of Both Pre-Creation & The Physical Creation

> 1 God COMMANDED in the very lowest *parts*, that visible things should come down from invisible, and **Adoil** came down **very great**, and I beheld him, and lo! He had a belly of great **light**.
>
> 2 And I said to him: 'Become undone, Adoil, and let the visible *come* out of thee.'
>
> 3 And he came undone, and a great light came out. And I *was* in the midst of the great light, and as there is born light from light, there came forth a great age, and showed all creation, which I had thought to create.
>
> 4 And I saw that *it was* good.
>
> 5 And I placed for myself a throne, and took my seat on it, and said to the light: 'Go thou up higher and fix thyself high above the throne, and be a foundation to the highest things.'
>
> 6 And above the light there is nothing else, and then I bent up and looked up from my throne.

C.1 What are these 6 verses talking about? These verses certainly sound very mysterious and somewhat confusing at first glance.

C.2 In spite of there being only 6 verses in this chapter of the Secrets of Enoch, we are told a lot of information about Pre-Creation times and what went on.

VERSE 1: **A)** God COMMANDED in the **very lowest** *parts*, that **B) visible** things should come down from **invisible**, and **C) Adoil** came down **very great**, and I beheld him, and lo! **D)** He had a **belly of great light**.

C.3 I have divided up this verse 1 into 4 distinct parts: **A, B, C and D** for the sake of clarification

C.4 VERSE 1: A) 'very lowest *parts*'. Why does it say that God commanded the very lowest parts both in this chapter and in the very next one that visible should come down from invisible.

C.5 This chapter is about Light, and the next chapter 26 is about Darkness?

VERSE 1: **A** 'God COMMANDED in the very lowest *parts*,' –

This is making a distinction between the upper parts of light and the lower parts of Darkness.

C.6 VERSE 1: B 'Visible things should come down from invisible' -This is talking about God creating the physical universe before it had ever happened and bringing His creations down from the spiritual dimensions to the physical.

C.7 VERSE 1: C Adoil- who is Adoil? Is this entity male or female? By the description of it it sounds female and when you happen to know that the Holy Spirit is female then it would make more sense to state a 'she' and not 'he in the text.

C.8 VERSE 1: D 'I beheld him, and lo! He had a belly of great **light**.' -This is the mysterious part as this being or entity is either very fat or perhaps pregnant as other writers have also suggested. It says that this entity is a 'he'?

C.9 He had a great belly of light. Males do not get pregnant. That is an entirely female trait both in the physical world and in the much vaster spiritual world. Male and Female are in fact eternal traits! Other writers have stated that this verse seems to be talking about the female trait of being pregnant with many things of light and with many creations that are waiting to be born or created. Why call the entity male if it is most obviously female? See my write up on this topic at the end of this very chapter.

VERSE 2 And I said to him: 'Become undone, Adoil, and let the visible *come* out of thee.'

C.10 ADOIL – Unlike other early Enoch writings, the (Slavonic) Apocalypse of Enoch depicts a unique story of primordial creation, revealing an elaborate course of events that preceded the visible creation of the world. The importance of this mystical account is underlined by the fact that it was delivered to the seventh antediluvian hero Enoch by God himself.

VERSE 2 And I said to him: 'Become undone, Adoil, and let the visible *come* out of thee.' Here we see the INVISIBLE becoming VISIBLE

C.11 From chapter 1 **'conceived love for him'** – this sounds like a **feminine expression** for love. Why does it state it is this way? What if we have **God the Father and God the Holy Spirit Mother and God the Son.** Then the above expression would make a lot more sense. There are many people today who believe that the Holy Spirit is female.

C.12 Author: Let's imagine for a moment that the ancient Hebrew writings were correct and that the New Testament Jewish Christians were correct - who all stated that the Holy Spirit is female. Jewish law stated in the Old Testament that the 'testimony of two men was true'.

John 8:17: It is also written in your law, that the testimony of two men is true.

C.13 I was also very impressed by a woman's comment on my audio/visual site on YouTube when I was mentioning that my research had caused me to conclude that we have a Trinity of God the Father, and God the Mother, and God the Son - Jesus. That woman commented: 'How could an 'all male' Trinity be able to design a woman?' She was right!

C.14 Now as other scholars have wisely stated, if we all could see Creation as it really is and how it was formed then everything else would make a lot more sense as everything in the nature is both male and female. What about the spirit world behind this physical world? Isn't that also both male and female? And if those who made Creation itself were indeed male and female then it would mean that male and female are not just a sexual distinction confined to just the physical world.

C.15 The opposite is true as the physical world is a temporal version of an eternal reality. If you were born as a man here in the physical realm then you would be a man in the spiritual realm as your spirit is masculine. The same goes for the female.

C.16 Women can rejoice in the fact that they have a wonderful and fully compassionate Mother in the spirit world -The Holy Spirit, and she is God the Mother, the Father's wife. Jesus is their Son.

C.17 I suppose a good question would be why is Jesus the only Son of God the Father and the Holy Spirit Mother and who is Himself also God or almighty? A fascinating topic indeed!

C.18 Why are there only 3 in the Trinity of the religions and not 4 or more Gods? That is also a very interesting question. God simply states in the Bible that before Him there was no other God. Why is there not a Daughter of God but only the Son of God? The answer to that question is found in the Bride of Christ.

Isaiah 45.5 "I am the Lord, and there is no other;
Besides Me there is no God. I will gird you, though you have not known Me;

Exodus 20.3 "You shall have no other gods before Me

C.19 When God states 'I am the lord and there is no other' He is also talking on behalf of the entire trinity of God: God the Father, the Holy Spirit Mother and Jesus the only begotten Son of God and the Creator.

1 John 5.7 For there are **three** that bear record in heaven, the Father, the Word (Jesus), and the Holy Ghost (Mother): and these three are one.

C.20 In this Slavic version of 2nd Enoch this chapter shows something very interesting as it mentions a being that would appear to be pregnant -Adoil ! ? As far as I know only woman or the feminine side of nature can get pregnant. I am not saying that I know the whole picture, but it appears to me that the physical world is a reflection of the much vaster spiritual world.

C.21 In our physical world we distinctly see male and female in all of Creation but these are temporal values are they not? That is what is taught. What if male and female are actually eternal values and that they never change. What if this chapter of Enoch is doing a clumsy job of trying to state the following:

C.22 In Pre-Creation times there was Almighty God the Father and He was married to a Feminine Goddess of God the Mother. He loved her very much and as women do, she got pregnant. I know this is just a simple illustration as God and the Holy Spirit are infinite and who am I to try and describe them, but I am trying to the best of my ability to make it easier for others to understand, instead of having the concepts of God the Father and the Holy Spirit and God the Son having been made too complicated by the religious institutions - which shy away from many realities of the spirit world.

C.23 Religious people spiritually speaking seem to me like a person who walks on the beach and gets his toes wet in the sea-water, but who never ventures out into the ocean, which is just full of adventure and amazing discoveries. Tradition tells them to stay on the beach and not dive into the waters. Why? Because religious people in general don't ask the right questions of Jesus, God and His Holy Spirit. They tend not to have a personal link with God, where they can ask questions and get answers from God. No, the religious person is too much in a box of traditions to venture out into new possibilities. If anyone suggest something different might be the truth - he is immediately shouted down as being a blasphemer or worse. Just because the majority of religious people believe one thing is right, does not make it right. What does God Himself say about these things?

'Prove Me saith the Lord God'. God likes us to challenge Him as to why things are the way they are.

Malachi 3.10 Bring ye all the tithes into the storehouse, that there may be meat in mine house, and **prove me** now herewith, saith the Lord of hosts, if I will not open you the windows of heaven, and **pour you out a blessing**, that there shall not be room enough to receive it.

Isaiah 45.11 Thus saith the Lord, the Holy One of Israel, and his Maker, 'Ask me of things to come concerning my sons, and concerning the work of my hands **command ye me**'.

Matthew 7.7 "Ask, and it shall be given you; seek, and ye shall find; knock, and it shall be opened unto you:"

John 14.14 If ye shall ask anything in My name (Jesus) I will do it.

C.24 THE 2ND BOOK OF ENOCH CLEARLY SHOWS A FEMININE 'PREGNANT' BEING IN THE GODHEAD

In working on the Book of 2nd Enoch and researching what has been said by theologians and writers it becomes evident that many writers are far too complicated for the average reader to understand.

Many so-called expert or professional writers of the past are simply making things far too complicated.

For example, others have not noticed the simple fact that there is a feminine reference to the Godhead in Chapter 25 of 2nd Enoch as it mentions that 'he' has a big belly and later a writer mentions the entity sounds pregnant.

Even a small child used to be able to tell you that it is the feminine being that gets pregnant and has babies.

I don't know what on earth they are teaching the little children today to the point that there is no longer any male or female and that men can have babies!?. What utter madness.

Satan and his ilk are always trying to corrupt the truth and say that 'it aint necessarily so' to suit an agenda whether it is history or science or organized religions or finance.

I think that the problem is that the basics of Creation have not been properly established due to bias in Judeo/Christian beliefs which give the impression that God the Father and God the Holy Spirit and God the Son are all masculine.

Many religionists obviously don't like the idea that there is a female member of the Trinity in the Holy Spirit Mother.

That should be natural to understand and believe as the rest of God's amazing Creation.

All of Creation is male and female and for a very good reason. Satan and the modernists are trying to teach modern man that you don't have to be male or female and that having children is not important.

God's very first command to the very first man and woman was to procreate and fill the earth with people.

Today the powers that be are trying to get rid of the populations of the earth through nasty eugenics programs.

Man has departed from the simplicity of Christ and the simplicity that existed in the beginning of Creation before the son of Satan known as Cain came along and committed the very first murder.

According to the Jewish Historian in circa 100 AD, Josephus stated that Cain was the first to use weights and measures. Cain was in fact the very first deceptive merchant. Josephus goes on to state that Cain increased his substance by lying and cheating and teaching mankind to stray away from the original simplicity that God had taught them.

Education has often educated man out of faith and into disbelief. To have faith in God one has to believe the Word of God and not put up with the adulterated truths. There are certain basics to believe in if one is to believe in and follow the Bible for our education.

It is very important to stick with what the apostle Paul stated in the New Testament

2 Corinthians 11.3 'I fear least by any means the Serpent beguiled Eve through his subtlety that your minds should be corrupted from the simplicity that is in Christ..

C.25 SUMMARY SO FAR: What was going on in the Pre-Creation times before God had created the spirit world or the physical world or all the beings of heaven and earth. Well, some scholars or writers try to make this chapter too intangible or ethereal or imaginary for my liking, when it seems plain that the story of Adoil and Archas, which you will read about in the next chapter, it is not just talking about an age of time (intangible) but talking about entities that have the direct authority from God to be in charge of things. There is something similar in the next or 26 chapter talking about the dark dimensions. God has made one entity in charge of the Light and higher dimensions and another in charge of all the lower dimensions or the Darkness These entities appear to be female by virtue of the fact that it states that they were pregnant. Male beings do not get pregnant, that we know for certain. That is what chapters 25-26 appear to be saying.

C.26 Spiritually speaking in simple physical language, God is love according to the Bible, I think that in eternity God the Father and God the Holy Spirit loved each other very much and the result was that the Holy Spirit got pregnant. Not necessarily in the physical way we think, but as someone has wisely mentioned when a man and woman are together, and they love each other. Then often the woman gets pregnant. The man or husband is thinking of a few things like the woman and perhaps how to take care of her. The woman however is thinking of 20 other relevant things such as where are they going to live, if children come along, and how will they best take care of themselves and what will they dress them in, and where to go and buy the clothes for the children; and where will they go to school etc?

C.27 Since God is an eternal being and likewise so is also the Holy Spirit, what if in Eternity, God the Father and God the Holy Spirit Mother went through stages of love such as we humans, who are reflections of God go through?

C.28 Such as love when we are young or even teenagers and then when love gets a bit more serious and the women is ready for pregnancy. This is the most important time for the woman. She needs her man's protection more than ever before, and His supply and his assurance and comfort. She is happy to be pregnant but she needs constant reassurance.

C.29 This chapter of 2nd Enoch seem to state that a time came when the Holy Spirit was pregnant with millions of creations that as yet had not been made manifest, and so God the Father stated 'Let's make a dimension where all of your creations can become a reality and thus both the Spirit world first of all, and as a reflection the physical world was also created.

C.30 The Bible states that Jesus was the beginning of the Creation of God. Then God the Father and the Trinity created the angels and spiritual beings and heaven itself. Once that was all established eventually, they created the physical dimensions.

C.31 All the feminine creations were also manifest in these creations, so as to make the Creation itself very colourful and well-balanced.

C.32 Creation could not have been made by an all male Godhead. That does not make any sense.

C.33 It is the woman's touches that make all the difference in a home.

VERSE 5 And I placed for myself a throne, and took my seat on it, and said to the light: 'Go thou up higher and fix thyself high above the throne, and be a foundation to the highest things.'

God the Father talking to his Son Jesus, telling him to be in charge of the LIGHT and all the higher dimensions. This all happened before the Creation of the physical dimensions. Jesus stated that He was the 'light of the world' in John chapter 8.

C.34 I am convinced that it was Jesus who was the creator of the physical world, but that He had a lot of help from His Mother the Holy Spirit in creating things to get the right colours and to make the male/female balance as stated so well in Genesis 'Let us create man in our image and male and female created He them.' Who was God talking to unless it was a female – the Holy Spirit Mother?

Genesis 1.26-27 And God said, **Let us** make man in our image, after our likeness: and let them have dominion over the fish of the sea, and over the fowl of the air, and over the cattle, and over all the earth, and over every creeping thing that creepeth upon the earth. So God created man in his own image, in the image of God created he him; **male and female** created he them.

C.35 I think this explanation has some merit. We all know that the Gospel of John states that in the beginning was the Word and the Word was with God and the Word was God. Jesus was the Creator of this physical universe as He is also known as the Son of God. If the Holy Spirit is thus His divine Mother then it would have been Jesus with the help of His Holy Spirit Mother and Father doing the original creation of the physical world. It would appear that it was God the Father and the Holy Spirit Mother that created the spiritual world. The Bible teaches that Jesus was the beginning of the Creation of God.

VERSE 5 And I placed for myself a throne, and took my seat on it, and said to the light: 'Go thou up higher and fix thyself high above the throne, and be a foundation to the highest things.'

C.36 In this chapter it seems to also show God talking to the Light entity -Jesus and telling Him to rule over all the higher levels of Heaven. Strangely in the very next chapter it seems to mention the Lord of the Underworld. – Archas. How is that even possible? A person in charge of the underworld?

C.37 MORE ABOUT THE UNFLUENCE OF THE STARS ON THE CREATION OF MAN: A similar correspondence between the sevenfold cosmology and the sevenfold anthropogony appears in several Gnostic texts, including the Apocryphon of John, where the seven components of Adam's body correspond to the seven anthropogonic agents associated with planetary spheres and responsible for the fashioning of the first human's body. Thus, the Apocryphon of John unveils the identities of seven rulers and their role in the creation of the psychic body of Adam [Editor: The Apocryphon of John mentions that the Holy Spirit is female in nature and Mother of all]

> 3 And he came undone, and a great light came out. And I *was* in the midst of the great light, and as there is born light from light, there came forth a great age, and showed all creation, which I had thought to create.

> 4 And I saw that *it was* good.
>
> 5 And I placed for myself a throne, and took my seat on it, and said to the light: 'Go thou up higher and fix thyself high above the throne, and be a foundation to the highest things.'
>
> 6 And above the light there is nothing else, and then I bent up and looked up from my throne.

C.38 For example, others have not noticed the simple fact that there is a feminine reference to the Godhead in Chapter 25 of 2nd Enoch as it mentions that 'he' has a big belly and later a writer mentions the entity sounds pregnant.

Even a small child used to be able to tell you that it is the feminine being that gets pregnant and has babies.

I don't know what on earth they are teaching the little children today in the West to the point that there is no longer any male or female and that men can have babies!?. What utter madness.

Satan and his ilk are always trying to corrupt the truth and say that 'it aint necessarily so' to suit an agenda whether it is history or science or organized religions or finance.

I think that the problem is that the basics of Creation have not been properly established due to bias in Judeo/Christian beliefs which give the impression that God the Father and God the Holy Spirit and God the Son are all masculine.

C.39 Many religionists don't like the idea that there is a female member of the Trinity in the Holy Spirit Mother.

It was not difficult to find lots of evidence that the Holy Spirit is in fact female.

That should be natural to understand and believe as the rest of God's amazing Creation.

All of Creation is male and female and for a very good reason. Satan and the modernists are trying to teach modern man that you don't have to be male or female and that having children is not important.

God's very first command to the very first man and woman was to procreate and fill the earth with people.

It is very important to stick with what the apostle Paul stated in the New Testament

2 Corinthians 11.3 'I fear least by any mean the Serpent beguiled Eve through his subtlety that your minds should be corrupted from the simplicity that is in Christ..

The Earliest Christians Viewed the Holy Spirit as Female! - Jason's Voyage (jasonsvoyage.com)

C.40 With the concept of the Holy Spirit being the perfect Mother everything makes much more sense in looking at the Creation itself. It states in Genesis that God created us in His image and then succinctly states and in make and female created He them. Who was God talking to if not the female Holy spirit His eternal companion. Thinking like this brings a whole new reality to love and romance and love itself. Everyone needs to taste of love itself and it is my hope and prayer that eventually everyone who is godly will find the perfect soul-mate.

C.41 If Jesus was the one who created the physical dimension, one thing for sure is that He had lots of help not just from God the Father but from God the Mother who put her beautiful myriad of touches to Creation with all of its thousands of variety of flowers and trees and creatures with all of their amazing colours. Macho religions have pushed our precious Holy spirit Mother completely out of the picture which simply does not work. Love is everything in this universe in its many forms. Without the female side of things there is no future! It is as simple as that.

Isaiah 65.18 But be ye glad and rejoice for ever in that which I create: for, behold, I **create Jerusalem a rejoicing, and her people a joy.**

C.42 Summarizing THE SECRETS OF ENOCH INSIGHTS CHAPTER 25

There are so many very interesting details in the 2nd Book of Enoch that are just fascinating. None more so that the Pre-Creation Story. It is sad that many of the religionists and the scholars of religion are so tied up in ancient dogma of 'male religion dominance' that they can't even work it out that **only women give birth to babies** and that **CREATION** itself has a Mother in the form of the **Holy Spirit Mother** as mentioned in 2nd Enoch chapter 25, which is not very difficult to prove.

C.43 Two scholars who have totally nailed this topic are Marianne Widmalm and Ally Kateusz. Both of these women are Hebrew scholars. They both prove beyond a shadow of a doubt that all the early Christians addressed the Holy Spirit as Mother as did all the apostles and even Jesus Himself. The Holy Spirit's gender was gradually changed by scribes from feminine to masculine from the 4th to the 7th centuries AD. Why did the scribes change the gender of the Holy Spirit? Because of the dictums of Rome and in particular the Roman Catholic church.

C.44 According to Hebrew scholars the main reason the Holy Spirit's gender was changed from feminine to masculine was when the Bible was translated from Hebrew into Greek and then Latin. The pronouns are used differently in Greek and Latin. Well, that is how it started. I covered this topic of the Holy Spirit being feminine, and I do recommend that readers get a hold of the books by Marianne Widmalm – 'Our Mother the Holy Spirit' and Ally Kateusz – 'Finding Holy Spirit Mother'

C.45 I believe there are other angles as to why this happened, and I think one has to go back to Pre-Flood times in order to fully understand the real problem. It goes all the way back to the fallen angels.

C.46 I must state here that it is essential to realize that of course God the Father has a wife and companion in the Holy Spirit Mother and always has done. These are eternal values. As other scholars have rightly stated when you look at the Bible through the lenses of the Holy Spirit being the Mother in the so-called Trinity everything else makes perfect sense. Now why on earth would this information be withheld from believers for the past 1600 years until now?

C.47 Did you know that Origen whose books were the basis of the Catholic church religion and who incidentally lived in the 3rd century warned the Catholic church that if they did not change their ways they would become infested with demons or the children of the Fallen angels otherwise known as the 'disembodied spirits' of the giants.

C.48 It would seem that that is exactly what happened from the 4th century onwards as the Catholic church burned at the stake anyone who did not agree with their religious dictums of the moment.

C.49 The Catholic church has a lot of blood on their hands including that of Joan of Arc. They martyred her and 20 years later declared her as one of their saints.

C.50 Between 300-400 AD at the council of Laodicea women were banned from being bishops and spiritual leaders. Many were burned alive in their own churches for not following papal orders.

C.51 There has been a strong hatred of women throughout history as they have been blamed for many things in the past, where society has tried to push women into subservient roles in most religions.

C.52 Why did this happen? Is there a strong reason? I think it all stems from Pre-Flood times and that men after the Great Flood did not want their women to behave as the daughters of Cain ever again. They also did not want the women to abandon the normal human men in favour of 'Fallen angels' as happened in Genesis 6 and Enoch 6, Jasher ,5, Jubilees 4.

C.53 I also think that there is a strong argument as to why the Fallen angels and Satan ended up hating women in particular as they hated the Holy Spirit Mother.

C.54 Satan and 'The Fallen angels' chose the ways of total rebellion against God, but they obviously were not too smart after all, as their plans all failed.

The fallen angels thought that they would go down to earth to cohabitate with the beautiful women on the earth and begat children by them.

However, they forgot one very important thing. Creation is by God the Father and by God the Mother and by Jesus their Son.

C.55 According to Genesis God the Father and God the Mother were talking together when in Genesis1 God stated:

Genesis 1 ' Let us make man in our image and male and female created He them.

God was obviously talking with a female and that was the Holy Spirit Mother.

C.56 The Fallen angels left out 'God the Mother', who was the one who created all the females in God's Creation.

C.57 When the Fallen angels had sex with the women on the earth, that is why they could only have sons and no daughters. No wonder their sons the giants went crazy and berserk with no women around that were giants. After co-habitating with the women for a while then the Fallen angels started mating with animals and other creatures and created chimeras. This was possible as angels are shape-shifters. They also did this with other creatures. Such a total horror and aberration of God's original Creation. The evil spirit world is now therefore very perverse and they do not according to nature, or stick to male and female relationships.

C.58 This is also why our planet is having such problems to this day. Everything of real value is being destroyed. It used to be simple that a man is a man and woman is a woman, but now they can't even define what a woman is! This is 'newspeak' as mentioned by George Orwell in his dystopian book '1984'. If things continue the way that they are going one day people won't even be able to understand each other's speech as all the words will mean something else. What madness

C.59 Here is a very interesting article about CREATION shows a GEO-CENTRIC view of our universe, or the fact that the sun rotates around the earth and not Helio-central that the earth rotates around the sun. This article also mentioned pregnancies in the Bible and their great significance concerning Creation itself.

Revelation 12:1-3 "And there appeared a great wonder in heaven; a woman clothed with the sun, and the moon under her feet, and upon her head a crown of twelve stars: And she being with child cried, travailing in birth, and pained to be delivered. And she brought forth a man child, who was to rule all nations with a rod of iron: and her child was caught up unto God, and to his throne."

Here we see a pregnant woman in heaven about to give birth to a man child who is to "rule all nations with a rod of iron". We know this prophecy has not been fulfilled and will not be fulfilled until the second coming of Jesus. He certainly did not rule all nations with a rod of iron upon His first coming.

Psalm 2:9 speaks of this same event:

Psalm 2:9 "Thou shalt break them with a rod of iron; thou shalt dash them in pieces like a potter's vessel."

Luke 1:30-35 "And the angel said unto her, Fear not, Mary: for thou hast found favour with God. And, behold, thou shalt conceive in thy womb, and bring forth a son, and shalt call his name Jesus. He shall be great, and shall be called the Son of the Highest: and the Lord God shall give unto him the throne of his father David: And he shall reign over the house of Jacob for ever; and of his kingdom there shall be no end. Then said Mary unto the angel, How shall this be, seeing I know not a man? And the angel answered and said unto her, The Holy Ghost shall come upon thee, and the power of the Highest shall overshadow thee: therefore also that holy thing which shall be born of thee shall be called the Son of God."

Continuing in Luke 1, one of the first things Mary does after receiving this message from Gabriel is to visit her cousin Elisabeth who is six months pregnant with John the Baptist. As soon as Elisabeth hears Mary's greeting the babe leaped in her womb.

Luke 1 "And it came to pass, that, when Elisabeth heard the salutation of Mary, the babe leaped in her womb; and Elisabeth was filled with the Holy Ghost."

Obviously the "womb" is of tremendous importance both spiritually and physically. Three other verses in which "womb" could almost be interpreted as somewhat of an enigma are:

Psalm 110:3 "Thy people shall be willing in the day of thy power, in the beauties of holiness from the womb of the morning."

Job 38:8,29 "And I shut up the sea with gates, when it rushed out, coming forth out its mother's womb." "Out of whose womb comes the ice?"

Genesis 25:23 "And the Lord said to her, There are two nations in thy womb."

Here we have the Lord speaking of the sea coming out of its mother's womb, ice coming out of a womb and two nations coming from Rachel's womb. Very mysterious occurrences. When you think about two nations coming from the womb of a woman it sounds, well, unusual.

Obviously, pregnancy, the womb, and deliverance both spiritually and physically are absolutely fundamentally essential for our redemption. Before wrapping this up we wanted to share a few verses from Proverbs, chapter eight, regarding the Holy Spirit, the third member of the Godhead. "Thou shalt proclaim wisdom, that understanding may be obedient to thee. For she is on lofty eminences, and stands in the midst of the ways. For she sits by the gates of princes, and sings in the entrances. The Lord made me the beginning of his ways for his works. He established me before time was in the beginning, before he made the earth: even before he made the depths; before the fountains of water came forth: before the mountains were settled, and before all hills, he begets me. The Lord made countries and uninhabited tracks, and the highest inhabited parts of the world. When he prepared the heaven, I was present with him; and when he prepared his throne upon the winds: and when he strengthened the clouds above; and when he secured the fountains of the earth: and when he strengthened the foundations of the earth: I was by him, suiting myself to him, I was that wherein he took delight; and daily I rejoiced in his presence continually."

Wisdom, as is very clear, is definitely referred to in the feminine pronoun. Those of you familiar with this web site will know that we believe the Holy Spirit to be the female representative of the trinity. Incidentally the Shekiniah Glory, which rested between the wings of the Cherubim on the mercy seat atop the Ark of the Covenant, was a feminine representation of the glory of God.

Genesis 1:26-27 "And God said, Let us make man according to our image and likeness, and let them have dominion over the fish of the sea, and over the flying creatures of heaven, and over the cattle and all the earth, and over all the reptiles that creep on the earth. And God made man, according to the image of God he made him, male and female he made them."

Let's go back to the idea of a finite geocentric universe. If the Bible is to be taken literally, outside the universe is some type of water surrounding the universe.

Genesis 1:6-8 "And God said, Let there be a firmament in the midst of the water, and let it be a division between water and water, and it was so. And God made the firmament, and God divided between the water which was under the firmament and the water which was above the firmament. And God called the firmament Heaven, and God saw that it was good, and there was evening and there was morning, the second day."

Genesis 7:11 "In the six hundredth year of the life of Noe, in the second month, on the twenty-seventh day of the month, on this day all the fountains of the abyss were broken up, and the flood-gates (windows) of heaven were opened."

Is it possible that the water that exists around the universe is representative or could actually be the womb of the Holy Spirit which the whole creation is groaning and travailing in pain together waiting to be delivered through the redemption by the second coming of Jesus the Messiah? The womb of the universe, seen and unseen.

C.60 HOLLOW EARTH

Job 38:8,29 "And I shut up the sea with gates, when it rushed out, coming forth out its mother's womb." "Out of whose womb comes the ice?"

This verse is mentioned by the writer of the last article. In studying this verse it appears to be talking about the Northern entrance or (where the North Pole is supposed to be). There are in fact holes at the poles which descend inside a hollow earth with seas on the underside of the earth. In the Northern opening there is an ice barrier of several hundred feet high in the area where one cannot see either the outer sun or the inner sun. There are many scientific reports about these facts. Including the explorer Admiral Byrd of the USA back in 1926 and 1947.

C.61 The apocryphal book of 2nd Esdras, was in the KJV of the Bible until the 19th century. God mentions in this amazing book that the earth is hollow. This book was written by the prophet Ezra circa 500 BC. Here are some verses from that book which you will also find in my book '**Esdras Insights**', which came out August 2023.

2ND ESDRAS CH 4.23 And I said," No lord, it cannot". And he said to me, "In Hades the chambers of the souls are like the **womb**" "For just as a woman who is in travail makes haste to escape the pangs of birth, so also do these places hasten to give back those things that were committed to them from the beginning; then the things that you desire to see will be disclosed to you.

2ND ESDRAS CH 5.30 He said to me 'Even so have I given the **womb of the earth** to those who from time to time are **sown in it**, for as an infant does not bring forth, and a woman who has become not does not bring forth and longer, so have I organized the world that I have created.

C.62 THE APOCRYPHON OF JOHN which was written before 185 AD states the following about the Holy Spirit – 'And His (God the Father) thought performed a deed and she came forth, namely she who had appeared before him in the shine of His light.'

This is the first power which was before all of them and which came forth from his mind, She is the forethought of the All - her light shines like His light -the perfect power which is the image of the invisible, virginal Spirit who is perfect.

This inevitably reminds us of the Wisdom texts in Proverbs, which describe her as God's first Creation or emanation, and a reflection, or radiance, of His light and an image of His goodness. It goes on to say 'she became the womb of everything for it is she who is prior to them all. Christ is described as the Word and the Light following the John Gospel. The Holy Spirit is the Mother of all living. Sophia which is the Greek word for Wisdom is also called 'Life which is the Mother of all living.' – [excerpt from Our Mother the Holy Spirit by Marianne Widmalm -2019]

CHAPTER 26

THIS CHAPTER IS ABOUT THE DARKNESS & DESCENT INTO DARKNESS

C.1 ARCHAS - definition: Greek - ἀρχὰς - Rulers, Principalities, '**Beginning of Creation**'; 'In the Beginning has laid the **FOUNDATION**'- Mentioned in the Bible in certain editions: Luke 12.11; Ephesians 6.12;Colossians 2.15; Hebrews 1.12 - **SOURCE:** Greek Concordance: ἀρχὰς (archas) -- 4 Occurrences (biblehub.com)

> AND I summoned the very lowest a **second time**, and said: 'Let Archas come forth hard,' and **he** came forth hard from the invisible.
>
> 2 And Archas came forth, hard, **heavy**, and very **red.**
>
> 3 And I said: 'Be opened, Archas, and let there be **born** from thee,' and he came undone, an age came forth, very great and very dark, bearing the creation of all lower things, and I saw that *it was* good and said to him:
>
> 4 'Go thou down below, and make thyself firm, and be for a foundation for the lower things,' and it happened and he went down and fixed himself, and **became the foundation for the lower things, and below the darkness there is nothing else**.

C.2 There are only 4 verses in this chapter but they give an amazing amount of information which I will dra out in this chapter about the darkness.

C.3 It states here in verse 3 that Archas is giving birth to the things of the 'heavy and red' things of the underworld. What things are heavy and red? like perhaps Satan who is known as a red Devil or red Dragon which would tend to suggest that this entity is female.

VERSE 4 'Go thou down below, and make thyself firm, and be for a foundation for the lower things,' and it happened and he went down and fixed himself, and became the foundation for the lower things, and below the darkness there is nothing else.

C.4 Who is this talking about? It is not Lucifer or Satan. However Satan has become the ruler of the nether worlds or at least one of its captives, but there would appear to be a greater power than Satan or Lucifer in charge of the lower dimensions which also contains Hell, the Lake of Fire and Parsadise. Who or what exactly is Archas, now that is a very good question? It would seem that Satan likes to act as if he is so powerful and in charge of the nether regions, but in real terms he is one of the inmates of the lower regions and is becoming confined more and more to the lower regions when he is thrown into the 'Bottomless Pit' by an angel of God as mentioned in **Revelation 20.1-3**. How could a pit be Bottomless? I answered that question in another of my books.

REVELATION 20.1-3
1"And I saw an angel come down from heaven, having the key of the bottomless pit and a great chain in his hand."

2 And he laid hold on the dragon, that old serpent, which is the Devil, and Satan, and bound him a thousand years,

3 And cast him into the bottomless pit, and shut him up, and set a seal upon him, that he should deceive the nations no more, till the thousand years should be fulfilled: and after that he must be loosed a little season.

C.4 We know that Jesus, after He died went down to the underworld and fought against Satan and took away from Satan the Keys of Death and the Keys of Hell. Surely Lucifer or Satan is not the appointed Lord of the underworld?

Revelation 1.17-18 And when I saw him, I fell at his feet as dead. And he laid his right hand upon me, saying unto me, Fear not; I am the first and the last: 18 I am he that lives, and was dead; and, behold, I am alive for evermore, Amen; and have the keys of hell and of death.

Matthew 12.40"For as Jonah was three days and three nights in the belly of the great fish, so will the Son of Man be three days and three nights in the heart of the earth."

1Peter 3.18-20 "For Christ also died for sins once for all, the just for the unjust, in order that He might bring us to God, having been put to death in the flesh, but made alive in the spirit; in which also He went and made proclamation to the spirits now in prison, who once were disobedient, when the patience of God kept waiting in the days of Noah, during the construction of the ark, in which a few, that is, eight persons, were brought safely through the water."

What Is the Harrowing of Hell?

Jesus' descent into the place of the dead is referred to in the Apostles' Creed and the Athanasian Creed, which state that Jesus "descended into the underworld." His descent to the underworld is mentioned in the New Testament in 1 Peter 4:6, which states that the "*gospel was preached even to those who are now dead*" (see below). The Catholic Catechism interprets Ephesians 4:9, which states that "[Christ] descended into the lower parts of the earth," as also supporting this interpretation. The Harrowing of Hell is commemorated in the liturgical calendar on Holy Saturday.

According to the apocryphal Gospel of Nicodemus, the Harrowing of Hell was foreshadowed by Christ's raising of Lazarus from the dead preceding his own crucifixion. The hymns of Easter weekend mention that as he did on earth, John the Baptist prepared the way for Jesus in Hell by prophesying to the spirits held there that Christ would soon save them.

C.5 It would seem that Satan is going to end up being one of the inmates of hell and the Lake of fire but initially the Bottomless Pit. So, who is in charge of the underworld? Is there something that we are unaware of concerning the underworld? Who is in charge of the underworld when Satan is an inmate?

Revelation 1.8 I am he that lives, and was dead; and, behold, I am alive for evermore, Amen; and have the keys of hell and of death.

C.6 In summary for this chapter it would seem that logos or the Word of God or Jesus was in charge of the light and all things of light and that darkness was a sort of dark reflection of the light, but who is in charge of the darkness? The following verse makes it very clear that it is God or the Lord that has created the darkness:

Isaiah 45.7 "I form the light, and create darkness: I make peace, and create evil: I the LORD do all these *things*.

C.7 God in stating that he creates darkness could be referring to the physical darkness of the night and not necessarily the great spiritual darkness but then.. Perhaps the point here is that God was creating choice. The choice for light or for darkness. Therefore, one became a reflection of the other or an upside down, inside out image, that shrinks downwards. These are words used by other writers to describe what they call the negative upside-down shrinking world of hell and the underworld.

C.8 Having said that, has the Lord put some being or archangel in charge of the nether regions with the description of Archas. Notice that like Adoil in the last chapter this being Archas could actually also be feminine, as it also mentions the same description of this being very heavy or 'pregnant' and very 'red' with dark creations or ideas. Is the darkness just the inverse of the light or a shadowy reflection.

C.9 This is a big mystery, but there is plenty of evidence of feminine goddesses and beings like the SPHINX and MEDUSA not to mention that 1 Enoch mentions that the women that the Fallen angels cohabited with became the SIRENS which are very dangerous dark creatures. It is stated that the sirens were the ancestors of the mermaids. I think of many dangerous goddesses that people have worshipped through time such as Astaroth and some terrible beings to which the nations paid homage and made idols to and did all kinds of horrors in homage of demon gods and goddesses.

C.10 Disclaimer by the author: I don't begin to think that I know all the answers about this intriguing topic as to the question: Are there powerful feminine spirits in charge of the negative spirit world or the underworld?

C.11 However, just as I found out many years ago that contrary to religious traditions that the Holy Spirit is in fact feminine, then it is also possible that there are some very powerful <u>negative female spirits</u> that <u>control the darkness of the underworld</u>? Do they often control the souls of men through seduction in all forms. Just a thought that needs a lot more investigation.

C.12 We know that it was God who allowed the Light to be created but that he also allowed the Darkness to be created. So, I guess that the angels of God take care of the nether realms just like they take care of the sun the moon and the stars and the moon and planets. We know that there is an angel that takes care of Hell, but it is not Satan. Satan himself will end up in the Bottomless Pit and then the Lake of Fire.

C.13 The Book of Solomons Proverbs reveals a lot of interesting information on this topic as it keeps mentioning the powerful spirit of WISDOM herself and an exact opposite feminine spirit of unrighteousness, foolishness, shallowness, licentiousness and personified as a lusty whore.

C.14 WISDOM

Proverbs 3:13-18 - Happy is the man that finds wisdom, and the man that gets understanding.

Proverbs 2:6 - For the Lord giveth wisdom: out of his mouth cometh knowledge and understanding.

Ephesians 5:15-16 - See then that ye walk circumspectly, not as fools, but as wise, Redeeming the time, because the days are evil.

James 1:5 - If any of you lack wisdom, let him ask of God, that giveth to all men liberally, and upbraideth not; and it shall be given him.

Colossians 3:16 - Let the word of Christ dwell in you richly in all wisdom; teaching and admonishing one another in psalms and hymns and spiritual songs, singing with grace in your hearts to the Lord.

C.15 The Proverbs mention repeatedly that there is this evil feminine spirit which is the opposite of the Holy Spirit herself and that this anti-thesis of the Holy Spirit or Wisdom is very dangerous and seductive and leads people straight down to HELL.

C.16 This evil seductive female spirit sounds like one of the infamous seductive Sirens, and their descendants the mermaids, that used to lure sailors to their deaths on the rocks with their sweet hypnotic melodious voices as shown in Greek mythology in the story of Jason and the Argonauts. Apparently, some of these creatures looked like women with fishy tails but acted more like a deceptive and alluring shark ready to devour mankind.

Proverbs 2.16-19 Whose ways *are* crooked, and *they* froward in their paths: To deliver thee from the **strange woman**, even from the stranger which flatters with her words; Which forsakes the guide of her youth, and forgets the covenant of her God.

For her house inclines unto death, and her paths unto the dead. None that go unto her return again, neither take they hold of the paths of life.

Proverbs 6:24-27: To keep thee from the evil woman, from the flattery of the tongue of a strange woman. Lust not after her beauty in thine heart; neither let her take thee with her eyelids. For by means of a whorish woman a man is brought to a piece of bread: and the adulteress will hunt for the precious life. Can a man take fire in his bosom, and his clothes not be burned?

Proverbs 5:3-5: For the lips of a strange woman drop as an honeycomb, and her mouth is smoother than oil: But her end is bitter as wormwood, sharp as a two-edged sword. Her feet go down to death; her steps take hold on hell.

Proverbs 7:4-5: Say unto wisdom, Thou art my sister; And call understanding thy kinswoman: That they may keep thee from the strange woman, From the stranger which flatters with her words.

C.17 Did you know that the KJV of the Bible mentions a staggering **403** times the words '**strange woman**'. **Wisdom** is mentioned around **63** times. Obviously, God was trying to warn men about certain types of women, who are dangerous as they carry a familiar spirit or evil spirit of seduction that can lead the soul straight down to Hell.

C.18 Sadly, the main religious establishments have tried to subjugate women for millennia and often blame the women for the 'fall of man' and give not honour to the women because of what the daughters of Cain did before the great Flood.

C.19 Those woman who co-habited with the Fallen angels in Pre-Flood times became sirens. Those sirens became the spirits of extreme lust and destructive violence and perversion.

C.20 This is from the Apocryphal book: **'TEACHING OF THE 12 APOSTLES'** Here it is describing the Darkness and Death:-

V. 'But the path of death is this. First of all, it is evil and full of cursing; there are found murders, adulteries, lusts, fornication, thefts, idolatries, soothsaying, sorceries, robberies, false witnessings, hypocrisies, double-mindedness, craft, pride, malice, self-will, covetousness, filthy talking, jealousy, audacity, arrogance; there are they who persecute the good—lovers of a lie, not knowing the reward of righteousness, not cleaving to the good nor to righteous judgment, watching not for the good but for the bad, from whom meekness and patience are afar off, loving things that are vain, following after recompense, having no compassion on the needy, nor labouring for him that is in trouble, not knowing him that made them, murderers of children, corrupters of the image of God, who turn away from him that is in need, who oppress him that is in trouble, unjust judges of the poor, erring in all things. From all these, children, may ye be delivered.'

C.21 Perhaps because of Pre-Flood happenings mankind became afraid of the women yielding to such evil spirits of lust and perversion. Sadly, this fear of what women could do in choosing evil such as being an evil witch has led to much misunderstanding about things mentioned in the **Book of Remedies** given to Moses by the angels of the Presence which showed remedies for every known disease known to mankind.

C.22 The Book of Remedies was removed by Hezekiah in around 720 BCE at God's behest as people started worshipping this **Book of Remedies** more than God. Later I think others got copies of that book, which became the **Book of Spells** or at least part of it and used it to devise **spells and incantations** which are used by witches and wizards of the dark realms even to this day. [Book of Remedies is mentioned in the Apocryphal books:

C.23 In ancient times herbs were the main source of remedies. According to the **Book of *Jubilees (10:12)**, the angels revealed the various remedies to Noah, who wrote them down in a book: Medicinal Herbs (jewishvirtuallibrary.org) BOOK OF REMEDIES | outofthebottomlesspit.co.uk]

C.24 A VISION OF LIGHT AND DARKNESS from the Apocryphal Book 'TEACHING OF THE 12 APOSTLES'

I. There are two paths, **one of life and one of death**, and the difference is great between the two paths.

C.25 This is similar to the **TESTAMENTS OF THE TWELVE PATRIACHS** from 3700 years ago in the Old Testament, in the case of Jacob the Patriarch's son Asher.

THE TESTAMENT OF ASHER -*The Tenth Son of Jacob and Zilpah.* - **CHAPTER1.3** 'Two ways hath God given to the sons of men, and two inclinations, and two kinds of action, and two modes of action, and two issues. For there are two ways of **good and evil**.

C.26 Continuing from the Apocryphal Book: **'TEACHING OF THE 12 APOSTLES'**

II. But the second commandment of the teaching is this. Thou shalt not kill; thou shalt not commit adultery; thou shalt not corrupt youth; thou shalt not commit fornication; thou shalt not steal; thou shalt not use soothsaying; thou shalt not practise sorcery; thou shalt not kill a child by abortion, neither shalt thou slay it when born.

III. My child, fly from everything that is evil, and from everything that is like to it. Be not wrathful, for wrath leadeth unto slaughter; be not jealous, or contentious, or quarrelsome, for from all these things slaughter ensues. My child, be not lustful, for lust leadeth unto fornication; be not a filthy talker; be not a lifter up of the eye, for from all these things come adulteries. My child, be not an observer of omens, since it leadeth to idolatry, nor a user of spells, nor an astrologer, nor a travelling purifier, nor wish to see these things, for from all these things idolatry arises. My child, be not a liar, for lying leadeth unto theft; be not covetous or conceited, for from all these things thefts arise. My child, be not a murmurer, since it leadeth unto blasphemy; be not self-willed or evil-minded, for from all these things blasphemies are produced; but be thou meek, for the meek shall inherit the earth;

Now the path of life is this—first, thou shalt love the God who made thee, thy neighbour as thyself, and all things that thou would should be done unto thee, do not thou unto another. And the doctrine of these maxims is as follows. Bless them that curse you and pray for your enemies.

XV And then shall the 'Deceiver of the world' appear as the Son of God, and shall do signs and wonders, and the earth shall be delivered into his hands; and he shall do unlawful things, such as have never happened since the beginning of the world.

2 Thessalonians 2.1-12 Now we beseech you, brethren, by the coming of our Lord

Jesus Christ, and by our gathering together unto him. That ye be not soon shaken in mind, or be troubled, neither by spirit, nor by word, nor by letter as from us, as that the day of Christ is at hand. Let no man deceive you by any means: for that day shall not come, except there come a falling away first, and that man of sin be revealed, the son of perdition. Who opposes and exalts himself above all that is called God, or that is worshipped; so that he as God sits in the temple of God, shewing himself that he is God. For the mystery of iniquity doth already work: only he who now let will let, until he be taken out of the way. And then shall that Wicked be revealed, whom the Lord shall consume with the spirit of his mouth, and shall destroy with the brightness of his coming: Even him, whose coming is after the working of Satan with all power and signs and lying wonders, And with all deceivableness of unrighteousness in them that perish; because they received not the love of the truth, that they might be saved. And for this cause God shall send them strong delusion, that they should believe a lie. That they all might be damned who believed not the truth but had pleasure in unrighteousness.

DESCENT INTO DARKNESS IN THE 4TH TO 5TH CENTURY AD, as the Holy Roman Catholic church rose to power on the ashes of the Roman Empire and continued the authoritarian absolute control for a 1000 years.

C.27 THE DEADLY COUNCIL OF LAODICEA - 364 AD At the origin of the Catholic church, the Catholic church came up with 60 canonical edicts, the disobedience to which many of these edicts would result in offenders being burned at the stake.

The Books of Enoch were banned including 2nd Enoch and the punishment for having a copy of this book was indeed to be burned at the stake. This law was kept for a 1000 years by the Catholic church. Why were they so afraid of Enoch's books? Because it showed that the powers behind the Catholic church were the same devils as the disembodied spirits of the giants or sons of the Fallen angels from Pre-Flood times.

C.28 Strangely although Wikipedia mentions the Council of Laodicea in 364 AD, it ends up minimizing it, when it should have told the truth as to the beginning of 'absolute control' of what people were allowed to read. Watch out for Wikipedia as it does not have that name for no reason. It is a site for rubbishing the truth when it can get away with, it by allowing interesting information and then stating as Satan did in the Garden of Eden saying 'It ain't necessarily so' and thus casting doubt on what you have just read. That is known as modern scepticism, but it is most definitely satanic in nature and does not engender faith in God, His Word and the Truth.

C.29 Origen, called one of the founding fathers of Christianity whose Christian philosophies were largely followed by the Catholic church around 100 years after they had martyred Origen himself. He himself warned the church that they would be taken over by the same devils and demons as mentioned in the Book of Enoch, if they continued with slaughtering the innocent and martyring people like himself. The catholic church has been infamous for martyring its victims and later digging them up as saints to worship as in the case of both Origen and much later in time Joan of Arc.

C.30 Women leaders and bishops banned

Between 300-400 AD at the council of Laodicea women were banned from being bishops and spiritual leaders. Many were burned alive in their own churches for not following papal orders.

C.31 The sect of the Cathars were slaughtered in the 13th century by the Catholic church to the tune of 100,000 in the French city of Beziers in Southern France. When the general in charge of the slaughter asked the Pope or king in charge 'what about the 30,000 Catholics living in the town, he was informed to 'kill them all' as God knows his own. This attitude by the Papal powers showed their attitude towards God -total rebellion against the laws of Christ. The papal powers are certainly not Christian but often satanic.

C.32 Christ himself had nothing good to say about the church of Laodicea in the Book of Revelation

Revelation 3.14-19 And unto the angel of the church of the Laodiceans write; These things saith the Amen, the faithful and true witness, the beginning of the creation of God;

15 I know thy works, that thou art neither cold nor hot: I would thou wert cold or hot.

16 So then because thou art lukewarm, and neither cold nor hot, I will spue thee out of my mouth.

17 Because thou sayest, I am rich, and increased with goods, and have need of nothing; and knowest not that thou art wretched, and miserable, and poor, and blind, and naked:

18 I counsel thee to buy of me gold tried in the fire, that thou mayest be rich; and white raiment, that thou mayest be clothed, and *that* the shame of thy nakedness do not appear; and anoint thine eyes with eyesalve, that thou mayest see.

C.33 Enoch himself warned in the book of Enoch that the (church) devils who burned people at the stake would themselves be punished by a burning much worse than physical fire, so I would not want to be all those popes of the Catholic church during the 1000 year Inquisition where millions of people were murdered, tortured and burned at the stake. Here is an official list of a few famous martyrs, not to mention the millions of innocents slaughtered.

List of Christian martyrs: List of Christian martyrs - Wikipedial

Enoch 91.5-12

5 For I know that violence must increase on the earth,
And a great chastisement be executed on the earth,
And all unrighteousness come to an end:
Yea, it shall be cut off from its roots,
And its whole structure be destroyed.

6 And unrighteousness shall again be consummated on the earth,
And all the deeds of unrighteousness and of violence
And transgression shall prevail in a twofold degree.

7 And when sin and unrighteousness and blasphemy
And violence in all kinds of deeds increase,
And apostasy and transgression and uncleanness increase,
A great chastisement shall come from heaven upon all these,
And the holy Lord will come forth with wrath and chastisement
To execute judgement on earth.

8 In those days violence shall be cut off from its roots,
And the roots of unrighteousness together with deceit,
And they shall be destroyed from under heaven.

9 And all the idols of the heathen shall be abandoned,
And the temples burned with fire,
And they shall remove them from the whole earth,
And they (the heathen) shall be cast into the judgement of fire,
And shall perish in wrath and in grievous judgement for ever.

10 And the righteous shall arise from their sleep,
And wisdom shall arise and be given unto them.

11 And after that the roots of unrighteousness shall be cut off, and the sinners shall be destroyed by the sword and the blasphemers destroyed in every place,

12 And those who plan violence and those who commit blasphemy shall perish by the sword.

C.34 Origen warned the Catholic church when he himself was tortured by them that they were becoming just like those described in the Book of Enoch of being the reprobate wicked who killed the innocent. This was probably why the Books of Enoch were banned around 100 years after the death of Origen in 230 AD. According to scholars and historians Origen died from the torturous wounds afflicted on him by the Catholic church a few years after his inquisition. Again, we have another example where the Catholic church murdered a person and then later acknowledged them as a saint or hero like Joan of Arc in the 14th century. Many of Origen's teachings became the backbone of theology of the Catholic church. Origen wrote around 6000 books and articles and taught in the most prestigious places of the Roman Empire. He was very famous in his day and was known as a Christian philosopher. Observers stated that he spoke the Word of God with great conviction and was very persuasive in teaching Christianity.

Author: Today I wanted to sum up some of my thoughts about this book of 2nd Enoch.

C.35) One needs to have read the 1st Book of Enoch in order to have a better grasp of the meaning of the 2nd Book of Enoch. I have written about 1st Enoch and 2nd Enoch in my INSIGHTS books: Book 1: Enoch Insights; Book 2: Secrets of Enoch Insights

C.36) There is a lot of excellent scholarly material out there about the Books of Enoch:

One cannot understand about Pre-Creation as mentioned in this 2nd Book of Enoch without first knowing that the Holy Spirit is female or the Mother of God. This is the reason why the 25th chapter about Adoil seems so strange and confusing when one first reads it.

Instead of the name Adoil I would say (excuse the pun) (Ad the oil) of the feminine Holy Spirit to your knowledge, and thus have great Wisdom.

C.37) Adoil is the Holy Spirit in my opinion also known as Wisdom in the Hebrew Old Testament. She is Wisdom as mentioned clearly in Proverbs 8 and many other Proverbs as well as other passages in the KJV Bible. The Holy Spirit is Mother God and the mother of Jesus. In fact She is Mother and Creator of all the female side of the Creation.

C.38) There was God the Father and God the Mother according to 25th chapter of 2nd Enoch and then was a sort of birth and then born the Son of God Jesus who was made in charge of all the higher realms or dimensions of light

38) Chapter 26 tells of another female entity and another sort of birth of yet another obviously female being that God the Father makes in charge of all the lower regions or dimensions. Who is this female entity? I don't think that it is Satan as he ends up as an inmate of the Bottomless Pit in the nether worlds and he and his fallen angels end up in the lake of fire. This female entity of darkness seems to be a direct dark reflection of the female Holy Spirit. I must say it is difficult to fathom exactly what Enoch was talking about. I would say that the dark reflection of the Holy Spirt being is an anti-Holy Spirit being in every sense of the word. Is this negative female entity participant in the lives of mankind? Who is she? Well, we certainly don't have all the answers. There have certainly been some very powerful dark female entities mentioned throughout history such as Astaroth, but I don't think we can find one that could be described as 'in charge of all the lower dimensions? Chapter 26 of 2nd Enoch is in fact very mysterious and I would say incomplete and somewhat hidden from view because the scribes that put it together did not acknowledge that the Holy Spirit is female and the wife of God the Father and Mother of Jesus so that they talk about a 'He' that is pregnant which is insane! Only the female gets pregnant by God's design.

C.39) When we say God in Hebrew it uses the word Elohim meaning 'gods'. So when we are talking about God we are really talking about a couple -God the Father and God the Mother.

C.40) From the Bible it tells us that there is an angel in charge of the Bottomless Pit in Revelation 20.

It also tells us in the Hebrew Book of 1st Book of Enoch that Uriel or Ariel has one of his responsibilities is being in charge of the Lake of Fire. What this is telling me is that God the Father is ultimately totally in charge of the higher dimensions and the Lower dimensions, but he has his guardians in charge of different realms within His vast kingdom

1st ENOCH Chapter 20.1-2 And these are the names of the angels who watch: Uriel one of the holy angels who is over the world and Tartarus. Raphael who is over the spirits of men. Raguel one of the holy angels who takes vengeance on the world of the luminaries. Michael one of the holy angels, to wit, he that is set over the best part of mankind and over chaos. Saraquael one of the holy angels who is set over the spirit who sin in the spirit: Gabriel one of the holy angels, who is over paradise and the serpents and the Cherubim: Remiel one of the holy angels whom God has set over those who rise. (are resurrected)

1st ENOCH Chapter 40.8-9 After that I asked the angel of peace who went with me and showed me everything that was hidden; 'Who are these four presences, which I have seen and whose words I have heard and written? And he said to me, 'This is Michael the merciful and long-suffering (commander of the Lords hosts) and the second who is set over all the diseases and all the wounds of the children of men is Raphael; and third, who is set over the powers is Gabriel; and the fourth is set over repentance unto hope of those who inherit eternal life is called Phanuel. These are the four angels of the Lord of spirits and the four voices I heard in those days.

C.41) I know that Hell itself has an overseer, but it is certainly not Satan as he is destined to become one of the inmates.

C.42) Enoch mentions in 1st Enoch in chapter 22 - 3-4 vast hollow areas inside the earth which must be massive, to contain all the souls who have died throughout history or many billions of people. We know that the earth is hollow and not solid from many studies of both science and scripture.

C.43) We know from scripture that one day all the lower dimensions will be done away with after they have served their complete purpose.

Revelation 20.14 'Death and hell were cast into the lake of fire'

C.44) How many lower dimensions are there? Now that is a good question. Going strictly from scriptures whether in the KJV Bible or from the Apocryphal and Hebrew books of old we come to the following conclusions.

Sheol or the unseen state where all people who die go to first of all Enoch mentions 3-4 different levels. There is also Hell and the Lake of Fire. So, I can count at least 6 lower levels. The Catholics according to the Book Dante's Inferno mention around 10 lower levels. They have different levels for different crimes and iniquities that man has committed. Of course, there could be many more lower levels. Only God knows the truth about that.

C.45) I read an amazing book about Hell one time, where each person was re-living that hell that they had created whilst on the earth and each life has a whole situation tailed just jro them. So that would suggest infinite possibilities in hell. Here is a quote from that amazing book. You can find a lot more info about the conditions in Hell by reading my 1st book Out of the Bottomless Pit chapter 16 TRIPS TO HELL -THE GREEN DOOR

C.46) MY IST BOOK OUT OF THE BOTTOMLES PIT -Chapter 16

'Everything everybody was doing was totally futile and useless and just a waste of time! They were all very busy accomplishing nothing. Everything was not only endless and fruitless and futile, but sort of backwards. I had a feeling that things were either inside out or upside down, so peculiar!. I thought to myself 'Wow this must be Hell! I thought what could be worse than that for the wicked -an extension of 'life after death' for the wicked would be just a hellish extension of the same meaningless, purposeless, fruitless existence, painful existence, sorrowful existence, sad existence! Each person was continuing in their own private Hell of his former existence without any relief, no surcease, no hope of it ever ending, and yet all absolutely useless. Hell is the extension, multiplication, amplification, continuation, endless continuation of the same monotonous lives that the wicked people of the world live even right now. The writer of this book who visited hell mentioned that **Hell had an angelic over-seer.**

C.47) According to the Apocryphal Book of 2nd Esdras God told Esra to make 25 of the books available for the general public and the rest of the book around 70 in number are just for the initiated

C.48) Another very important point is that books such as the Books of Enoch cannot be understood unless you have the Key to opening the books.

C.49) The Key is to have received Jesus the Saviour and Messiah into your heart and to have asked for the Holy Spirit to fill you with Her Wisdom as in Proverbs 8. Also all the early Christians were anointed by the Holy Spirit Mother to enable them to be a witness for Jesus and thus preach the Gospel about Jesus the Saviour.

C.50) Here is a simple prayer of Salvation 'Dear Jesus please forgive me my sins, come into my heart and save me and fill me up with your Holy Spirit and help and empower me to love others and tell others about the truth of salvation. Amen

C.51) In the times before Christ when people died they all went down into the earth or SHEOL which is a waiting place for the spirits -when it is decide where they deserve to go .

C.52) After Christ came and died for mankind the righteous or saved no longer go down into the earth to the wayfaring station in Sheol, but they go straight upwards to the Heavenly city as mentioned in the Book of Revelation. Jesus also stated in John

John 14 2-6. In My Father's house are many mansions; if it were not so, I would have told you. I go to prepare a place for you. And if I go and prepare a place for you, I will come again and receive you to Myself; that where I am, there you may be also. And where I go you know, and the way you know."

C.53) IN CONCLUSION FOR CHAPTERS 25 & 26 ABOUT LIGHT & DARKNESS.

It is very important to realize that most of the TRUTH has been deliberately hidden from the view of the public since the time of Creation by devils and demons working in the darkness and lower regions and also the Prince of the Air-Satan in the atmosphere above us.

We live in a sort of negative Matrix, where we have to diligently search for the truth. The world is currently descending into total darkness, lawlessness and chaos just like in pre-Flood times According to the Bible Evil itself will be personified in the character of the ANTI-CHRIST who will come on the scene to supposedly rescue man from the mayhem.

There will be a 7-year Peace Pact based in Jerusalem between Jews, Muslims and Christians. A third Temple will be built in Jerusalem. This will give a plastic Peace for 3 and a half years until the Antichrist declares himself god and demands that all the world worship him as god. He will by then be Satan incarnate.

Then will begin 3 and a half years of GREAT TRIBULATION. The infamous Mark of the beast of Revelation 13 will come to fruition as well as the worship of the Image of the Beast.

After a reign of terror for 3 and half years Jesus will return and take the righteous home to heaven and he will destroy all of Satan's forces.

Then will be poured out the Wrath of God (Revelation 14) upon the earth as well as the Battle of Armageddon. Finally, all evil and spiritual hordes of darkness of devils and demons and other critters will get locked up in the Bottomless Pit according to Revelation 20.

The Golden Age of the Millennium will begin with Christ as King of Kings and Lord of Lords for 1000 years.

After the 1000 years of Golden Age of Peace, Satan will be loosed out of the Bottomless Pit with his evil entourage for a little season according to Revelation 20 and will go out to deceive the nations once more.

Finally, God gets totally fed up with them and fire comes down from heaven to destroy them all. Satan himself then gets thrown into the Lake of Fire according to Revelation 20.

Then comes the Great White Throne Judgment where all the souls who have ever lived who were not saved by Christ are judged. If they are not found in the Book of Life they are thrown into the Lake of Fire.

After that comes the eternal age where there is no more evil or darkness and where Death & Hell are cast into the Lake of Fire. Then God's wonderful Heavenly Crystal city will descent to the earth and the heavenly life will begin for all where there is no more war only joy and peace forever after and where all of your dreams really do come true. Heaven is a wonderful place where we can all be happy and one day it will come down to the surface of the earth at the end of the Golden Age.

It will then be a world in the light with Christ, and His Holy Spirit Mother and God the Father with no more in the darkness of Satan, demons and evil mankind. What about those who went into the Lake of fire? Will they repent? According to some of the chapters of this book of 2nd Enoch it looks like many of them finally will repent.

Unfortunately for Satan, according to the **Book of Isaiah chapter 14, Satan is to be made an end of** and probably all the ruling spiritual powers that exist today and who rule the world through their puppets on the earth insane demon-possessed leaders and controllers of the earth in finance and politics.

CHAPTER 27

> AND I commanded that there should be taken from light and darkness, and I said: 'Be thick,' and it became thus and I spread it out with the light, and it became water, and I spread it out over the darkness, below the light, and then I made firm the waters, that is to say the bottomless, and I made foundation of light around the water, and created seven circles from inside, and imaged it (*sc.* the water) like crystal wet and dry, that is to say like glass, *and* the circumcession of the waters and the other elements, and I showed each one of them its road, and the seven stars each one of them in its heaven, that they go thus, and I saw that it was good.

C.1 Now what on earth is this verse talking about as one can't build the planet without earth and rocks etc This above verse mentions 7 stars and waters but no earth?

C.2 Circumcession -def. I could not find a definition for this word, but it would seem to mean 'circulation' or 'flow'. The earth according to Creation Science is made with a Canopy of water above it, about 100 miles up in the sky, which used to protect the earth from UV and cosmic rays and was the reason people used to live for 900 years before the Great Flood.

C.3 The earth is also strongly influenced by the stars which are taken care of by God's angels of light.

C.4 Why was the canopy 100 miles up in the sky? This is the location apparently where gravity and centrifugal forces cancel each other out in opposite directions and thus the canopy would just float there at that level protecting the earth from harm from radiation.

Genesis 1.6-8 And God said 'Let there be a firmament in the midst of the waters and let it divide the waters from the waters. And God made the firmament and divided the waters that were **under** the firmament from the waters that were **above** the firmament; and it was so. And God called the firmament Heaven

Job 37.18 Hast thou with him spread out the <u>sky</u>, which is strong, and as a molten <u>looking glass</u>?

C.5 This above verse in Job is clearly stating that the waters above the sky used to look like a mirror or a 'looking glass' in Pre-Flood times and before the canopy of waters was destroyed.

C.6 The firmament of Heaven here is talking about the sky. God is stating here that at the beginning of creation he made the land and seas. Far above the sky he also placed waters which are known as the Canopy.

C.7 It is estimated that the water canopy above the earth was between 1- 5 meters thick and circulated around the entire globe. I also believe that the earth was created hollow and there would have also been a canopy of waters above the undersurface of the earth for the exact same reason. According to ancient Hebrew texts the Garden of Eden was located inside a Hollow Earth which is reflected in the Jewish mystical book the Zohar along with other books.

C.8 It shows God creating the land and seas in Genesis 1.9-10 and makes a distinction from the waters above the sky or firmament of heaven.

Genesis 1.9-10 Then God said, "Let the waters under the heavens be gathered together into one place, and let the dry land appear"; and it was so. And God called the dry land Earth, and the gathering together of the waters He called Seas. And God saw that it was good.

C.9 It sounds like God is explaining how He made the earth, and he mentions the 'bottomless'. Well, I explained in a video some 5 years ago that when God created the earth that perhaps it was similar to a pottery class. I used to do pottery when at school. All God had to do was put His hands through from another dimension of the spiritual dimensions and with a gigantic piece of clay in his hands set it spinning. In pottery one has a spinning wheel and you the student are given a limp of clay. You then put the clay in the middle of the spinning wheel and your hands are forced outwards as a vessel automatically is created. You notice right away that the vessel is hollow and has holes at the top and bottom. I think that is also what God is describing here, that He created a hollow earth in mentioning the 'bottomless' which is **inside** the earth. See my video on YOUTUBE: (917) 'HOLLOW EARTH' & 'HOLES AT THE POLES' - PARANORMAL - -by S.N.Strutt VIDEO 1 - YouTube

C.10 'created **seven circles** from inside' There was a famous scientist called Symmes some hundreds of years ago claiming that the earth was both hollow and that there were globes one inside the other inside the earth with holes at their poles and that each glove could support life. See my book **'OUT OF THE BOTTOMLESS PIT 1'** about the Hollow Earth Theory:

In 1818, 'John Cleves Symmes (1780-1829) circulated a flyer announcing his theory of Earth's structure and polar geography. Declaring that Earth is "hollow, and habitable within; containing a number of solid concentric spheres, one within the other, and that it is open at the poles 12 or 16 degrees," Symmes solicited ".one hundred brave men" for an expedition north of the 82nd parallel in search of "a warm and rich land, stocked with thrifty vegetables and animals, if not men." So began the history of American polar exploration. Symmes's idea attracted general ridicule, but it also tapped a vein of cultural patriotism, national pride, and expansionist ambition that won him a group of loyal followers. Chief among Symmes's supporters was Jeremiah Reynolds, who played a key role in obtaining congressional funding for the Great American Exploring Expedition of 1838-1842. In this paper, I recount the story of Symmes's theory and trace its influence on the establishment of a wholly American scientific enterprise and American literature and fringe culture.'

SOURCE: (PDF) Hollow and Habitable Within: Symmes's Theory of Earth's Internal Structure and Polar Geography (researchgate.net)

C.11 Did you know that Satan stated to God that he was going 'to and fro' in the earth and 'up and down' IN the earth: It sounds like the earth is hollow:

Book of Job 1.6-7 Now there was a day when the sons of God came to present themselves before the Lord, and Satan came also among them.

And the LORD said unto Satan, 'Whence comest thou? Then Satan answered the LORD, and said, From going to and fro in the earth, and from walking up and down in it.

C.12 Genesis 1.2 And the earth was without form and void; And darkness was upon the face of the deep.

This verse in Genesis seems to be describing the original mass that God had in His hands while making the earth. 'Without form and 'void'.

Void can mean emptiness or an empty place.

In simple terms of the Potter - God had a mass of material and set it spinning and a vessel appeared rather like in pottery when a spinning wheel is used, and you put a lump of clay on the wheel and the spinning motion forces the clay in your hands outwards and forms a vessel which is both hollow with holes at the top and bottom.

In the case of the earth, we have Hollow earth and the 'Holes at the Poles'.

C.13 In summary according to science before 1950 concerning the Creation of the earth: 1) A canopy of water around the earth 2) The land and seas on the outer crust and its mountains. 3) Hollow earth with the crust around 300-500 miles thick 4) Underworld crust of the earth also with lands and seas and high mountains, many of which are volcanic. 5) Above the surface of the inner earth a canopy of water 6) A central sun in the middle of the earth around 600 miles in diameter.

Psalm 136.5-6 To Him that by wisdom made the heavens. To Him that stretched out the earth **above** the waters

C.14 What waters could be contained below the earth? Apparently, science is finding out that there are indeed vast oceans below the surface of the earth that are even bigger than the ones on the surface of the earth. It is stated that circa 300 miles down in the earth are great caverns or massive seas and reservoirs of waters.

C.15 If one takes all of the above information on board it makes this 1st and 2nd verses of this chapter make a lot more sense as to its strange description of Creation made from light and darkness.

C.16 By examining carefully different Bible verses we find that it is mentioned that there are 1) waters above the firmament of the sky and 2) waters in which the earth and lands appear and that also there are 3) waters under the earth as well.

Jeremiah 10.12-13 He hath made the earth by his power, he hath established the world by his wisdom, and hath stretched out the heavens by his discretion. When he utters his voice, there is a multitude of waters in the heavens, and he causes the vapours to ascend from the ends of the earth; he maketh lightnings with rain, and bringeth forth the wind out of his

C.17 These above verses reveal a lot about Creation. 1) stretched out the heavens 2) multitude of waters in the heavens 3) vapours to ascend from the ends of the earth 4) maketh lightnings with rain 5) bringeth forth the wind 6) treasures.

JOB 26.5 Dead things are formed from under the waters, and the inhabitants thereof.

C.18 'Dead things are formed from under the waters'. Now what could that be referring to? And the inhabitants thereof. What inhabitants live under the sea? Now there is a good question?!

JOB 26.6 Hell is naked before him, and destruction hath no covering.

C.19 'Hell is naked before him and destruction hath no covering'. Clearly it is stating that God is in control of Hell and knows all that is going on there. Destruction hath no covering. All the destructions going on by mankind are all known to God. Is God inferring that the earth is hollow as Hell needed a place to be inside the earth?

JOB 26.7 He stretches out the north over the empty place and hangs the earth upon nothing.

C.20 Now this verse is the clincher of Creation: *'He stretches out the North over the empty space'* As I mentioned before in pottery whilst making a vessel, one sets it upon a spinning wheel and places a piece of clay in the middle of the spinning wheel and the clay is forced out in all directions leaving a 'hollow forming vessel', which also has 'holes in the top and bottom'. So, it is also with the planet. There are holes at the poles of around 1500 miles in diameter. They are cloaked by clouds most of the time. This is clearly mentioned in Job 26.8. The clouds are caused by the extremes of temperature in those regions.

JOB 26.8 He binds up the waters in his thick clouds; and the cloud is not rent under them.

C.21 *'And hangs the earth upon nothing'* This part of the verse is amazing, as you could only observe this if you were an observer in outer space looking down on the North Pole, and seeing the earth hanging in space and perhaps noticing that it is spinning but that nothing is attached to the top of the earth, as there is a hole there, and nothing can be attached to the North Pole as in fact it is but a giant hole leading to the Inner Earth. So how does the earth just sit and spin in space so perfectly, without any thing attached to the very top of it. It does not even wobble! That seems to be the observation of this Bible verse given to Job by God.

JOB 26.9 He holds back the face of his throne and spreads his cloud upon it.

C.22 JOB 26.9 - This verse is stating that God was sitting on His throne whilst he was creating the earth, and when he created all the clouds. Clouds according to science cover from 5 to 90% of the earth's atmosphere at any given time and that the clouds are created by the difference in the temperatures of the moving or circulating seas.

C.23 God 'sitting on His throne' whilst 'making His creation' is also mentioned in this very Book of "2nd Enoch - in an earlier chapter.

[10] **JOB 26.10** He hath compassed the waters with bounds, until the day and night come to an end.

C.24 All these verses in the Book of Job are to do with Creation and how God formed the earth. It is very important to know that the earth is in fact hollow if we are to understand the weather correctly, which modern science cannot, because they teach that the earth is solid. What is the difference?

C.25 Well, if the earth is in fact hollow, and that there is an under crust to the earth which also has seas, then the climate of the Inner Earth would affect the climate on the outside.

C.26 We now know that the seas are in circulation and go through the poles into the inner earth through the North Pole and eventually come out of the Southern Pole which affects the temperatures of the seas and affects the climate of the outer earth.

C.27 Because attention to the above facts is not taken seriously by modern science, this could explain the many strange occurrences on our planet, and why man can never predict the weather correctly well in advance. Simply put, there are too many factors that science simply does not take into consideration whilst trying to predict the weather forecast.

> 2 And I separated between light and between darkness, that is to say in the midst of the water hither and thither, and I said to the light, that it should be the day, and to the darkness, that it should be the night, and there was evening and there was morning the first day.

C.28 ROUND EARTH - THE EARTH IS ROUND ACCORDING TO THE BIBLE!

Isaiah 40.22 It is he that sits upon the **circle** of the earth, and the inhabitants thereof are as grasshoppers; that stretches out the heavens as a curtain, and spreads them out as a tent to dwell in:

Job 26: 7 He stretches out the north over the empty place and hangs the earth upon nothing.

C.29 "The flat Earth model is an archaic conception of the Earth's shape as a plane or disk. Many ancient cultures subscribed to a flat Earth cosmography, including Greece until the classical period, the Bronze Age and Iron Age civilizations of the Near East until the Hellenistic period, India until the Gupta period (early centuries AD) and China until the 17th century. That paradigm was also typically held in the aboriginal cultures of the Americas, and the notion of a flat Earth domed by the firmament in the shape of an inverted bowl was common in pre-scientific societies.

C.30 The idea of a spherical Earth appeared in Greek philosophy with Pythagoras (6th century BC), although most Pre-Socratics retained the flat Earth model.

Aristotle provided evidence for the spherical shape of the Earth on empirical grounds by around 330 BC. Knowledge of the spherical Earth gradually began to spread beyond the Hellenistic world from then on.

Ancient Near East In early Egyptian and Mesopotamian thought the world was portrayed as a flat disk floating in the ocean. A similar model is found in the Homeric account of the 8th century BC in which "Okeanos, the personified body of water surrounding the circular surface of the Earth, is the begetter of all life and possibly of all gods."

C.31 The Israelites likely had a similar cosmology, with the earth as a flat disc floating on water beneath an arced firmament separating it from the heavens. The Pyramid Texts and Coffin Texts reveal that the ancient Egyptians believed Nun (the Ocean) was a circular body (a term meaning "dry lands" or "Islands"), and therefore believed in a similar Ancient Near Eastern circular earth cosmography surrounded by water.

C.32 Early Christian Church The influential theologian and philosopher Saint Augustine, one of the four Great Church Fathers of the Western Church, similarly objected to the "fable" of an inhabited Antipodes: But as to the fable that there are Antipodes, that is to say, men on the opposite side of the earth, where the sun rises when it sets to us, men who walk with their feet opposite ours that is on no ground credible. And, indeed, it is not affirmed that this has been learned by historical knowledge, but by scientific conjecture, on the ground that the earth is suspended within the concavity of the sky, and that it has as much room on the one side of it as on the other: hence they say that the part that is beneath must also be inhabited.

But they do not remark that, although it be supposed or scientifically demonstrated that the world is of a round and spherical form, yet it does not follow that the other side of the earth is bare of water; nor even, though it be bare, does it immediately follow that it is peopled.

For Scripture, which proves the truth of its historical statements by the accomplishment of its prophecies, gives no false information; and it is too absurd to say, that some men might have taken ship and traversed the whole wide ocean, and crossed from this side of the world to the other, and that thus even the inhabitants of that distant region are descended from that one first man.

The view generally accepted by scholars of Augustine's work is that he shared the common view of his contemporaries that the Earth is spherical, in line with his endorsement of science in De Genesi ad litteram.

That view was challenged by noted Augustine scholar Leo Ferrari, who concluded that he was familiar with the Greek theory of a spherical earth, nevertheless, (following in the footsteps of his fellow North African, Lactantius), he was firmly convinced that the earth was flat, was one of the

two biggest bodies in existence and that it lay at the bottom of the universe.
Apparently, Augustine saw this picture as more useful for scriptural exegesis than the global earth at the centre of an immense universe. Diodorus of Tarsus, a leading figure in the School of Antioch and mentor of John Chrysostom, may have argued for a flat Earth; however, Diodorus' opinion on the matter is known only from a later criticism.

Chrysostom, one of the four Great Church Fathers of the Eastern Church and Archbishop of Constantinople, explicitly espoused the idea, based on scripture, that the Earth floats miraculously on the water beneath the firmament. Athanasius the Great, Church Father and Patriarch of Alexandria, expressed a similar view in Against the Heathen.

Severian, Bishop of Gabala, wrote that the Earth is flat and the sun does not pass under it in the night, but "travels through the northern parts as if hidden by a wall".

"And they said, Come, let us build to ourselves a city and tower, whose top shall be to heaven, and let us make to ourselves a name, before we are scattered abroad upon the face of all the earth." Genesis 11

The Bible clearly stated that the earth is round and a globe in the Book of Job and Isaiah and proverbs:

Job 26.7,10 He stretches out the north over the void and hangs the earth on nothing. He has inscribed a circle on the face of the waters at the boundary between light and darkness.

Isaiah 40.21 Do you not know? Do you not hear? Has it not been told you from the beginning? Have you not understood from the foundations of the earth? It is he who sits above the circle of the earth, and its inhabitants are like grasshoppers; who stretches out the heavens like a curtain, and spreads them like a tent to dwell in;
Isaiah 40.22 'It is he who sits above the **circle** of the earth, and its inhabitants are like grasshoppers; who stretches out the heavens like a curtain, and spreads them like a tent to dwell in'

Proverbs 8.27 When he established the heavens, I was there; when he drew a circle on the face of the deep.

This book of the 'Secrets of Enoch' or otherwise known as the 2nd Book of Enoch also clearly states that the earth is round; as does also the 1st Book of Enoch

C.32 It is hard to understand how mankind has so often been devoid of understanding when it comes to the truth in science when it was clearly made known to man in the Bible thousands of years ago that the earth is round?

CHAPTER 28

> *The week in which God showed Enoch all his wisdom and power, throughout all the seven days, how he created all the heavenly and earthly forces and all moving things even down to man.*
>
> AND then I made firm **the heavenly circle**, and *made* that the **lower water** which is under heaven collect itself together, into one whole, and that the chaos become dry, and it became so.

C.1 The heavenly circle? This seems to be talking about the canopy of water that used to surround the entire planet some 100 miles up in the atmosphere, where the forces of gravity and centrifugal forces cancelled each other out.

C.2 This canopy was destroyed at the time of the Great Flood of Noah. Some say the canopy could have been ice rather than water.

C.3 In order to maintain the amazing light qualities of water of reflection, refraction and ability to also act as a magnifying lens, I personally think that the canopy was made of water and stayed as water as those waters were always moving, and thus did not freeze out there in space or around 100 miles high above the earth.

C.4 This bit is talking about the seas on the earth: 'made that the lower water which is under heaven collect itself together, into one whole, and that the chaos become dry, and it became so.'

> 2. Out of the waves I created rock hard and big, and from the rock I piled up the dry, and the dry I called earth, and the midst of the earth I called abyss, that is to say the bottomless, I collected the sea in one place and bound it together with a yoke.

C.5 'midst of the earth I called abyss, that is to say the bottomless' What a verse - clearly showing that God created the earth hollow! The word Bottomless Pit is mentioned.

There are abysses descending through the crust of the earth. When the Great Flood came the seas and waters were descending into these abysses, which are mentioned to be bottomless. Why does it say bottomless? If the earth was solid it would not use the word 'bottomless'. Bottomless – definition without a bottom or endless

ABYSS - Definition: The bottomless Pit is translated from the Greek word "abusos," or in English "abyss." In the Greek Old Testament, it refers to the formless earth before Creation:

Genesis 1:1, 2 "And the earth was without form and void and darkness was upon the face of the deep"

Luke 8:31 "And they begged Him that He would not command them to go out into the abyss."

C.6 This above verse refers to a place where demons have no one to possess or use.

Revelation 20:1-3 "Then I saw an angel coming down from heaven, having the key to the bottomless pit and a great chain in his hand. He laid hold of the dragon, that serpent of old, who is *the* Devil and Satan, and bound him for a thousand years; and he cast him into the bottomless pit, and shut him up, and set a seal on him, so that he should deceive the nations no more till the thousand years were finished. But after these things he must be released for a little while"

> 3 And I said to the sea: 'Behold I give thee *thy* eternal limits, and thou shalt not break loose from thy component parts.›
>
> 4 Thus I made fast the firmament. This day I called me the first-created.

C.7 'The Bottomless Pit' as defined in Revelation 20

If the earth is hollow, and has a crust of around 500 miles thick, then the centre of gravity of the planet would be in the middle of the crust and not in the centre of the planet. If one opened up an Abyss in the crust of the earth that was bottomless pit how could it be bottomless? If one could dig a very deep pit of hundreds of miles deep, any object thrown into the pit would keep falling until it came close to the centre of gravity of the crust of the earth and would pass the centre of gravity until the gravity changed direction and what had been down was now up and this would slow down the object until it fell in the opposite direction. Therefore, the perfect place for a bottomless pit would be in the 500 miles of the crust of the earth.

C.8 Any person like Satan of the Fallen angels thrown into such a place would simply oscillate back and forth for 1000 years. Of course, this is just a physical illustration of a spiritual occurrence.

C.9 Geo-centrism and Helio-centrism

Romans 8:22 For we know that the whole creation groans and travails in pain together until now.

C.10 The geocentric universe is limited in size as opposed to a heliocentric universe which may be limitless in size. Below are some verses that we think could help to lend support to the hypothesis we plan to put forth.

Romans 8:21-23 Because the creature itself also shall be delivered from the bondage of corruption into the glorious liberty of the children of God. For we know that the whole creation groaneth and travaileth in pain together until now. And not only they, but ourselves also, which have the firstfruits of the Spirit, even we ourselves groan within ourselves, waiting for the adoption, to wit, the redemption of our body.

C.11 In these verses we wanted to point out the word "delivered" in verse 21. and also how it is the entire creation, not just the earth, that is groaning and travailing in pain in verse 22. and in Colossians 1:16-17 The Creation not only seems to include the earth but the entire universe both seen and unseen. "For by him were all things created, that are in heaven, and that are in earth, visible and invisible, whether they be thrones, or dominions, or principalities, or powers: all things were created by him, and for him. And he is before all things, and by him all things consist."
So, when does this deliverance take place?

C.12 Romans 8:23 is very specific as to when this happens, at the time of the redemption of our body.

1Corinthians 15.52 "In a moment, in the twinkling of an eye, at the last trump: for the trumpet shall sound, and the dead shall be raised incorruptible, and we shall be changed."

1 Thessalonians 4:16: "For the Lord himself shall descend from heaven with a shout, with the voice of the archangel, and with the trump of God: and the dead in Christ shall rise first."

Revelation 10:7: "But in the days of the voice of the seventh angel, when he shall begin to sound, the mystery of God should be finished, as he hath declared to his servants the prophets."

C.13 The whole creation groaning and travailing in pain waiting to be delivered sounds to us very similar to a woman who is pregnant and about to give birth.

Luke 21:8-11,25-28 "And there shall be signs in the sun, and in the moon, and in the stars; and upon the earth distress of nations, with perplexity; the sea and the waves roaring; Men's hearts failing them for fear, and for looking after those things which are coming on the earth: for the powers of heaven shall be shaken. And then shall they see the Son of Man coming in a cloud with power and great glory. And when these things begin to come to pass, then look up, and lift up your heads; for your redemption draweth nigh."

C.14 Luke 21:28 like Romans 8:23 again uses the word "redemption" at the time of the second coming of Jesus.

Revelation 12:1-3 "And there appeared a great wonder in heaven; a woman clothed with the sun, and the moon under her feet, and upon her head a crown of twelve stars: And she being with child cried, travailing in birth, and pained to be delivered. And she brought forth a man child, who was to rule all nations with a rod of iron: and her child was caught up unto God, and to his throne."

C.15 Here we see a pregnant woman in heaven about to give birth to a man child who is to "rule all nations with a rod of iron". We know this prophecy has not been fulfilled and will not be fulfilled until the second coming of Jesus. He certainly did not rule all nations with a rod of iron upon His first coming.

Psalm 2:9 "Thou shalt break them with a rod of iron; thou shalt dash them in pieces like a potter's vessel."

Luke 1:30-35 "And the angel said unto her, Fear not, Mary: for thou hast found favour with God. And, behold, thou shalt conceive in thy womb, and bring forth a son, and shalt call his name Jesus. He shall be great, and shall be called the Son of the Highest: and the Lord God shall give unto him the throne of his father David: And he shall reign over the house of Jacob for ever; and of his kingdom there shall be no end. Then said Mary unto the angel, How shall this be, seeing I know not a man? And the angel answered and said unto her, The Holy Ghost shall come upon thee, and the power of the Highest shall overshadow thee: therefore also that holy thing which shall be born of thee shall be called the Son of God."

C.16 Continuing in Luke 1, one of the first things Mary does after receiving this message from Gabriel is to visit her cousin Elisabeth who is six months pregnant with John the Baptist. As soon as Elisabeth hears Mary's greeting the babe leaped in her womb. "And it came to pass, that, when Elisabeth heard the salutation of Mary, the babe leaped in her womb; and Elisabeth was filled with the Holy Ghost."

C.17 Obviously the "womb" is of tremendous importance both spiritually and physically. Three other verses in which "womb" could almost be interpreted as somewhat of an enigma are:

Psalm 110:3 "Thy people shall be willing in the day of thy power, in the beauties of holiness from the womb of the morning." (KJV)

Job 38:8,29 "And I shut up the sea with gates, when it rushed out, coming forth out its mother's womb." "Out of whose womb comes the ice?"

Genesis 25:23 "And the Lord said to her, There are two nations in thy womb."

C.18 Here we have the Lord speaking of the sea coming out of its mother's womb, ice coming out of a womb and two nations coming from Rachel's womb. Very mysterious occurrences. When you think about two nations coming from the womb of a woman it sounds, well, unusual. Obviously, pregnancy, the womb, and deliverance both spiritually and physically are absolutely fundamentally essential for our redemption.

C.19 Before wrapping this up we wanted to share a few verses from Proverbs, chapter eight, regarding the Holy Spirit, the third member of the Godhead. "Thou shalt proclaim wisdom, that understanding may be obedient to thee. For she is on lofty eminences, and stands in the midst of the ways. For she sits by the gates of princes, and sings in the entrances. The Lord made me the beginning of his ways for his works. He established me before time was in the beginning, before he made the earth: even before he made the depths; before the fountains of water came forth: before the mountains were settled, and before all hills, he begets me. The Lord made countries and uninhabited tracks, and the highest inhabited parts of the world. When he prepared the heaven, I was present with him; and when he prepared his throne upon the winds: and when he strengthened the clouds above;

and when he secured the fountains of the earth: and when he strengthened the foundations of the earth: I was by him, suiting myself to him, I was that wherein he took delight; and daily I rejoiced in his presence continually." Wisdom, as is very clear, is definitely referred to in the feminine pronoun. Those of you familiar with my views will know that I believe the Holy Spirit to be the female representative of the Trinity. Incidentally the Shekiniah Glory, which rested between the wings of the Cherubim on the mercy seat atop the Ark of the Covenant, was a feminine representation of the glory of God.

Genesis 1:26-27 "And God said, 'Let us' make man according to our image and likeness, and let them have dominion over the fish of the sea, and over the flying creatures of heaven, and over the cattle and all the earth, and over all the reptiles that creep on the earth. And God made man, according to the image of God he made him, male and female he made them." Let's go back to the idea of a finite geocentric universe. If the Bible is to be taken literally, outside the universe is some type of water surrounding the universe.

Genesis 1:6-8 "And God said, Let there be a firmament in the midst of the water, and let it be a division between water and water, and it was so. And God made the firmament, and God divided between the water which was under the firmament and the water which was above the firmament. And God called the firmament Heaven, and God saw that it was good, and there was evening and there was morning, the second day."

Genesis 7:11 "In the six hundredth year of the life of Noe, in the second month, on the twenty-seventh day of the month, on this day all the fountains of the abyss were broken up, and the flood-gates (windows) of heaven were opened." Is it possible that the water that exists around the universe is representative or could actually be the womb of the Holy Spirit which the whole creation is groaning and travailing in pain together waiting to be delivered through the redemption by the second coming of Jesus the Messiah? The womb of the universe, seen and unseen.

CHAPTER 29

> *Then it became evening, and then again morning, and it was the second day. [Monday is the first day.] The fiery Essence.*
>
> AND for all the heavenly troops I imaged the image and essence of fire, and my eye looked at the very hard, firm rock, and from the gleam of my eye the lightning received its wonderful nature, *which is both fire in water and water in fire, and one does not put out the other, nor does the one dry up the other, therefore the lightning is brighter than the sun, softer than water and firmer than hard rock.*
>
> 2 And from the rock I cut off a great fire, and from the fire I created the orders of the incorporeal ten troops of angels, and their weapons are fiery and their raiment a burning flame, and I commanded that each one should stand in his order.

C.1 'from the fire I created the orders of the incorporeal ten troops of angels' Here God is stating that He created angels out of fire. Well, that is spiritual fire obviously as the physical world was brought into being after the angels were created.

C.2 therefore the lightning is brighter than the sun – The 1st book of Enoch mentions that the angels are as stars and sometimes they can change their form into lightning.

C.3 'incorporeal ten troops of angels': Incorporeal definition: - *not composed of matter; having no material existence:* In other words, the angels are not physical but spiritual.

C.4 incorporeal ten troops of angels' -God created 10 troups of angels. Definition of a troup? Since it is known that there are millions of angels, it would be difficult to define a troup. Perhaps these troups were only the very first angels to have been created and that God created millions more as time went by for specific purposes

Here Satanail with his angels was thrown down from the height.

> 3 And one from out the order of angels, having turned away with the order that was under him, conceived an impossible thought, to **place his throne higher than the clouds above the earth, that he might become equal in rank to my power.**

C.5 Satan rebels against God as evidenced in the following Bible verses

Ezekiel 28.1 The word of the LORD came again unto me, saying, 'Son of man, say unto the prince of Tyrus, Thus saith the Lord God; Because thine heart is lifted up, and thou hast said, I am a God, I sit in the seat of God, in the midst of the seas; yet thou art a man, and not God, though thou set thine heart as the heart of God.'

C.6 Satan through history has possessed many of its arrogant kings and leaders and emperors as is the case here where Satan for a while possessed the king of Tyre which was a might city and empire which has the biggest sailing fleet of ships in its time.

Ezekiel 28.3-17 Behold, thou *art* wiser than Daniel; there is no secret that they can hide from thee:

4 With thy wisdom and with thine understanding thou hast gotten thee riches, and hast gotten gold and silver into thy treasures:

2 Peter 2.3 "And through covetousness shall they with feigned words make merchandise of you: whose judgment now of a long time lingers not, and their damnation slumbers not."

5 By thy great wisdom *and* by thy traffick hast thou increased thy riches, and thine heart is lifted up because of thy riches:

C.7 'Traffick' or traffic is talking about the fleet of many ships that the King of Tyre had, that travelled all around the world to make merchandise with the nations of the earth

6 Therefore thus saith the Lord GOD; Because thou hast set thine heart as the heart of God;

7 Behold, therefore I will bring strangers upon thee, the terrible of the nations: and they shall draw their swords against the beauty of thy wisdom, and they shall defile thy brightness.

8 They shall bring thee down to the pit, and thou shalt die the deaths of *them that are* slain in the midst of the seas.

Revelation 20.1-3 20 And I saw an angel come down from heaven, having the key of the bottomless pit and a great chain in his hand. And he laid hold on the dragon, that old serpent, which is the Devil, and Satan, and bound him a thousand years. And cast him into the bottomless pit, and shut him up, and set a seal upon him, that he should deceive the nations no more, till the thousand years should be fulfilled: and after that he must be loosed a little season.

9 Wilt thou yet say before him that slayeth thee, I *am* God? but thou *shalt be* a man, and no God, in the hand of him that slayeth thee.

10 Thou shalt die the deaths of the uncircumcised by the hand of strangers: for I have spoken *it*, saith the Lord GOD.

11 Moreover the word of the LORD came unto me, saying,

C.8 God's description of Satan when God first created him:-

12 Son of man, take up a lamentation upon the king of Tyrus(Satan) , and say unto him, Thus saith the Lord GOD; Thou seal up the sum, full of wisdom, and perfect in beauty.

13 Thou hast been in Eden the garden of God; every precious stone *was* thy covering, the sardius, topaz, and the diamond, the beryl, the onyx, and the jasper, the sapphire, the emerald, and the carbuncle, and gold: the workmanship of thy tabrets and of thy pipes was prepared in thee in the day that thou wast created.

14 Thou *art* the anointed cherub that covereth; and I have set thee *so*: thou wast upon the holy mountain of God; thou hast walked up and down in the midst of the stones of fire.

15 Thou *wast* perfect in thy ways from the day that thou wast created, till iniquity was found in thee.

16 By the multitude of thy merchandise they have filled the midst of thee with violence, and thou hast sinned: therefore I will cast thee as profane out of the mountain of God: and I will destroy thee, O covering cherub, from the midst of the stones of fire.

17 Thine heart was lifted up because of thy beauty, thou hast corrupted thy wisdom by reason of thy brightness: I will cast thee to the ground, I will lay thee before kings, that they may behold thee.

18 Thou hast defiled thy sanctuaries by the multitude of thine iniquities, by the iniquity of thy traffick; therefore will I bring forth a fire from the midst of thee, it shall devour thee, and I will bring thee to ashes upon the earth in the sight of all them that behold thee.

19 All they that know thee among the people shall be astonished at thee: thou shalt be a terror, and never *shalt* thou *be* any more.

C.9 Notice that this verse seems to indicate that the days are coming when Satan shall be no more or that Satan will cease to exist anymore! In chapter 18 of 2nd Enoch it seemed to show the Fallen angels after they had 'been through' the Lake of fire, but there is no direct mention of Satan in that chapter. It would appear according to the Bible that in the case of Satan he will be totally destroyed as he was created as a very powerful cherub whom all the fallen angels are afraid of and they are forced to do Satan's bidding at the present time.

7 And when the thousand years are expired, Satan shall be loosed out of his prison,

8 And shall go out to deceive the nations which are in the four quarters of the earth, Gog, and Magog, to gather them together to battle: the number of whom is as the sand of the sea.

9 And they went up on the breadth of the earth, and compassed the camp of

the saints about, and the beloved city: and fire came down from God out of heaven, and devoured them.

[10] And the devil that deceived them was cast into the lake of fire and brimstone, where the beast and the false prophet are, and shall be tormented day and night for ever and ever.

C.10 It is essential for God to destroy the origin of evil and pride and arrogance if God is to be able to build a much better world as described in Revelation 21-22.

C.11 If there is no more Satan, then - no more Evil.

C.12 None of us want to think of the possibility that evil might just creep slowly back into the Heavenly City of the future. Then Evil will not exist in any form and will not even be an option of choice for men and angels or other beings.

C.13 Thank God for His great wisdom and omnipotence. He has been very longsuffering with all the shenanigans of mankind and the Devil and his fallen angels for the past 6000 years or even longer.

C.14 It makes sense that God will totally eradicate Satan and perhaps many of the worst of the Fallen angels for all the evil that they have done to mankind and their great offense unto God and His precious Holy Spirit and against Jesus their Son

> 4 And I threw him out from the height with his angels, and he was flying in the air continuously above the bottomless.

C.15 Why does it state 'and he was flying in the air continuously 'above the bottomless.' The only place on earth that I can think of that sounds remotely like this description is the air directly above the poles or what others call the 'holes in the poles', that that lead through gigantic holes into the inner earth and that location could be defined as 'bottomless'. Why does God have Satan and his angels 'flying in the air continuously above the bottomless.' Was it to remind them that they were going to end up in a bottomless pit if they did not repent?

Revelation 12.9 And the great dragon was cast out, that old serpent, called the Devil, and Satan, which deceives the whole world: he was cast out into the earth, and his angels were cast out with him.

C.16 More descriptions of Satan from the book of Isaiah chapter 14

Isaiah 14.9-17 Hell from beneath is moved for thee to meet *thee* at thy coming: it stirreth up the dead for thee, *even* all the chief ones of the earth; it hath raised up from their thrones all the kings of the nations.

10 All they shall speak and say unto thee, Art thou also become weak as we? art thou become like unto us?

11 Thy pomp is brought down to the grave, *and* the noise of thy viols: the worm is spread under thee, and the worms cover thee.

12 How art thou fallen from heaven, O Lucifer, son of the morning! *how* art thou cut down to the ground, which didst weaken the nations!

13 For thou hast said in thine heart, I will ascend into heaven, I will exalt my throne above the stars of God: I will sit also upon the mount of the congregation, in the sides of the north:

14 I will ascend above the heights of the clouds; I will be like the most High.

15 Yet thou shalt be brought down to hell, to the sides of the pit.

16 They that see thee shall narrowly look upon thee, *and* consider thee, *saying, Is* this the man that made the earth to tremble, that did shake kingdoms;

17 *That* made the world as a wilderness, and destroyed the cities thereof; *that* opened not the house of his prisoners?

CHAPTER 30

> ON the third day I commanded the earth to make grow great and fruitful trees, and hills, and seed to sow, and I planted Paradise, and enclosed it, and placed as armed *guardians* flaming angels, and thus I created renewal.

Genesis 1.11-13 And God said, Let the earth bring forth grass, the herb yielding seed, and the fruit tree yielding fruit after his kind, whose seed is in itself, upon the earth: and it was so. And the earth brought forth grass, and herb yielding seed after his kind, and the tree yielding fruit, whose seed was in itself, after his kind: and God saw that it was good. And the evening and the morning were the third day.

C.1 *'Great and fruitful trees'.* Here it is stating that the trees before the Great Flood at the very beginning of Creation were very tall trees and that they bore an exceptional amount of fruit.

C.2 *'I planted Paradise and enclosed it'.* Paradise had actually been already created in other slightly higher dimension of the spirit according to the apocryphal book of The Lost Books of Adam and Eve. [See my book Eden Insights]

Genesis 2.8a And the Lord God planted a garden eastward in Eden.

C.3 *'guardians flaming angels'* The Garden of Eden was indeed guarded by Cherubim with flaming swords according to the Bible.

C.4 *'I created renewal'* God is stating that the Garden of Eden was a place of renewal. Or a place where souls get refreshed and inspired and comforted and renewed.

> 2 Then came evening and came morning the fourth day.
>
> 3 [Wednesday]. On the fourth day I commanded that there should be **great lights** on the **heavenly circles.**

C.5 This is very interesting information, as it is stating that there were heavenly circles on the which God created the stars in orbit. If one considers the earth as the centre of God's Creation. Then imagine many fixed circular orbits of stars going further and further away from the earth but in definite planned orbits. The stars were not randomly created from chaos as taught by science in modern times and as the Bible calls 'Science falsely so-called'.

1 Timothy 6:20 Avoiding profane and vain babblings, and oppositions of science falsely so called.

> 4 On the first uppermost circle I placed the stars, Kruno, and on the second Aphrodit, on the third Aris, on the fifth **Zeus**, on the sixth

> Ermis, on the seventh lesser the moon, and adorned it with the lesser stars.

C.6 According to a scientific article which uses this same name Kronos is a star very far away indeed. I don't know if it is talking about the exact same star as mentioned in this 2nd Book of Enoch but anyway the article seemed intriguing:

Kronos: The eater of planets

A Sun-like star in our galaxy has likely eaten over a dozen of its rocky inner planets, earning it the nickname Kronos. The lead author of the study, Semyeong Oh, explained that Kronos — named after the mythological Greek Titan who ate his own children — is the most obvious and dramatic example yet of a Sun-like star consuming its own planets. It is located some 350 light years from earth.

Source: Kronos: The eater of planets (astronomy.com)

C.7 'and on the second Aphrodit'. Aphrodite is an ancient Greek goddess associated with love, lust, beauty, pleasure, passion, procreation, and as her syncretized Roman goddess counterpart *Venus*, desire, sex, fertility, prosperity, and victory.

C.8 There is a planet named after her in Roman culture as Venus. However, a star which is far away with the name of Aphrodit? I have not found such a name yet.

C.9 *'Aris, on the fifth Zeus, on the sixth Ermis'* - These other names are names of Roman and Greek gods.

> 5 And on the lower I placed the sun for the illumination of day, and the moon and stars for the illumination of night.
>
> 6 The sun that it should go according to each animal), **twelve**, and I appointed the succession of the months and their names and lives, their thunderings, and their hour-markings, how they should succeed.

C.10 Stars and constellations that represent the **12 Signs of the Zodiac** are mentioned as having influence over the earth and in particular over mankind.

Genesis 1.14-19 And God said, 'Let there be lights in the firmament of the heaven to divide the day from the night; and let them be for signs, and for seasons, and for days, and years: And let them be for lights in the firmament of the heaven to give light upon the earth.': and it was so. And God made two great lights; the greater light to rule the day, and the lesser light to rule the night: he made the stars also. And God set them in the firmament of the heaven to give light upon the earth, And to rule over the day and over the night, and to divide the light from the darkness: and God saw that it was good. And the evening and the morning were the **fourth day.**

> 7 Then evening came and morning came **the fifth day.**
>
> 8 [Thursday]. On the fifth day I commanded the sea, that it should bring forth fishes, and feathered birds of many varieties, and all animals creeping over the earth, going forth over the earth on four legs, and soaring in the air, male sex and female, and every soul breathing the spirit of life.

Genesis .1.20-23 God said, "I command the ocean to be full of living creatures, and I command birds to fly above the earth." So, God made the giant **sea monsters** and all the living creatures that swim in the ocean. He also made every kind of bird. God looked at what he had done, and it was good. Then he gave the living creatures his blessing—he told the ocean creatures to increase and live everywhere in the ocean and the birds to increase everywhere on earth. And the evening and the morning were the fifth day.

> 9 And there came evening, and there came morning the sixth day.
>
> 10 [Friday]. On the sixth day I commanded my wisdom to create man from seven consistencies: one, his flesh from the earth; two, his blood from the dew; three, his eyes from the sun; four, his bones from stone; five, his intelligence from the swiftness of the angels and from cloud; six, his veins and his hair from the grass of the earth; seven, his soul from my breath and from the wind.
>
> 11 And I gave him seven natures: to the flesh hearing, the eyes for sight, to the soul smell, the veins for touch, the blood for taste, the bones for endurance, to the intelligence sweetness (*sc.* enjoyment).
>
> 12 I conceived a cunning saying to say, I created man from invisible and from visible nature, of both are his death and life and image, he knows speech like some created thing, small in greatness and again great in smallness, and I placed him on earth, a second angel, honourable, great and glorious, and I appointed him as ruler to rule on earth and to have my wisdom, and there was none like him of earth of all my existing creatures.

Psalm 8.5 "For thou hast made him a little lower than the angels, and hast crowned him with glory and honour."

C.11 *'I created man from invisible and from visible nature'* This chapter tells us a lot about how God created Adam. In verse 12 it reveals that man has

both a body and a spirit.
And the evening and the morning were the fifth day.

Genesis 1.24-31 And God said, 'Let the earth bring forth the living creature after his kind, cattle, and creeping thing, and beast of the earth after his kind': and it was so.

And God made the beast of the earth after his kind, and cattle after their kind, and everything that creeps upon the earth after his kind: and God saw that *it was* good.

Genesis 1.26-27 And God said, 'Let us make man in our image, after our likeness: and let them have dominion over the fish of the sea, and over the fowl of the air, and over the cattle, and over all the earth, and over every creeping thing that creeps upon the earth.' So God created man in his *own* image, in the image of God created he him; male and female created he them.

Genesis 1.28-29 And God blessed them, and God said unto them, 'Be fruitful, and multiply, and replenish the earth, and subdue it: and have dominion over the fish of the sea, and over the fowl of the air, and over every living thing that moves upon the earth.' And God said, 'Behold, I have given you every herb bearing seed, which is upon the face of all the earth, and every tree, in the which is the fruit of a tree yielding seed; to you it shall be for meat. And to every beast of the earth, and to every fowl of the air, and to everything that creeps upon the earth, wherein there is life, I have given every green herb for meat: and it was so'.

Genesis 1.30 And God saw everything that he had made, and, behold, it was very good. And the evening and the morning were the sixth day.

> 13 And I appointed him a name, from the four component parts, from east, from west, from south, from north, and I appointed for him four special stars, and I called his name Adam, and showed him the two ways, the light and the darkness, and I told him:
>
> 14 'This is good, and that bad,' that I should learn whether he has love towards me, or hatred, that it be clear which in his race love me.
>
> 15 For I have seen his nature, but he has not seen his own nature, therefore *through* not seeing he will sin worse, and I said 'After sin *what is there* but death?'
>
> 16 And I put sleep into him and he fell asleep. And I took from him a rib, and created him a wife, that death should come to him by his wife, and I took his last word and called her name mother, that is to say, Eva.

C.12 Eva is the Latin for Eve.

Genesis 2.22-25 "And the rib, which the LORD God had taken from man, made he a woman, and brought her unto the man." and brought her unto the man. "And Adam said, This *is* now bone of my bones, and flesh of my flesh: she shall be called Woman, because she was taken out of Man." Therefore shall a man leave his father and his mother, and shall cleave unto his wife: and they shall be one flesh. And they were both naked, the man and his wife, and were not ashamed.

CHAPTER 31

> ADAM has life on earth, and I created a garden in Eden in the east, that he should observe the testament and keep the command.

Genesis 2.8-9 And the LORD God planted a garden eastward in Eden; and there he put the man whom he had formed. And out of the ground made the LORD God to grow every tree that is pleasant to the sight, and good for food; the tree of life also in the midst of the garden, and the tree of knowledge of good and evil.

C.1 What was the 'testament' and 'the command'? The Testament was to obey God. The command was not to touch the Tree of the Knowledge of Good and Evil. We know from Genesis that God told Adam and Eve that they could eat of all of the trees in the Garden of Eden except the Tree of the knowledge of Good and Evil. God also stated clearly that in the day that they ate of the Tree of the Knowledge of Good and Evil that they would surely die.

Genesis 2.8-9 And the LORD God commanded the man, saying, Of every tree of the garden thou mayest freely eat: But of the tree of the knowledge of good and evil, thou shalt not eat of it: for in the day that thou eatest thereof thou shalt surely die.

C.2 When they ate the apple they did die - spiritually and everything they were used to seeing from the spiritual realm faded away and disappeared.

> 2 I made the **heavens open to him**, that he should **see the angels** singing the **song of victory**, and the gloomless light.

C.3 The Garden of Eden was on a celestial plane or a realm between the incorruptible (spiritual) and the corruptible (physical) where Adam and Eve could see the angels and the things of light in heaven and could directly communicate with God, Jesus and His Holy Spirit as well as the angels.

> 3 And he was continuously in paradise, and the devil understood that I wanted to create another world, because Adam was lord on earth, to rule and control it.

C.4 See my book 'Eden Insights' for a lot more details about what it was like in the Garden of Eden before Adam and Eve fell.

C.5 This verse clearly shows that Satan was around before the creation of the physical earth.

> 4 The devil is the evil spirit of the lower places, as a fugitive he made Sotona from the heavens as his name was **Satanail**, thus he became different from the angels, *but **his nature** did not change **his intelligence*** as far as *his* understanding of righteous and sinful *things*.

C.6 Satan was cast out of the heavenly realms and he came to dwell in the lower regions from which he launched his attacks on mankind.

Revelation 12.7-8 And there was war in heaven: Michael and his angels fought against the dragon; and the dragon fought and his angels. And prevailed not; neither was their place found any more in heaven.

> 5 And he understood his condemnation and the sin which he had sinned before, therefore he conceived thought against Adam, in such form he entered and **seduced Eva**, but did not touch Adam.

C.7 This verse seems to allude to Satan having had sex with Eve, from whom Cain the very first murderer was born. This above verse also mentions that Satan did not touch Adam in the way he touched Eve. Well, thank God for that! Of course, later on in time, satanic rituals and perversions became rampant which was one of the reasons why God destroyed most of humanity and all the chimeras and other aberrations of God's Creation.

> 6 But I cursed ignorance, but what I had blessed previously, those I did not curse, I cursed not man, nor the earth, nor other creatures, but man's evil fruit, and his works.

C.8 God is separating man from his sin and evil works in verse 6. Why does He state that? It is because He wants mankind to know that a Saviour of the world is coming who would be able to save mankind from all of their sins if they embrace Him -Jesus.

C.9 VERSE 5 'And he understood his condemnation and the sin which he had sinned before, therefore he conceived thought against Adam, in such form he entered and seduced Eva, but did not touch Adam.'

The serpent beguiled Eve states the Bible. In this 2nd book of Enoch however, it states that a lot more than Eve eating an apple went on near the Tree of Good and Evil. It states that the serpent seduced Eve, not beguiled her. Maybe Satan did both & thus the birth of the first human - Cain was born by Satan & that is why he murdered his brother Abel - as Satan's goal has always been to destroy God's creation and especially mankind. This started what is known as 'Satan's Seed' on the earth. Later the fallen angels showed up to also create chaos in breeding with the licentious daughters of Cain which eventually brought total destruction in the Pre-Flood world.

"The LORD God said unto the woman, What is this that thou hast done? And the woman said, The serpent beguiled me, and I did eat." (Genesis 3:13)

C.10 What is the difference between beguile and seduce? Here is a definition of these words:

Seduce = entice (someone) into **sexual** activity:

An example of the word **seduce** was the story of Samson and Delilah, where Delilah had sexual relations with Samson using her beauty and charm to both beguile and seduce Samson. This caused Samson to get into big trouble with

Israel's enemies - the Philistines.

Beguile = charm or enchant (someone), often in a deceptive way

C.11 Here is an example of **beguile:**

In second Corinthians, chapter eleven, Paul states: "I fear, lest by any means, as the serpent beguiled Eve through his subtilty, so your minds should be corrupted from the simplicity that is in Christ."

The dictionary definition of **"beguile" is deceive**. From the very beginning original sin entered into the world through Eve falling for a deceitful lie. Can this happen to people of God? Absolutely.

C.12 As Paul warned the Christians in Corinth not to be deceived through subtilty. Subtilty being an old English word, today spelt subtly, meaning amongst other things slyness in design; cunning.

C.13 In Jesus' famous End Time discourse in Matthew 24, He warned four times in verses 4,5,11, and 24, not to be deceived. Who is He warning? At the very least it would be anyone who would have read Matthew 24, and most likely those readers who would have been believers in His words.

C.14 We live in an age of great deception.

2 Timothy 3:13 "Evil men and seducers shall wax worse and worse, deceiving, and being deceived."

C.15 Paul also states concerning the soon coming world dictator, the Antichrist: **2 Thessalonians 2:9** "Even him, whose coming is after the working of Satan with all power and signs and lying wonders.

C.16 Jesus shows John in Revelation it is through deceit, subtly, lies, etc. that the image of the beast, antichrist, is created, which leads ultimately to the infamous 666 mark of the beast.

Revelation 13:13-14 "He, (the false prophet), doeth great wonders, so that he maketh fire come down from heaven on the earth in the sight of men, And deceives them that dwell on the earth by the means of those miracles which he had power to do in the sight of the beast."

C.17 We know of course that we are in a great spiritual warfare between good and evil:

Ephesians 6:12 "For we wrestle not against flesh and blood, but against principalities, against powers, against the rulers of the darkness of this world, against spiritual wickedness in high places."

C.18 However, this spiritual warfare is definitely manifested in our physical world between God's representatives and Satan's representatives, with Satan's ultimate representative being the Antichrist. This is clearly mentioned in many chapters in the Bible. Jesus also warned us:

Matthew 7.15 'Beware of false prophets, which come to you in sheep's clothing, but inwardly they are ravening wolves.'

C.19 Shockingly, I heard, that the current Pope Francis made the statement on a worldwide scale that Christians should stop worshipping Jesus Christ and start worshipping Satan. [Pope Francis Orders Christians To 'Pray to Satan' for 'Real Enlightenment' (planet-today.com) } He is forbidding Catholics from telling others about Jesus and he talking specifically against people knowing Jesus personally. The Pope was stating that Lucifer is God and Christ is his son. What utter blasphemy! Does that make the Pope the False Prophet? So, who will be the coming Antichrist.

C.20 The current Pope is a communist from Argentina and is also obviously a Luciferian. Some people are saying that he leader of the World Economic Forum - Klaus Shuab is a good candidate for the Antichrist as he is into a lot of self-worship and Luciferian glorification. I don't know if the Pope is the False prophet as mentioned in Revelation chapter 11, but he certainly is a devil. Here are some amazing verses about the coming satanic evil and the Rise of the Antichrist. I certainly think that we are about to see the **Rise of the Antichrist.** See my **YOUTUBE** videos: @stephenstrutt

2 Thessalonians 2.3-4 Let no man deceive you by any means: for that day (Of Christ's 2nd Coming) shall not come, except there come a falling away (from faith -apostasy) first, and that man of sin be revealed, the son of perdition; "Who opposes and exalts himself above all that is called God, or that is worshipped; so that he as God sits in the temple of God, shewing himself that he is God."

C.21 Satanic practices from before the Great Flood are returning, as mentioned in Genesis 6, when the Fallen angels breed with the women on the earth and bore giants and then in their depravity they started messing around with the DNA of animals, birds and other creatures upon the earth to create the chimeras.

MIXTURE OF SPECIES -MIXING THE DNA OF ANIMALS AND OTHER CREATURES WITH MANKIND – THE FALLEN ANGELS -THE BOOK OF ENOCH

Genesis 6 talks about the same thing as Jubilees 5 and Jasher 4 and 1 Enoch 6

Jashur 4:18 "Their judges and rulers went to the daughters of men and took their wives by force from their husbands according to their choice, and the sons of men in those days took from the cattle of the earth, the beasts of the field and the fowls of the air, and taught the mixture of animals of one species with the other, in order therewith to provoke the Lord; and God saw the whole earth and it was corrupt, for all flesh had corrupted its ways upon earth, all men and all animals."

C.22 Apparently, the transhumanist movement is not something new but was in existence before God destroyed the world with a flood, and is one of the primary reasons for the flood.

Ecclesiastes 1:9 "That which has been is what will be, That which is done is what will be done, And there is nothing new under the sun."

C.23 "Noah was a just man, perfect (Perfect of course was not meaning sinless. Romans 3:23) in his generations. Noah walked with God.

Genesis 6:9, 12 "Noah was a just man, perfect in his generations. Noah walked with God. So, God looked upon the earth, and indeed it was corrupt; for all flesh had corrupted their way on the earth."

C.24 The book of **Jashur** is mentioned in the Bible in Joshua 10:13 and 2 Samuel 1:18 lending credence as to the authenticity of this book.

C.25 The transhumanist movement and all of its contributing occult science, as this does concern all of us.

Book Of Jubilees 1:5-10. "And it came to pass when the children of men began to multiply on the face of the earth and daughters were born unto them, that the angels of God saw them on a certain year of this jubilee, that they were beautiful to look upon; and they took themselves wives of all whom they chose, and they bare unto them sons and they were giants. And lawlessness increased on the earth and all flesh corrupted its way, alike men and cattle and beasts and birds and everything that walks on the earth −all of them corrupted their ways and their orders, and they began to devour each other, and lawlessness increased on the earth and every imagination of the thoughts of all men (was) thus evil continually. And God looked upon the earth, and behold it was corrupt, and all flesh had corrupted its orders, and all that were upon the earth had wrought all manner of evil before His eyes. And He said that He would destroy man and all flesh upon the face of the earth which He had created. But Noah found grace before the eyes of the Lord. And against the angels whom He had sent upon the earth, He was exceedingly wroth, and He gave commandment to root them out of all their dominion, and He bade us to bind them in the depths of the earth, and behold they are bound in the midst of them, and are (kept) separate. And against their sons went forth a command from before His face that they should be smitten with the sword, and be removed from under heaven. And He said 'My spirit shall not always abide on man; for they also are flesh and their days shall be one hundred and twenty years'. And He sent His sword into their midst that each should slay his neighbour, and they began to slay each other till they all fell by the sword and were destroyed from the earth. And their fathers were witnesses (of their destruction), and after this they were bound in the depths of the earth for ever, until the day of the great condemnation, when judgment is executed on all those who have corrupted their ways and their works before the Lord."

C.26 1ST ENOCH - THE WORLD WAS CHANGED

Enoch 8:1 "And The World Was Changed"

In **Genesis, chapter six**, the Bible tells us that during the time of Noah, that giants came into existence because of fallen angels who cohabited with the daughters of men. Today this is now a much more widely understood and accepted subject than in past years. Below is where we find the account of these happenings in the book of Genesis.

Genesis 6.2-5 "And it came to pass when men began to be numerous upon the earth, and daughters were born to them, that the sons of God having seen the daughters of men that they were beautiful, took to themselves wives of all whom they chose. And the Lord God said, My Spirit shall certainly not remain among these men for ever, because they are flesh, but their days shall be an hundred and twenty years. Now the giants were upon the earth in those days; and after that when the sons of God were wont to go in to the daughters of men, they bore children to them, those were the giants of old, the men of renown."

There is a fuller account of this event described in the **Book of Enoch**, even naming the names of many of the fallen angels. "And it came to pass, when the sons of men had increased, that in those days there were born to them fair and beautiful daughters. And the Angels, the sons of Heaven, saw them and desired them. And they said to one another: "Come, let us choose for ourselves wives, from the children of men, and let us beget, for ourselves, children." And Semyaza, who was their leader, said to them: "I fear that you may not wish this deed to be done and that I alone will pay for this great sin." And they all answered him and said: "Let us all swear an oath, and bind one-another with curses, so not to alter this plan, but to carry out this plan effectively." Then they all swore together and all bound one another with curses to it. And they were, in all, two hundred and they came down on Ardis, which is the summit of Mount Hermon. And they called the mountain Hermon because on it they swore and bound one another with curses."

Enoch 6:1-6 (Emphasis added) In 1869 Charles Warren made an interesting discovery on the top of Mount Hermon. There is a sacred building made of hewn blocks of stone on the summit of Mount Hermon. Known as Qasr Antar, it was the highest temple of the ancient world, sitting at 2,814 feet (858 m) above sea level. It was documented by Sir Charles Warren in 1869. Warren described the temple as a rectangular building, sitting on an oval, stone plateau without roof. He removed a limestone stele from the northwest of the oval, broke it into two pieces and carried it down the mountain and back to the British Museum, where it currently resides. An inscription on the stele was translated by George Nickelsburg to read "According to the command of the greatest and Holy God, those who take an oath (proceed) from here." Nickelsburg connected the inscription with oath taken by the angels under Semjaza who took an oath together, bound by a curse in order to take wives.

Book of Enoch (1 Enoch 6:6). Hermon was said to have become known as "the mountain of oath" by Charles Simon Clermont-Ganneau. The name of God was supposed to be a Hellenized version of Ba'al or Hadad and Nickelsburg connected it with the place name of Baal-Hermon (Lord of Hermon) and the deity given by Enoch as "The Great Holy One".[Eusebius recognized the religious importance of Hermon in his work "Onomasticon", saying "Until today, the mount in front of Panias and Lebanon is known as Hermon and it is respected by nations as a sanctuary" (Emphasis added) It has been pretty much established that the fallen angels, or Watchers as they are also known, entered our world from the spiritual realm, another dimension on the summit of Mount Herman. It could be said that at the summit of mount Herman there was or is a portal or star-gate to another world.

C.27 Nimrod was aware of this type of phenomenon when he commissioned the building of the **Tower of Babel** which was to reach onto heaven. This is also what projects like **CERN** are hoping to achieve. They want to open a portal to another dimension.. Besides producing giants, which are often referred to as Nephilim, there were other unpleasant consequences that took place on earth because of the fallen Watchers.

C.28 One particular **Watcher** named **Azazel** really did some major damage. "And Azazel taught men to make swords, and daggers, and shields, and breastplates. And he showed them the things after these, and the art of making them; bracelets, and ornaments, and the art of making up the eyes, and of beautifying the eyelids, and the most precious stones, and all kinds of coloured dyes. And the world was changed. See then what Azazel has done; how he has taught all iniquity on the earth and revealed the eternal secrets that are made in Heaven. And the whole Earth has been ruined by the teaching of the works of Azazel; and against him write: ALL SIN." - **Enoch 8:1, 9:6, 10:8**

C.28 AZAZEL THE SCAPEGOAT

An interesting side note is that Azazel is the name of the scapegoat in the Torah which was used to take away the sins of the nation of Israel. "The scapegoat was a goat that was designated (Hebrew לַעֲזָאזֵל (la-aza'zeyl; either "for absolute removal" (Brown-Driver-Briggs Lexicon) or possibly "for Azazel" (some modern versions taking the term as a name) an outcast in the desert as part of the ceremonies of the Day of Atonement, that began during the Exodus with the original Tabernacle and continued through the times of the temples in Jerusalem.

C.29 ATONEMENT Throughout the year, the sins of the ancient Israelites were daily transferred to the regular sin offerings as outlined in the Torah in Leviticus Ch 16. Once a year, on the tenth day of the seventh month in the Jewish calendar, the Day of Atonement, the High Priest of Israel sacrificed a bull for a sin offering for his own sins. Subsequently he took two goats and presented them at the door of the tabernacle with a view to dealing with the corporate sins of God's people — the nation of Israel. Two goats were chosen by lot: one to be "The Lord's Goat", which was offered as a blood sacrifice, and the other to be the "Azazel" scapegoat to be sent away into the wilderness. The blood of the slain goat was taken into the Holy of Holies behind the sacred veil and sprinkled on the mercy seat, the lid of the ark of the covenant. Later in the ceremonies of the day, the High Priest confessed the sins of the Israelites to Yahweh placing them figuratively on the head of the other goat, the Azazel scapegoat, who "took them away" never to be seen again. The sin of the nation was thus "atoned for" (paid for) by the "The Lord's Goat" and "The Azazel Goat".

C.30 Going back to the point that it would seem that the summit of Mount Hermon was a portal into another world, we would like to speculate on a possibility of a verse out of Revelation.

Revelation 12:9 "And the great dragon was cast out, that old serpent, called the Devil, and Satan, which deceives the whole world: he was cast out into the earth, and his angels were cast out with him."

The question that we wanted to think about was where would the Devil be cast out onto the earth? What geographical location? He is not omnipotent, so it has to be a single place. Could it be the summit of **Mount Hermon**, as there has already been a precedent of that mountain being the location of a doorway of the fallen angels, Watchers? "

C.30 Mount Hermon is 33 Degrees Latitude and 33 longitude

Another interesting observation are the ruins of an ancient temple on the summit of Mount Hermon. "In 1666, Louis XIV of France, authorized the building of an observatory in Paris to measure longitude. This was the beginning of the Paris Zero Meridian. Believe it or not, according to the "Paris Zero Meridian" Mount Hermon (and the ancient territory of Dan) is located at 33 degrees east of the Paris Zero Meridian (longitude), and 33 degrees north of the Equator (latitude)! The 33rd degree became an important part of Freemasonry, probably due to a history that dates back to the Knights Templar, the French Merovingian Dynasty, and their family ties to the Danites"

C.31 What does the ancient tribe of Dan have to do with any of this? The tribe of Dan bordered Mount Hermon and according to Judges 17, were completely given over to idolatry and the worship of Baal. In Genesis, chapter 49, Jacob prophesied over all of his sons and their role in the last days.

Genesis 49:1, 17 "And Jacob called his sons, and said to them, Assemble yourselves, that I may tell you what shall happen to you in the last days. And let Dan be a serpent in the way, besetting the path, biting the heel of the horse (and the rider shall fall backward)"

C.32 The Antichrist will come out of Israel

There are many Bible prophecy teachers who have speculated that the Antichrist would come out of Israel, specifically the tribe of Dan.

Even Winston Churchill made this observation. "In an article written by Winston Churchill and published in the Sunday Herald Newspaper on February 8th, 1920 titled "A struggle for the soul of the Jewish people," Churchill said the following: "And it may well be that this same astounding people may at the present moment be in the actual process of producing another system of morals and philosophy, as malevolent as Christianity was benevolent, which, if not arrested, would shatter irretrievably all that Christianity has rendered possible. "It would almost seem as if the gospel of Christ and the gospel of Anti-Christ were destined to originate among the same people; and that this mystic and mysterious people had been chosen for the supreme manifestations, both of the divine and the diabolical..."

C.34 PANIAS & THE BOTTOMLESS PIT

Revelation 9:1-2,11 "And the fifth angel sounded, and I saw a star fall from heaven unto the earth: and to him was given the key of the bottomless pit. And he opened the bottomless pit; and there arose a smoke out of the pit, as the smoke of a great furnace; and the sun and the air were darkened by reason of the smoke of the pit. And they had a king over them, [which is] the angel of the bottomless pit, whose name in the Hebrew tongue [is] Abaddon, but in the Greek tongue hath [his] name Apollyon."

There are other versions of the Bible that also use the term shaft and Abyss. It has been proven that Abaddon or Apollyon is the Devil. So, what does Panias have to do with any of this? Josephus writes in "Wars of the Jews" 1.21.3 "And when Caesar had further bestowed upon him another additional country, he built there also a temple of white marble, hard by the fountains of Jordan: the place is called Panium (Panias, Caesarea Philippi), where is a top of a mountain that is raised to an immense height, and at its side, beneath, or at its bottom, a dark cave opens itself; within which there is a horrible precipice, that descends abruptly to a vast depth: it contains a mighty quantity of water, which is immovable; and when anybody lets down anything to measure the depth of the earth beneath the water, no length of cord is sufficient to reach it." It is interesting to note that the cave at Panias has never been fully excavated and explored.

C.35 What the ancient historian Josephus described was corroborated by the discovery of such a chasm outside the entrance, in the excavated area (although the grotto (cave) has not been excavated yet). Here, the partial collapse of a Roman vaulted substructure revealed a chasm . . . the chasm reaches all the way to the underground water level. It is likely, therefore, that a similar hollow once existed inside the cave and formed a **'sacred well' to the Paneion**.

C.36 The Hellenistic arrangement of the grotto awaits the clearing of the cave floor, presently covered by the collapse of the cave's roof in the 1837 earthquake. Few Hellenistic remains were uncovered in the excavation outside the cave, and it seems that in this period the cult place was confined to the natural cave."

C.37 "Gates of Hades"

This means there is much more evidence buried in the remains. Ancient descriptions and archaeology indicate a **passage way** into the earth. The descriptions of a passage to the underworld may be confirmed by an inscription that says "Gates of Hades" to match Jesus' description of this place. Pan's Grotto at the base of Mount Hermon

C.38 ABOUT PANIAS: In the Book of Matthew, chapter 16, Jesus said something very interesting while visiting Caesarea Philippi which is Panias.

Matthew 16:13-16 "When Jesus came into the coasts of Caesarea Philippi, he asked his disciples, saying, Whom do men say that I the Son of man am? And they said, Some [say that thou art] John the Baptist: some, Elias; and others, Jeremias, or one of the prophets. He saith unto them, But whom say ye that I am? And Simon Peter answered and said, Thou art the Christ, the Son of the living God. And Jesus answered and said unto him, Blessed art thou, Simon Barjona: for flesh and blood hath not revealed [it] unto thee, but my Father which is in heaven. And I say also unto thee, That thou art Peter, and upon this rock I will build my church; and the gates of hell shall not prevail against it."

C.39 DRAGON

If the dragon of Revelation 12 were cast out onto the earth at the summit of Mount Hermon and given the key to the bottomless which he opens, could that pit be at the bottom of Mount Hermon at Panias at the "Gates of Hades"? Of course, the dragon and especially his angels would not just be confined to this area as Revelation 12:9 makes clear.

Revelation 12:9 "And the great dragon was cast out, that old serpent, called the Devil, and Satan, which deceives the whole world: he was cast out into the earth, and his angels were cast out with him."

C.40 One last point; the present war in Syria. Israel today controls the base of Mount Hermon where Panias is located, but Syria controls the summit where the watchers entered earth's realm. Another interesting point to note is that the highest United Nations outpost in the world is located on the summit of Mt. Hermon. These types of locations are very important to the world's most important elites who are also some of the worlds top occultists. When the United States invaded Iraq it was widely under reported that one very important mission they conducted was what was believed to be a visit to the tomb of Gilgamesh – Nimrod to retrieve a sample of his DNA

C.41 The truth is that many bottomless pits have been found on our planet including in Lucerne in Switzerland where the CERN particle-collider was built. There are apparently other locations in the USA, and I am sure that there are many entrances into the underworld all over the world. These locations are bottomless, dangerous and are indeed dimensional gates. Strange goings on are found at these locations on the planet. [See my books on the paranormal – **Out of the Bottomless Pit 1 & 2**]

CHAPTER 32

> I SAID to him: 'Earth thou art, and into the earth whence I took thee thou shalt go, and I will not ruin thee, but send thee whence I took thee.

Genesis 3.19 In the sweat of thy face shalt thou eat bread, till thou return unto the ground; for out of it was thou taken: for dust thou art, and unto dust shalt thou return.

> 2 Then I can again take thee at **My second coming**!

C.1 Christ's 2nd Coming is also mentioned many times in the Lost Books of Adam and Eve.

The Lost Books of Adam and Eve were translated from Hebrew into Greek around 100-300 BCE at the Library in Alexandria. This is amazing that the Lord Himself in verse 2 is mentioning His 2nd Coming, when He had not yet come the 1st time when born in Bethlehem as the only begotten Son of God unto Mary and Joseph. Only God could possibly know that very advanced information over 5000 years ago in the time of Enoch or over 5000 before Christ's 2nd Coming. It is good that this verse is telling us this, as it also shows that time is running out as it is now around 6000 years since Creation. It won't be long until Christ Jesus arrives at His glorious 2nd Coming. The Rapture is what we all look forward to.

1 Thessalonians 4.16-17 For the Lord himself shall descend from heaven with a shout, with the voice of the archangel, and with the trump of God: and the dead in Christ shall rise first: Then we which are alive and remain shall be caught up together with them in the clouds, to meet the Lord in the air: and so shall we ever be with the Lord.

Revelation 11.15 The seventh angel sounded his trumpet, and there were loud voices in heaven, which said: "The kingdom of the world has become the kingdom of our Lord and of his Messiah, and he will reign for ever and ever."

> 3 And I blessed all my creatures visible and invisible. **And Adam was five and half hours in paradise.**

C.2 According to the Hebrew Book of Jubilees' Adam and Eve lived 7 years in the Garden of Eden until Satan showed up and seduced Eve.

Jubilees 3.17-18a 'And after the completion of 7 years, which he had completed there, seven years exactly, [8.AM] and in the 2nd month, on the seventeenth day (of the month), the serpent came and approached the woman, and serpent said unto the woman, 'Hath God commanded you, saying 'Ye shall not eat of every tree of the Garden.

C.3 A similar time-frame of 5½ is mentioned in the Lost Books of Adam and Eve, except it mentions 5 and a half days - not hours.

C.4 The 5 and a half days in the Lost Books of Adam and Eve which was in Greek just like the Septuagint, are supposed to be 5500 of years from the Creation until the coming of Christ as mentioned in the Septuagint or Greek version of the Old Testament.

C.5 Some of the words in this book of the Secrets of Enoch are from Latin though originally from Hebrew then Greek and then Latin and finally English. The Septuagint holds to it having been 5500 years from Creation to Christ.

C.6 The King James version of the Bible holds to 4000 years from Creation to Christ. The Protestants and Catholic church hold to the 4000 years from Creation to Christ and the Orthodox holds to the Greek version of the Septuagint Old Testament putting the time from Creation unto Christ at 5500 years.

C.7 I explain why there is a time difference in my Insights books and in particular in my book 'Eden Insights', which is based on the Lost Books of Adam and Eve.

> 4 And I blessed the seventh day, which is the Sabbath, on which he rested from all his works.

Genesis 2.1-3 Thus the heavens and the earth were finished and the host of them. And on the seventh day God ended his work which he had made; and he rested on the seventh day from all his work which he had made.

And God blessed the seventh day and sanctified it: because that in it he had rested from all his work which God created and made.

CHAPTER 33

> AND I appointed the eighth day also, that the eighth day should be the first-created after my work, and that *the first seven* revolve in the form of the seventh thousand, and that at the beginning of the **eighth thousand there should be a time of not-counting, endless, with neither years nor months nor weeks nor days nor hours. - ETERNITY**

C.1 Here it is stating that there would be 7000-year period for the physical Creation. 1000 years for every day of Creation. Then for the 8th millennium God would create the New Heaven and the New earth wherein dwelleth righteousness and evil will simply cease to exist forever and **time** should be no more.

C.2 The 8th millennium will restore the spirit world to the physical world as it used to be before man fell. One day you will be able to see the inner workings of the Spirit world as it will no longer be hidden from your eyes.

C.3 Just like the famous atomic physicist * Millikan answered the question if he believed in God he simply replied taking out his ornate pocket watch 'Just as behind this watch is an intricate machinery that makes it work but you cannot see it, so behind the face of this physical universe that has to be a Maker.

* **Robert Andrews Millikan** (March 22, 1868 – December 19, 1953) was an American experimental physicist who won the Nobel Prize for Physics in 1923 for the measurement of the elementary electric charge and for his work on the photoelectric effect.

C.4 Just imagine for a moment that you pray for someone and immediate you see an angel show up to take your prayers to God. How reassuring that would be. We are surrounded by happenings in the spirit world. One day when the world is totally beautiful again and there is no evil it will be wonderful to have our eyes open to the spiritual world as well as the physical with nothing scary to see around us.

> 2 And now, Enoch, all that I have told thee, all that thou hast understood, all that thou hast seen of heavenly things, all that thou hast seen on earth, and all that I have written in books by my great wisdom, all these things I have devised and created from the uppermost foundation to the lower and to the end, and there is no counsellor nor inheritor to my creations.

C.5 One day we will also get to see things such as Enoch saw. God will show us how He made the Creation and show how all things started. The Bible states 'Thy children shall be taught of the Lord and great shall be the peace of thy children. That is talking about the Golden Age of the Millennium when

Christ reigns and rules for 1000 years. It is coming soon!

> 3 I am self-eternal, not made with hands, and without change.

Malachi 3.6 "For I the L ORD do not change; therefore you, O children of Jacob, are not consumed.

> 4 My thought is my counsellor, my wisdom and my word are made, and my eyes observe all things how they stand here and tremble with terror.

C.6 God the Father is stating that His 'own thoughts' are his counsellors along with 'Wisdom' which is another name for the Holy Spirit Mother of Heaven and God the Father's wife, and His Word – the Creator which is Jesus their Son.

Proverbs 9.10 The fear of the Lord is the beginning of wisdom.

2 Esdras 8:21 'Whose Throne is inestimable, whose glory may not be comprehended, before whom the hosts of Angels stand with trembling'.

C.7 This apocryphal Book of **2ⁿᵈ Esdras** was in the KJV of the Bible from 1611 when it was originally published until 1885. Why take such an amazing book out of the Bible? It is still in the Catholic Bible. [See my last book, called Esdras Insights]

1 John 5.7-9 [7] For there are three that bear record in heaven, the Father, the Word, and the Holy Ghost: and these three are one. And there are three that bear witness in earth, the Spirit, and the water, and the blood: and these three agree in one. If we receive the witness of men, the witness of God is greater: for this is the witness of God which he hath testified of his Son.

> 5 If I turn away my face, then all things will be destroyed.

Deuteronomy 31.17 'Then My anger will be kindled against them in that day, and I will forsake them and **hide My face** from them, and they will be consumed, and many evils and troubles will come upon them; so that they will say in that day, 'Is it not because our God is not among us that these evils have come upon us?' But I will surely **hide My face** in that day because of all the evil which they will do, for they will turn to other gods.'

> 6 And apply thy mind, Enoch, and know him who is speaking to thee, and take thou the books which thou thyself hast written.

Revelation 1.19 I am Alpha and Omega, the first and the last: and, What thou see, write in a book, and send it unto the seven churches which are in Asia; unto Ephesus, and unto Smyrna, and unto Pergamos, and unto Thyatira, and unto Sardis, and unto Philadelphia, and unto Laodicea.

> 7 And I give thee Samuil and Raguil, who led thee up, and the books,

> and go down to earth, and tell thy sons all that I have told thee, and all that thou hast seen, from the lower heaven up to my throne, and all the troops.

C.8 Raguil is better known as Raguel and is mentioned in different Apocryphal books. Samuil stands for Samuel - not really known as an angel but a great prophet of God. Perhaps a prophet being a messenger can also act as an angel. Look at this strange story about gods and spirits and prophets in the Bible - about Samuel.

I Samuel 28.7-27 And King Saul disguised himself, and put on other raiment, and he went, and two men with him, and they came to the woman with a familiar spirit by night: and he said, I pray thee, divine unto me by the familiar spirit, and bring me him up, whom I shall name unto thee. [1] Then said the woman, 'Whom shall I bring up unto thee'? And he said, Bring me up Samuel. [3] And the king said unto her, Be not afraid: for what saw thou? And the woman said unto Saul, I saw gods ascending out of the earth. And he said unto her, What form is he of? And she said, An old man cometh up; and he is covered with a mantle. And Saul perceived that it was Samuel, and he stooped with his face to the ground, and bowed himself. [15] And Samuel said to Saul, Why hast thou disquieted me, to bring me up? And Saul answered, I am sore distressed; for the Philistines make war against me, and God is departed from me, and answers me no more, neither by prophets, nor by dreams: therefore I have called thee, that thou mayest make known unto me what I shall do. [16] Then said Samuel, Wherefore then dost thou ask of me, seeing the Lord is departed from thee, and is become thine enemy? [17] And the Lord hath done to him, as he spake by me: for the Lord hath rent the kingdom out of thine hand, and given it to thy neighbour, even to David: [18] Because thou obeyed not the voice of the Lord, nor executed his fierce wrath upon Amalek, therefore hath the Lord done this thing unto thee this day. [19] Moreover the Lord will also deliver Israel with thee into the hand of the Philistines: and tomorrow shalt thou and thy sons be with me: the Lord also shall deliver the host of Israel into the hand of the Philistines.

> 8 For I created all forces, and there is none that resists me or that does not subject himself to me. For all subject themselves to my monarchy, and labour for my sole rule.

Isaiah 66.5 Hear the word of the LORD, ye that tremble at his word; Your brethren that hated you, that cast you out for my name's sake, said, Let the LORD be glorified: but he shall appear to your joy, and they shall be ashamed.

2 Esdras 8:21 Whose Throne is inestimable, whose glory may not be comprehended, before whom the hosts of Angels stand with trembling,

C.9 All of God's Creation subjected themselves to God except Satan.

I Peter 5.8 "Be sober, be vigilant; because your adversary the devil, as a roaring lion, walketh about, seeking whom he may devour:"

> 9 Give them the books of the handwriting, and they will read *them* and will know me for the creator of all things and will understand how there is no other God but me.

Philippians 4.8-9 Finally, brethren, whatsoever things are true, whatsoever things are honest, whatsoever things are just, whatsoever things are pure, whatsoever things are lovely, whatsoever things are of good report; if there be any virtue, and if there be any praise, think on these things.

> 10 And let them distribute the books of thy handwriting - children to children, generation to generation, nations to nations.

Deuteronomy 6:7-9 And thou shalt teach them diligently unto thy children, and shalt talk of them when thou sit in thine house, and when thou walk by the way, and when thou lie down, and when thou rise up. And thou shalt bind them for a sign upon thine hand, and they shall be as frontlets between thine eyes.

I Timothy 4.15 "Meditate upon these things; give thyself wholly to them; that thy profiting may appear to all."

> 11 And I will give thee, Enoch, my intercessor, the archistratege Michael, for the handwritings of thy fathers Adam, Seth, Enos, Cainan, Mahaleleel, and Jared thy father.

C.10 From a literal standpoint, "archistratege" appears to be the combination of two ancient Greek words: ἀρχι (archi), which means chief, first, or primary (as in archbishop or archangel); and στρατηγός (stratēgos) which means general or more literally, army leader. Thus, "archistratege" would mean "First General" or more euphemistically, "Supreme Commander." This title is consistent with Michael's role as leader of Heaven's armies. What is the meaning of archistratege? - Answers

CHAPTER 34

> THEY have rejected my commandments and my yoke, worthless seed has come up, not fearing God, and they would not bow down to me, but have begun to bow down to vain gods, and denied my unity, and have laden the whole earth with untruths, offences, abominable lecheries namely one with another, and all manner of other unclean wickedness, which is disgusting to relate.

C.1 My yoke. Jesus stated in the New Testament 'My Yoke is easy, and my burden is light. Jeus was telling people to obey God and to forsake this present world and that God would take care of us and would not fail us.

Matthew 11.29-30 Take my yoke upon you, and learn of me; for I am meek and lowly in heart: and ye shall find rest unto your souls. My yoke is easy and my burden is light

C.2 Worthless seed – This is talking about the seed of Satan which started off with Cain. Did you know that those who think that they rule this planet and are very arrogant, like Klaus Schaub of the World Economic Forum stating that by the year 2030 everyone would own nothing and eat bugs. They have stated about themselves that they are descended from Cain who was a son of Satan, and yet they also think that they are gods and deny the God of Creation! What does that tell you about them? That they are satanists.

C.3 'Bowed down to vain gods.' Humanity has largely bowed down to other gods or what were the Fallen angels and Satan and worshipped them instead of God – whether it was mammon or Lucifer or Pan etc. People are lured into worshipping temporal things that have no eternal satisfaction. As Jesus said 'Love not the things of the world for the things of the worlds will pass away ..if a man love the world the love of the Father is not in him.'

C.4 'denied my unity' This is talking about who Satan and the Fallen angels and evil spirits under them deny the Trinity. That is the true Trinity of God the Father, and God the Holy Spirit Mother, and their Son Jesus the Messiah.
[See my audio on this topic on YOUTUBE: (1018) BRIDE OF CHRIST & FEMALE HOLY SPIRIT - YouTube

1 John 2.15-17 Love not the world, neither the things that are in the world. If any man loves the world, the love of the Father is not in him. For all that is in the world, the lust of the flesh, and the lust of the eyes, and the pride of life, is not of the Father, but is of the world. And the world passes away, and the lust thereof: but he that doeth the will of God abides for ever.

C.5 'Laden the earth with untruths'

John 8.44 Ye are of your father the devil, and the lusts of your father ye will do. He was a murderer from the beginning, and abode not in the truth, because there is no truth in him. When he speaks a lie, he speaks of his own: for he is a liar, and the father of it.

C.6 'abominable lecheries' -lecher

Definition: a man given to excessive sexual indulgence; a lascivious or licentious man. [See my book Eden Insights which covers the origin of these things]

C.7 'unclean wickedness'

Romans 1.24 Wherefore God also gave them up to **uncleanness** through the lusts of their own hearts, to dishonour their own bodies between themselves: 25 Who changed the truth of God into a lie, and worshipped and served the creature more than the Creator, who is blessed for ever. Amen.

C.8 Here is the incredible chapter of Romans chapter 1, which covers all of the above-mentioned topics.

Romans 1.17-32 And likewise also the men, leaving the natural use of the woman, burned in their lust one toward another; men with men working that which is unseemly, and receiving in themselves that recompense of their error which was meet.

17 For therein is the righteousness of God revealed from faith to faith: as it is written, The just shall live by faith.

18 For the wrath of God is revealed from heaven against all ungodliness and unrighteousness of men, who hold the truth in unrighteousness;

19 Because that which may be known of God is manifest in them; for God hath shewed *it* unto them.

20 For the invisible things of him from the creation of the world are clearly seen, being understood by the things that are made, *even* his eternal power and Godhead; so that they are without excuse:

21 Because that, when they knew God, they glorified *him* not as God, neither were thankful; but became vain in their imaginations, and their foolish heart was darkened.

22 Professing themselves to be wise, they became fools,

23 And changed the glory of the uncorruptible God into an image made like to corruptible man, and to birds, and four-footed beasts, and creeping things.

24 Wherefore God also gave them up to uncleanness through the lusts of their own hearts, to dishonour their own bodies between themselves:

25 Who changed the truth of God into a lie, and worshipped and served the creature more than the Creator, who is blessed for ever. Amen.

26 For this cause God gave them up unto vile affections: for even their women did change the natural use into that which is against nature:

27 And likewise also the men, leaving the natural use of the woman, burned in their lust one toward another; men with men working that which is unseemly, and receiving in themselves that recompence of their error which was meet.

28 And even as they did not like to retain God in *their* knowledge, God gave them over to a reprobate mind, to do those things which are not convenient;

29 Being filled with all unrighteousness, fornication, wickedness, covetousness, maliciousness; full of envy, murder, debate, deceit, malignity; whisperers,

30 Backbiters, haters of God, despiteful, proud, boasters, inventors of evil things, disobedient to parents,

31 Without understanding, covenant breakers, without natural affection, implacable, unmerciful:

32 Who knowing the judgment of God, that they which commit such things are worthy of death, not only do the same, but have pleasure in them that do them.

> 2 And therefore I will bring down a deluge upon the earth and will destroy all men, and the whole earth will crumble together into great darkness.

Genesis 6.17 And, behold, I, even I, do bring a flood of waters upon the earth, to destroy all flesh, wherein is the breath of life, from under heaven; and everything that is in the earth shall die.

1ST ENOCH 65.1 In those days Noah saw that the earth had sunk down and its destruction was night; and he arose from thence and went to the ends of the earth, and cried aloud to his grandfather Enoch… **[See my other book Enoch Insights]**

C.9 1ST ENOCH CH 6 – THE FALL OF THE ANGELS
Book of Jude mentions the prophet Enoch.

Jude 1:15-16 " And Enoch also, the seventh from Adam, prophesied of these, saying, Behold, the Lord cometh with ten thousands of his saints, To execute judgment upon all, and to convince all that are ungodly among them of all their ungodly deeds which they have ungodly committed, and of all their hard speeches which ungodly sinners have spoken against him."

C.10 The **Book of Enoch** was found in Abyssinia (Ethiopia) in 1773 after being lost for about 1600 years. It was translated into English in 1821.

The Book of Enoch was readily accepted by the early church fathers.

For the first three centuries A.D. it was accepted as scripture by the early church. It was eventually dismissed from the Scriptures at the Council of Laodicea in 365 AD. After that you could be burned alive at the stake for possessing this book by Catholic edict.

Fragments were also found along with the Dead Sea Scrolls. The first thirty six chapters of the book of Enoch gives much information about these fallen angels and even gives their specific names.

GENESIS 6.1-11 It happened after the sons of men had multiplied in those days, that daughters were born to them, elegant and beautiful.

And when the angels, 'The sons of heaven', beheld them, they became enamoured of them, saying to each other, Come, let us select for ourselves wives from the progeny of men, and let us beget children.

C.11 BOOK OF ENOCH 7.1-7

7:1 It happened after the sons of men had multiplied in those days, that daughters were born to them, elegant and beautiful.

7:2 And when the angels, (3) the sons of heaven, beheld them, they became enamoured of them, saying to each other, Come, let us select for ourselves wives from the progeny of men, and let us beget children.

7:3 Then their leader Samyaza said to them; I fear that you may perhaps be indisposed to the performance of this enterprise;

7:4 And that I alone shall suffer for so grievous a crime.

7:5 But they answered him and said; We all swear;

7:6 And bind ourselves by mutual execrations, that we will not change our intention, but execute our projected undertaking.

7:7 Then they swore all together, and all bound themselves by mutual execrations. Their whole number was two hundred, who descended upon Ardis, (4) which is the top of mount Armon.

C.12 "In the days of Jared" – (R.H. Charles, editor. and translator - The Book of Enoch [Oxford: Clarendon Press, 1893]). The Aramaic text reads 'Watchers' from a fragment of text from the Cumran cave – [oxford -Clarendon press 1976]

That mountain therefore was called Hermon, because they had sworn upon it, and bound themselves by mutual execrations. Mt. Armon, or Mt. Hermon, derives its name from the Hebrew word herem, a curse (R.H. Charles, p. 63 of -The Book of Enoch [Oxford: Clarendon Press, 1893).

These are the names of their chiefs: Samyaza, who was their leader, Urakabarameel, Akibeel, Tamiel, Ramuel, Danel, Azkeel, Saraknyal, Asael, Armers, Batraal, Anane, Zavebe, Samsaveel, Ertael, Turel, Yomyael, Arazyal. These were the prefects of the two hundred angels, and the remainder were all with them. The Aramaic texts preserve an earlier list of names of these Watchers: Semihazah; Artqoph; Ramtel; Kokabel; Ramel; Danieal; Zeqiel; Baraqel; Asael; Hermoni; Matarel; Ananel; Stawel; Samsiel; Sahriel; Tummiel; Turiel; Yomiel; Yhaddiel

C.13 Then they took wives, each choosing for himself; whom they began to approach, and with whom they cohabited; teaching them sorcery, incantations, and the dividing of roots and trees.

Genesis 6. And the women conceiving brought forth giants. And it came to pass, when men began to multiply on the face of the earth, and daughters were born unto them, that the sons of God saw the daughters of men that they were fair; and they took them wives of all which they chose. There were giants in the earth in those days; and also after that, when the sons of God came in unto the daughters of men, and they bare children to them, the same became mighty men which were of old, men of renown.

C.14 So, we can see that in the days before the flood, giants lived on the earth that were the progeny of fallen angels and human woman - hybrids.

Incidentally, Jesus refers to the flood as an actual historical event: "They did eat, they drank, they married wives, they were given in marriage, until the day that Noe entered into the ark, and the flood came, and destroyed them all. **Luke 17:27** "But as the days of Noe were, so shall also the coming of the Son of man be.

Matthew 24:37"

What were the days of Noah like? "The earth also was corrupt before God, and the earth was filled with violence.

Genesis 6:11"

C.15 Not only was the earth corrupt and filled with violence but there was also a hybrid race of giants called the Nephilim. Will this happen again in the "end times"?

"Lift up a standard on the mountain of the plain, exalt the voice to them, beckon with the hand, open the gates, ye rulers. I give command, and I bring them: giants are coming to fulfil my wrath, rejoicing at the same time and insulting. **Septuagint Isaiah 13:2-3**"

Enoch 15:8 "And now, the giants who were born from body and flesh will be called **Evil Spirits** on the Earth, and on the Earth will be their dwelling."

CHAPTER 35

> BEHOLD from their seed shall arise another generation, much afterwards, but of them many will be very insatiate.

C.1 Insatiate - definition = never satisfied = demonic

> 2 He who raises that generation, *shall* reveal to them the books of thy handwriting, of thy fathers, *to them* to whom he must point out the guardianship of the world, to the faithful men and workers of my pleasure, who do not acknowledge my name in vain.

C.2 reveal to them the books of thy handwriting, of thy fathers

Proverbs 22.28 Remove not the ancient landmark, which thy fathers have set.

Jeremiah 6.16 Thus saith the Lord, 'Stand ye in the ways, and see, and ask for the old paths, where is the good way, and walk therein, and ye shall find rest for your souls.' But they said, we will not walk therein.

C.3 'Guardianship of the world'. To know that it was God that created the world and not someone else or something else like the false teachings of Evolution and the big bang or some other god.

Genesis 1.1 In the beginning **God** created the haven and the earth.

> 3 And they shall tell another generation, and those *others* having read shall be glorified thereafter, more than the first.

John 6.63 It is the spirit that quickens, the flesh profits nothing. The words that I speak unto you they are spirit and they are life.

Daniel 12.3 They that be wise shall shine as the brightness of the firmament and they that lead many to righteousness as the stars forever and ever.

THE FALLEN ANGELS

'And the women also of the angels that went astray shall become sirens - 1st Enoch 19.2'

C.4 That they would have different **kinds** of **forms**. That is why the Locusts in Revelation are so terrifying. Anyways after studying Jeremiah and Isaiah closely you'll notice that when God smites the angels (Satan's rebellion) during the Tribulation period that heaven is rolled up as a scroll.

C.5 This is clearly seen in Revelation and Isaiah. Soon after the Sirens, Satyr's, Lilith, and the demons are cast into Babylon which in Revelation when it is burnt it continues to burn forever.

C.6 See ORIGINS of the SIRENS in C.10.

Jude 1:14-16 and countless other verses. With that said. Namaah seems to be the origin of the women who seduced the **Watchers** as mentioned in **Enoch 6.**

Genesis 6, **Jasher 4 and Jubilees 5**. We are told of what became of the male giants when they died as they became the disembodied spirits of the giants which are also called demons.

Enoch 15 Enoch tells Azazel the fallen Watcher (Leviticus 16) that the sons of the giants would become demons after death. but what of the women who for had intercourse with the angels?

C.7 Enoch 19:2 says that the woman who cohabitated with the fallen angels became **Sirens**. When Jesus comes back and judges the earth the Sirens weep.

Enoch 96:2 "And the sirens shall sigh because of you-and weep."

Mermaids and other Female Demons

(Exodus 20:4) "Thou shalt not make to thyself an idol, nor likeness of anything, whatever things are in the heaven above, and whatever are in the earth beneath, and whatever are in the waters under the earth." Waters Under The Earth

C.8 Is it to prove that **mermaids (Sirens)** do in fact exist and confirmed by a high ranking US Naval officer who revealed the US Navy had kept one alive in captivity for two to three years.

The Navy supposedly did DNA testing on the "mermaid" and found that their DNA was almost identical to humans.

In his enquiry he also expressed that if mermaids did in fact exist they would most likely be dangerous and harmful and wondered if any good hybrids existed.

It should be noted that every major culture in the world has references to "mermaids". The following was our response, we thought we would share with you.

Siren. Saint Jerome, who produced the Latin Vulgate version of the Bible, used the word sirens to translate Hebrew tannīm ("jackals") in Isaiah 13:22, and also to translate a word for "owls" in Jeremiah 50:39.

Sirens continued to be used as a symbol for the dangerous temptation embodied by women regularly throughout Christian art of the medieval era; however, in the 17th century, some Jesuit writers began to assert their actual existence, including Cornelius a Lapide, who said of woman, "her glance is that of the fabled basilisk, her voice a siren's voice—with her voice she enchants, with **her beauty she deprives of reason—voice and sight alike deal destruction and death**."

Micah 1:8 (Septuagint) "Therefore, shall she lament and wail, she shall go barefooted, and being naked she shall make lamentation as that of serpents, and mourning as of the daughters of sirens."

Enoch 29:2 "And the women also of the angels who went astray shall become sirens."

Enoch 96:2 2 "And the sirens shall sigh because of you-and weep."

Baruch 10.8 'I will call the Sirens from the sea."

C.9 Hybrids: Since Satan can only imitate what God has done perhaps he was attempting to imitate the following verses in Ezekiel and Revelation and also make a deliberate attempt to provoke God at the same time.

Jashur 4:18 "And their judges and rulers went to the daughters of men and took their wives by force from their husbands according to their choice, and the sons of men in those days took from the cattle of the earth, the beasts of the field and the fowls of the air, and taught the mixture of animals of one species with the other, in order therewith to provoke the Lord; and God saw the whole earth and it was corrupt, for all flesh had corrupted its ways upon earth, all men and all animals."

Ezekiel Chapter 1:5-12 "And in the midst as it were the likeness of four living creatures. And this was their appearance; the likeness of a man was upon them. And each one had four faces, and each one had four wings. And their legs were straight; and their feet were winged, and there were sparks, like gleaming brass, and their wings were light. And the hand of a man was under their wings on their four sides. And the faces of them four turned not when they went; they went everyone straight forward. And the likeness of their faces was the face of a man, and the face of a lion on the right of the four; and the face of a calf on the left of the four; and the face of an eagle to the four. And the four had their wings spread out above; each one had two joined to one another, and two covered their bodies. And each one went straight forward: wherever the spirit was going they went and turned not back."

Ezekiel Chapter 10:8-22 "And I saw the cherubs having the likeness of men's hands under their wings. And I saw, and behold, four wheels stood by the cherubs, one wheel by each cherub: and the appearance of the wheels was as the appearance of a carbuncle stone. And as for their appearance, there was one likeness to the four, as if there should be a wheel in the midst of a wheel. When they went, they went on their four sides; they turned not when they went, for whichever way the first head looked, they went; and they turned not as they went. And their backs, and their hands, and their wings, and the wheels, were full of eyes round about the four wheels. And these wheels were called Gelgel in my hearing. And the cherubs were the same living creature which I saw by the river of Chobar. This is the living creature which I saw under the God of Israel by the river of Chobar; and I knew that they were cherubs. Each one had four faces, and each one had eight wings; and under their wings was the likeness of men's hands. And as for the likeness of their faces, these are the same faces which I saw under the glory of the God of Israel by the river of Chobar: and they went each straight forward."

Revelation 4:6-9 "And before the throne [there was] a sea of glass like unto crystal: and in the midst of the throne, and round about the throne, [were] four beasts full of eyes before and behind. And the first beast [was] like a lion, and the second beast like a calf, and the third beast had a face as a man, and the fourth beast [was] like a flying eagle. And the four beasts had each of them six wings about [him;] and [they were] full of eyes within: and they rest not day and night, saying, Holy, holy, holy, Lord God Almighty, which was, and is, and is to come. And when those beasts give glory and honour and thanks to him that sat on the throne, who lives for ever and ever."

Revelation 5:13-14 "And every creature which is in heaven, and on the earth, and under the earth, and such as are in the sea, and all that are in them, heard I saying, Blessing, and honour, and glory, and power, [be] unto him that sits upon the throne, and unto the Lamb for ever and ever. And the four beasts said, Amen. And the four [and] twenty elders fell down and worshipped him that lives for ever and ever." Good hybrids?

Jashur 36:31-35 "And afterward about one hundred and twenty great and terrible animals came out from the wilderness at the other side of the sea, and they all came to the place where the asses were, and they placed themselves there. And those animals, from their middle downward, were in the shape of the children of men, and from their middle upward, some had the likeness of bears, and some the likeness of the keephas, with tails behind them from between their shoulders reaching down to the earth, like the tails of the ducheephath, and these animals came and mounted and rode upon these asses, and led them away, and they went away unto this day. And one of these animals approached Anah and smote him with his tail, and then fled from that place. And when he saw this work he was exceedingly afraid of his life, and he fled and escaped to the city. And he related to his sons and brothers all that had happened to him, and many men went to seek the asses but could not find them, and Anah and his brothers went no more to that place from that day following, for they were greatly afraid of their lives."

Jashur 61:15-S16 "And Zepho went and he saw and behold there was a large cave at the bottom of the mountain, and there was a great stone there at the entrance of the cave, and Zepho split the stone and he came into the cave and he looked and behold, a large animal was devouring the ox; from the middle upward it resembled a man, and from the middle downward it resembled an animal, and Zepho rose up against the animal and slew it with his swords. And the inhabitants of Chittim heard of this thing, and they rejoiced exceedingly, and they said, What shall we do unto this man who has slain this animal that devoured our cattle?" It would seem a case could be made to surmise the possibility that mermaids-sirens do exist

ORIGIN OF THE SIRENS
C.10 'I read somewhere that in order for these women to cope with bearing the offspring of the fallen angels they themselves were subjected to transformation which will explain their hybrid look, half bird half human, there are just too many depictions of the similar looking siren in antiquity with most famous of all the Sumerian goddess Inana'

Very interesting, as this is what I have been trying to find an answer for?: How did the human women who had been the wives of the Fallen angels in Pre-Flood times become Sirens?

Sirens were said to be the mothers of the mermaids. I don't know, but I was thinking that the Fallen Angels they themselves could escape at the time of the Great Flood, as they are eternal beings and dimensional shape-shifters.

C.11 What about their human wives or their descendant daughters close to the Great Flood. If the Fallen angels were as smart as I think they were in changing the DNA of creatures and able to make hybrid creatures like Chimeras, is it just possible that they altered their wives , who ended up being the Sirens, who some claim were bird-like chimeras and yet others say they were the mothers of the mermaids.

C.12 What if the Fallen Angels knew that the Great Flood was coming. The Flood only affected the creatures on the land, and in the air - however the sea creatures did not die at the time of the Great Flood. That does finally happen at the Wrath of God according to Revelation 16 'All creatures that were in the sea and had life died'. This could explain why so many mermaids have been spotted in the seas and that they are very dangerous, and beguiling to man. Perhaps ancient mythological so-called fables had some truth to them after all?

C.13 CHIMERAS In the Bible, centaurs go by the name of **Nephilim**. They are an Anakim race of **human-horse hybrids** associated with Benjamin and Judah. These creatures were warriors, often carrying bows, arrows, and shields, and traveling in large armies. **Cretan Centaur and Minotaur**: In ancient Egypt, the Cretan Centaur and Minotaur took on new forms. The Cretan Centaur, which was part human and part horse, transformed into what we now recognize as the **Egyptian Sphinx**. The Sphinx has the body of a lion and the head of a human. It guards sacred sites and symbolizes mystery and wisdom .

C.14 ORIGINS OF DEMONIC ACTIVITY

Isaiah 13.21 Septuagint: 'But wild animals will rest there, and the houses will be filled with noise; there sirens will rest, and there demons will dance.' "sirens", are mentioned in the Septuagint in six verses, including three times in Isaiah (13:21, 34:13, 43:20), yet English translations of the Hebrew use "jackals" or "wild goats".

The **sirens** became synonymous with **mermaids** down through the ages,

The First Siren: Naamah

GENESIS 4 And Lamech took two wives. The name of the one was Adah, and the name of the other Zillah. Adah bore Jabal; he was the father of those who dwell in tents and have livestock. His brother's name was Jubal; he was the father of all those who play the lyre and pipe. Zillah also bore Tubal-cain; he was the forger of all instruments of bronze and iron. The sister of Tubal-cain was **Naamah.**

SEE MY BOOK - EDEN INSIGHTS - about this topic, and how these three children of 'Lamech the blind' were cursed and possessed by Satan -being the 5th generation from Cain. - Lamech had killed Cain by accident and was cursed for it by God Himself.

Genesis 4.15 'Whoso kills Cain shall be cursed 7-fold'.

C.15 EVIL really started to run rampant from 'Lamech the Blind's children onwards in around 300-400 years after creation.

C.16 It is not hard to see how Naamah, a figure of great beauty and musical talent who descended from the evil satanic Cain, could become associated with the Greek idea of a Siren, an evil figure of great beauty and musical prowess.

Aramaic words for ostrich and Naamah are homophones, meaning they sound the same .

This passage outlines some of the descendants of Cain. At first glance, it does not seem to offer even the slightest clue as the where the Sirens came from. However, in the Targums which are authorized Aramaic paraphrases of the Torah read in synagogues, something very interesting happens: three of the four extant Targums expand the account, associating Naamah with singing.

And the sister of Tubal-cain was Naamah, the inventor of *qinin* and songs

The Rabbis said: Naamah was a woman who sang to the timbrel in honour of idolatry

Furthermore, previous research was able to equate Naamah with Norea, a figure of great beauty found in various apocryphal writings.

As such it is not hard to see how Naamah, a figure of great beauty and musical talent who descended from the evil Cain, could become associated with the Greek idea of a Siren, an evil figure of great beauty and musical prowess.

Isaiah 34:13-14 I will summon the Sirens from the sea; And you, Liliths, come from the desert, And (you), demons and jackals, from the forests:

C.17 Naamah becomes associated with a new figure named **Lilith**. For example, in the ***Zohar***:

'There was a certain male who came into the world from the spirit of the side of Cain, and they called him Tubal-cain. And a certain female emerged with him, and human beings go astray after her, and she was called Naamah... And Naamah makes a roaring noise and cleaves to her side, and she still survives. And her dwelling is among the breakers of the great sea, and she goes out and makes sport with men, warming herself on them in dreams with human desire, and cleaving to them... The sons that she bears from mortal men present themselves to the females among mankind and they become pregnant by them and bear spirits. And they all go to ancient Lilith and she rears them.'

In addition to the association between Lilith and Naamah, note that the description of Naamah sounds a lot like a Siren.

C.18 Prior to the translation of the Septuagint, a tradition had developed that associated **Naamah** with roughly the same attributes ascribed to **Sirens** - a sinister nature, musical/singing skill, and physical beauty. Contemporary with the translation, there was an Aramaic association with ostriches and Naamah based on paronomasia. The original Septuagint translators read the passages about ostriches as having this same double meaning - both the physical bird and the attributes of Naamah. They made a choice to capture the alluring musician meaning in their translation rather than the animal meaning, causing Siren to enter the text.

In the Book of Job, the central character, utterly forsaken by God, utters his heart-breaking lament over his own spiritual loneliness:

Job, 30. 29-30 I am a brother to sirens and a companion of ostriches. My skin is black and falleth from me and my bones are burned with heat.

C.19 Sirens here are mysterious creatures of the desert, into which the man who had been forsaken by God feels himself to have been thrust. This is even clearer in the wonderful verses of Isaiah in which the eerie loneliness of Babylon is depicted after its conquest by the Medes:

Isaiah 13. 21, 22 Now beasts make their homes there and an empty echo is heard in the houses. Sirens have their habitation there and demons dance. Ass-centaurs dwell there and hedgehogs breed in the halls.:.

The last verse is retranslated by Jerome: "And owls answer each other through the halls and sirens dwell in the temple of pleasure- *Et sirenes in delubris voluptatis*".

This is the only passage in which the Latin Christian heard of Sirens in his Bible, and Jerome promptly proceeds to give his own commentary on the passage in which he describes the demonic character of these beings, doing so wholly in the spirit of classical mythology:

"By sweet and yet death-bringing song (*dulci et mortifero carmine*) they snatch the souls into the abyss so that with the raging of the shipwreck they may be devoured by dogs and wolves."

C.20 Such were the siren symbols with which the Greek Christian could re-acquaint himself from his Bible, and there was little left here of the Sirens of Homer. The sirens of Holy Scripture are nocturnal, demonic bird figures that live in the desert, and it is interesting to note how such a writer as Cyril of Alexandria conceives the sirens to be a kind of night-owl, while the exegetes who follow him identify them with the king fisher, halcyon, or again with owls, and this because of the latter's melancholy song.

C.21 Connecting link with Homer: for the Biblical sirens are nocturnal and demonic beings, and it was held, wholly the spirit of the original myth— that the purpose of Scripture was in this case to express the fact that these God-forsaken places had been delivered over to the power of the demons. "It is certain demons, loathsome and savage spirits" that live there, says Eusebius, and immediately he remembers the Greek myth: "For the Greeks say that the Sirens are sweet-singing but deceptive creatures." Even Cyril, who, as we saw, tends to prefer an objective interpretation as of a nocturnal animal, is too much of a Greek to wholly escape the memory of his poets. In his commentary on Micah he writes: "The Greeks and those who follow them give the name 'Siren' to spirits who are able to sing most sweetly and so, as by magic, get those who hear them into their power." And he interprets the whole passage of Satan and his demon hosts.

C.22 Different types of Demons

Now if you put **Isaiah 13:21,34:13,43:20** together with with **Job 30:29, Micah 1:8, Jeremiah 50;39** you discover that there are different types of demons. The Satyr's (hairy demons goats?), Liliths, and daughters of the Sirens (translated owls or ostriches). All of these demons are different types. Just as **Enoch 19** tells us.

C.23 See my 1ST book **ENOCH INSIGHTS**:

'ENOCH INSIGHTS': Chapter 19.1-2 And Uriel said to me, "Here shall stand the angels who have connected themselves with women, and their spirits assuming many different forms are defiling mankind and shall lead them astray into sacrificing to demons as gods, (here shall they stand) till the day of the great judgment in which they shall be judged till they are made an end of.

C.24: Here it clearly shows that angels are able to be *shape-shifters*. All through history sacrificing to Demons as gods has been very common place, though it *still exists in modern times*, it is mostly camouflaged.

2 And the women also of the angels who went astray shall become **sirens**, and I, Enoch alone saw the vision, the ends of all things, and no man shall see as I have seen.

C.25 Enoch states that he alone saw this vision, and that no man shall see as he has seen. This statement in a very real sense, proves that it was Enoch himself, seventh from Adam that *originally wrote this book*.

CHAPTER 36

NOW, Enoch, I give thee the term. of thirty days to spend in thy house, and tell thy sons and all thy household, that all may hear from my face what is told them by thee, that they may read and understand, how there is no other God but me.

2 And that they may always keep my commandments and begin to read and take in the books of thy handwriting.

3 And after thirty days I send all send my angel for thee, and they will take thee from earth and from thy sons to me.

CHAPTER 37

AND the Lord called up one of the older angels, terrible and menacing, and placed him by me, in appearance white as snow, and his hands like ice, having the appearance of great frost, and he froze my face, because I could not endure the terror of the Lord, just as it is not possible to endure a stove's fire and the sun's heat, and the frost of the air.

C.1 It is mentioning older angels fierce and menacing and says that they were frost angels. These frost angels were as cold as fire is hot.

Wisdom of Solomon 16.22 "But snow and ice endured the fire, and melted not, that they might know that fire burning in the hail, and sparkling in the rain, did destroy the fruits of the enemies."

2 And the Lord said to me: 'Enoch, if thy face be not frozen here, no man will be able to behold thy face.'

CHAPTER 38

AND the Lord said to those men who first led me up: 'Let Enoch go down on to earth with you and await him till the determined day.'

C.1 'determined day.' =The day that Enoch would be translated to heaven.

2 And they placed me by night on my couch.

3 And Mathusal (Methusaleh) expecting my coming, keeping watch by day and by night at my couch, was filled with awe when he heard my coming, and I told him, 'Let all my household come together, that I tell them everything.'

CHAPTER 39

> Oh, my children, my beloved ones, hear the admonition of your father, as much as is according to the Lord's will.
>
> 2 I have been let come to you to-day, and announce to you, not from my lips, but from the Lord's lips, all that is and was and all that is now, and all that will be till judgement-day.

C.1 God gave Enoch a complete rundown of all 7000 years of man's history until the eternal age or the 8th Millennium.

> 3 For the Lord has let me come to you, you hear therefore the words of my lips, of a man made big for you, but I am one who has seen the Lord's face, like iron made to glow from fire it sends forth sparks and burns,

Revelation 1.14-15 His head and his hairs were white like wool, ad white as snow, and this eyes as a flame of fire. And his feet like unto fine brass, as if they burned in a furnace; and his voice as the sound of many waters.

> 4 You look now upon my eyes, *the eyes* of a man big with meaning for you, but I have seen the Lord›s eyes, shining like the sun›s rays and filling the eyes of man with awe.
>
> 5 You see now, my children, the right hand of a man that helps you, but I have seen the Lord's right hand filling heaven as He helped me.
>
> 6 You see the compass of my work like your own, but I have seen the Lord's limitless and perfect compass, which has no end.
>
> 7 You hear the words of my lips, as I heard the words of the Lord, like great thunder incessantly with hurling of clouds.
>
> 8 And now, my children, hear the discourses of the father of the earth, how fearful and awful it is to come before the face of the ruler of the earth, how much more terrible and awful it is to come before the face of the ruler of heaven, the controller of quick and dead, and of the heavenly troops. Who can endure that endless pain?

Hebrew 10.31 "It is a fearful thing to fall into the hands of the living God."

CHAPTER 40

> AND now, my children, I know all things, for this is from the Lord's lips, and this my eyes have seen, from beginning to end.

C.1 Enoch has stated that he wrote 366 books. We have only a couple of them. What happened to the hundreds of other books that he wrote? Or more precisely the other 364 books?

> 2 I know all things, and have written all things into books, the heavens and their end, and their plenitude, and all the armies and their marchings.

C.2 'Armies and their marchings' -This is talking about all the armies of angels.

> 3 I have measured and described the stars, the great countless multitude *of them.*

C.3 By what ability could an individual describe all the stars in the heavens which are innumerable? That had to be a miracle of God in the spirit world. We with our finite brain can't even compute such things. Only supernatural wisdom could make such a claim possible.

C.4 According to God's prophets, in the case of some of them - suddenly they 'were in the Spirit' and their eyes were opened, and they could both see and hear and experience things that no one else on earth could experience. They were shown such amazing things of God and His Creation, so that they could come back down to earth and write it all down; so that future generations like us would have the pleasure of seeing all of God's wonders.

> 4 What man has seen their **revolutions**, and their **entrances**? For not even the angels see their number, while I have written all their names.

C.5 Enoch mentions that not only has he seen the stars on the physical plane, but that he also saw what was behind them in the spirit world. How they are kept in perfect synchronization in their endless circuits through the heavens.

> 5 And I measured the sun's **circle**, and measured its rays, counted the hours, I wrote down too all' things that go over the earth I have written the things that are nourished, and all seed sown and unsown, which the earth produces and all plants, and every grass and every flower, and their sweet smells, and their names, and the dwelling-places of the clouds, and their composition, and their wings, and how they bear rain and raindrops.

C.6 How could clouds have 'wings' unless Enoch is referring to angels or beings that take care of the clouds. It would appear that everything in God's great Creation has angels or spirit being and creatures that care for and protect Gods Creation. It could be big angels or even things small like fairies. All of God's Creation is well-cared for.

Hebrews 12.1 Wherefore seeing we also are compassed about with so great a cloud of witnesses, let us lay aside every weight, and the sin which doth so easily beset us, and let us run with patience the race that is set before us,

> 6 And I investigated all things and wrote the road of the thunder and of the lightning, and they showed me **the keys** and **their guardians**, their rise, the way they go; it is let out in measure (*sc.* gently) by a chain, lest by a heavy chain and violence it hurl down the angry clouds and destroy all things on earth.

C.7 '**the keys** and **their guardians**' This would appear to be referring to the angels and their powers or Keys - to take care of the thunder and lightning and the storm clouds.

> 7 I wrote the **treasure-houses of the snow**, and the **store-houses of the cold** and the **frosty airs,** and I observed their season's **key-holder**, he fills the clouds with them, and does not exhaust the treasure-houses.
>
> 8 And I wrote the resting-places of the winds and observed and saw how their key-holders bear **weighing-scales** and **measures**; first, they put them in *one* weighing-scale, then in the other the weights and let them out according to measure cunningly over the whole earth, lest by heavy breathing they make the earth to rock.

C.8 Enoch is telling us that angels are weighing the measures of the clouds. It mentions that they must watch out about 'their' heavy breathing lest they 'make the earth to rock'. I presume that it means the 'great forces of the winds' must be kept in balance or they could be a danger to the earth in making it to 'rock back and forth'?

> 9 And I measured out the whole earth, its mountains, and all hills, fields, trees, stones, rivers, all existing things I wrote down, the height from earth to the seventh heaven, and downwards to the **very lowest hell**, and the judgement-place, and the very great, open and weeping hell.

C.9 The 10 levels of heaven, as mentioned in earlier chapters, includes levels going up to the highest heaven and also levels going down to the lowest levels of the darkest and deepest Hell.

> 10 And I saw how the **prisoners are in pain**, expecting the limitless judgement.

C.10 According to this very same book in an earlier chapter on level 2 or the 2nd Heaven - on of the 'lower dimensions' of Hell, the fallen angels were in prison and in great pain and grief and endless sorrow.

> 11 And I wrote down all those being judged by the judge, and all their judgements (*sc.* sentences) and all their works.

C.11 In order to know everything about everything you would have to be God Himself who is omniscient. I suppose for Enoch that it was like watching a movie where you are shown a lot of what has been created and what will yet be created. Just amazing. Perhaps the other some 364 books that Enoch wrote, and which today sadly are missing as far as we know - well, perhaps those books described a lot of the details of Creation and things that are yet to be. It must be that in the eternal world or the spirit world and Heaven that one is given so much more spiritual light to comprehend all of God's amazing Creations. Not to just describe them, but to fully experience them also. Heaven sounds like an awesome and exhilarating place.

CHAPTER 41

AND I saw all forefathers from *all* time with Adam and Eva, and I sighed and broke into tears and said of the ruin of their dishonour:

2. 'Woe is me for my infirmity and *for that* of my forefathers,› and thought in my, heart and said:

3 'Blessed *is* the man who has not been born or who has been born and shall not sin before the Lord›s face, that he come not into this place, nor bring the yoke of this place!

Romans 5.12 -21 [12] Wherefore, as by one man sin entered into the world, and death by sin; and so death passed upon all men, for that all have sinned:

[17] For if by one man's offence death reigned by one; much more they which receive abundance of grace and of the gift of righteousness shall reign in life by one, Jesus Christ.)

[19] For as by one man's disobedience many were made sinners, so by the obedience of one shall many be made righteous.

[21] That as sin hath reigned unto death, even so might grace reign through righteousness unto eternal life by Jesus Christ our Lord.

CHAPTER 42

> I SAW the key-holders and guards of the **gates of hell** standing, like **great serpents**, and their faces like extinguished lamps, and their eyes of fire, their sharp teeth. And I saw all the Lord's works, how they are right, while the works of man are some *good*, and others bad, and in their works are known those who **lie evilly**.

C.1 As the content of this verse is so detailed, I am separating the verse into 2 parts. The 1st part seems totally unrelated to the 2nd part, and I suspect that at one time there was a lot more writing in this verse or even verses and one verse has been pushed into the back of the first one. Let's examine the verse as two separate verses.

> 1a. I SAW the key-holders and guards of the **gates of hell** standing, like **great serpents**, and their faces like extinguished lamps, and their eyes of fire, their sharp teeth.
>
> 1b. And I saw all the Lord's works, how they are right, while the works of man are some *good*, and others bad, and in their works are known those who **lie evilly**.

C.2 This above verse 1a is telling us a lot about Hell and the Serpent creatures that guard the gates of Hell itself. It is stating that there are great serpents who guard the Gates of Hell.

C.3 Can we find evidence of this in either history or mythology. Why even mention mythology? We find from consistent research that a lot of so-called mythology is very close to the truth. How can you believe anything modern education teaches you when their whole plan of education is totally ungodly, based on the LIE of evolution and they are unbelieving of the real truth about God's Word? Let's investigate this topic and see what we can find.

C.4 In ancient Greek mythology, the role of guarding the gates of the underworld fell to **Cerberus**, a monstrous three-headed dog. His mane was made from several hundreds of poisonous snakes, and he was a loyal servant of the Greek god Hades. Cerberus stood at the gates of hell, gracefully guiding the dead into the underworld. His other duties included preventing the dead from escaping the underworld and stopping any living beings from entering without Hades' permission.

Why was Cerberus placed at the gates of Hell?

Revelation 12.3 "And there appeared another wonder in heaven; and behold a great red **dragon**, having seven heads and ten horns, and seven crowns upon his heads."

Revelation 20.1-3 And I saw an angel coming down out of heaven, having the key to the Abyss and holding in his hand a great chain. He seized the **dragon,** that ancient serpent, who is the **devil**, or **Satan**, and bound him for a thousand years. He threw him into the Abyss, and locked and sealed it over him, to keep him from deceiving the nations anymore until the thousand years were ended.

Revelation 20.7-10 And when the thousand years are expired, **Satan** shall be loosed out of his prison, And shall go out to deceive the nations which are in the four quarters of the earth, Gog, and Magog, to gather them together to battle: the number of whom is as the sand of the sea. And they went up on the breadth of the earth, and compassed the camp of the saints about, and the beloved city: and fire came down from God out of heaven, and devoured them. And the devil that deceived them was cast into the lake of fire and brimstone, where the beast and the false prophet *are*, and shall be tormented day and night for ever and ever.

C.5 From the Bible we find the Story of the Serpent talking with Eve in the Garden of Eden. What I have read about this that the serpent race was taken over by Satan in the Garden of Eden, and that they have been subservient to Satan ever since. Many snakes today are seen either as dangerous in one form or another or poisonous or even deadly poisonous. Some are small and some are very large. They are not creatures that can normally be reasoned with.

Genesis 3.1 "Now the serpent was more subtil than any beast of the field which the LORD God had made. And he said unto the woman, Yea, hath God said, Ye shall not eat of every tree of the garden?"

C.6 The Bible mentions the serpent or snake many times. Moses 'lifted up the snake in the wilderness'. Moses lifted up his staff with a golden image of the snakes that were terrorizing the children of Israel. When the people looked on his staff with the brazen snakes on it, they were healed.

Numbers 21.9 "And Moses made a serpent of brass, and put it upon a pole, and it came to pass, that if a serpent had bitten any man, when he beheld the serpent of brass, he lived."

C.7 This symbol of Moses staff with the snakes entwinned on it, has become the symbol of modern medicine or Pharmacia .

C.8 The angels who fell in early pre-flood times, were all shape-shifters, so what form did each of the ancient 'gods' take on? Sometimes, apparently, they appeared as very tall men or women with the head of a bird and human body, and other times like chimeras both human, animal and snakes, according to the hieroglyphics of ancient times. Some gods took on the form of snakes in some form or other, but mostly as human/animal chimeras. There is clear evidence for this from all the pictures and drawings from ancient empires and civilizations including pre-Egyptian or pre-Flood, Egypt, Assyria, Babylon, medio-Persia, Greece, Rome.

2 Peter 2.4 For if God spared not the angels that sinned, but cast them down to hell, and delivered them into chains of darkness, to be reserved unto judgment.

C.9 Going back to VERSE: 1a. 'I SAW the key-holders and guards of the

gates of hell standing, like **great serpents**, and their faces like extinguished lamps, and their eyes of fire, their sharp teeth.'

1) Key-holders 2) Guards 3) Gates of Hell 4) like great serpents 5) faces like extinguished lamps 6) eyes of fire 7) sharp teeth

Revelation 1.18 I am he that lives, and was dead; and, behold, I am alive for evermore, Amen; and have the **keys of hell and of death**.

C.10 According to the Bible in the Book of Revelation by the time the Messiah had died he took a 3 and a half day trip into the heart of Hell and fought against Satan and took the Keys of Death and Hell away. Christ defeated Satan and took away his power over death and the power as to who should be in Hell and who was allowed to get out again this shook up the foundations of the Darkness and the Netherworld.

C.11 Jesus' descent into the place of the dead is referred to in the Apostles' Creed and the Athanasian Creed, which states that Jesus "descended into the underworld." His descent to the underworld is mentioned in the New Testament.

1 Peter 4.5-6 Who shall give account to him that is ready to judge the quick and the dead. For this cause was the gospel preached also to them that are dead, that they might be judged according to men in the flesh, but live according to God in the spirit.

Ephesians 4.9 "Now that he ascended, what is it but that he also descended first into the lower parts of the earth?"

C.12 After His crucifixion Jesus invaded Hell with His angels, before He was seen to be resurrected. He had such a love for the lost souls to have a chance to be saved, that He first went down to Hell to preach unto the dead in Hell so that they could be released from the jaws of Death and from the Gates of Hell.

1 Peter 3.18-22 "For Christ also hath once suffered for sins, the just for the unjust, that he might bring us to God, being put to death in the flesh, but quickened by the Spirit:" By which also he went and preached unto the spirits in prison (Hell); which sometime were disobedient, when once the longsuffering of God waited in the days of Noah, while the ark was a preparing, wherein few, that is, eight souls were saved by water. The like figure whereunto *even* baptism doth also now save us (not the putting away of the filth of the flesh, but the answer of a good conscience toward God,) by the resurrection of Jesus Christ: Who is gone into heaven, and is on the right hand of God; angels and authorities and powers being made subject unto him.

C.13 According to the Bible, Satan is no longer in charge of Hell, but Christ is, and Satan will soon be locked up in the Bottomless Pit. I don't know what has happened to the snake-like original guardians of Hell's Gates? Somehow, things changed drastically after Christ took the keys of Death and Hell from Satan circa 2000 years ago. The good news is that as a result, the Darkness is already defeated, and it is just a matter of time, until the light comes back to our world, and all evil and darkness is banished for good.

C.14 Verse 1a pt 2: 'their faces like extinguished lamps, and their eyes of fire, their sharp teeth'. – 'Faces like extinguished lamps' = faces of Death.

There is a description like this of those fallen angels with faces like 'extinguished lamps in this very book of the secrets of Enoch in the chapter 18, where the Fallen angels are in the dungeon and hung up on the wall. Here is a quote from **Chapter 18 verse 1**:

'THE men (Angels) took me on to the fifth heaven and placed me, and there I saw many and countless soldiers (fallen angels), called Grigori, of human appearance, and their size was greater than that of great giants and their faces withered, and the silence of their mouths perpetual.'

C.15 Somehow their eyes are not totally darkened, and they still had **fire** in their eyes? I believe that both the angels and other spirit beings are actually made with some sort of 'spiritual fire' from 'within' as shown in the description of Jesus in Revelation 1.

Revelation 1.13-16 And in the midst of the seven candlesticks *one* like unto the Son of man, clothed with a garment down to the foot, and girt about the paps with a golden girdle. His head and his hairs were white as snow; and his eyes as a **flame of fire**. And his feet like unto fine brass, as if they **burned in a furnace**; and his voice as the sound of many waters. And he had in his right hand seven stars: and out of his mouth went a sharp two-edged sword: and his **countenance** *was* as the **sun** shineth in his strength.

C.16 You can also read in **1 Enoch about** the 'angels stepping on fire'.

1 Enoch 71.1 The translation of Enoch to heaven: And it came to pass after this that my spirit was translated, and it ascended into the heavens, and I saw the holy sons of God (angels). They were stepping on flames of fire: their garments were white, and their faces shone like snow. And I saw two streams of fire, and the light of that fire shone like hyacinth, and I fell on my face before the Lord.

C.17 Sharp teeth is not something one would normally see in an angel or human so this is talking about the serpentine hybrid of the Fallen angels where can morph their form at will but it would seem that change from angel to serpent or another human or animal hybrid like Cerberus the three headed dog with its fur made of snakes and with sharp teeth, as mentioned in Greek mythology or even a giant serpent creature. Creatures which intimidate and cause fear.

C.18 Going back to VERSE 1b. *'And I saw all the Lord's works, how they are right, while the works of man are some good, and others bad, and in their works are known those who lie evilly.'*

C.19 What is this 2nd part of the verse talking about? This is stating that 1) All the works of the Lord are righteous and good and that 2) the works of mankind are some good and some evil. 3) There are also those who lie for a living and 4) In extreme cases lie to deceive and destroy others for their personal gain.

C.20 Going back to the very beginning of this chapter 'I SAW the key-holders'.

On the positive side, Jesus gave 'The Keys of the Kingdom of God' to His disciples as stated in Matthew 16.19. The Keys of the Kingdom have a lot of power to give Wisdom, discernment, knowledge of the Truth and they help against any problems encountered by a true disciple of Christ. The keys do miracles.

Matthew 16.19 "And I will give unto thee the keys of the kingdom of heaven: and whatsoever thou shalt bind on earth shall be bound in heaven: and whatsoever thou shalt loose on earth shall be loosed in heaven."

C.21 Going back to VERSE 1a: 'like great serpents' This amazing and colourful verse of this chapter 42, also mentions that 'what' Enoch saw standing at the Gates of Hell guarding them 'appeared' to him to look like snakes.

This would suggest that in the region of Hell things are not always as they appear to our physical senses. There is much more to the 'picture' than is meeting the eye.

This phenomenon has showed up time and time again around the planet and throughout all time. I believe that it has to do with an area of dimensional shift or portals. The paranormal and supernatural is full of such things.

What is the difference between physical reality, spiritual reality, dreams, visions or even projected images from God or even sometimes from the negative spirit world? Our personal perception of them and what they mean to us is what matters and how we interpret what we see or perceive.

C.22 Have you ever seen something that looks sort of 'out of place' and it is very hard to explain? Someone has wisely stated: what do you define as real? I personally have seen many things that 'seem' out of place. I have related some of my experiences in my books of the paranormal '**Out of the Bottomless Pit**' books **1** & **2**.

C.23 Read more about this topic When Jesus went down to Hell to rescue all the souls from Creation unto Christ – the Gospel of Nicodemus

Gospel of Nicodemus
Part II.-The Descent of Christ into Hell or also known as the Harrowing of Hell
Chapter I

C.24 Author: See my commentary of this 'Gospel of Nicodemus', at the end of this amazing story. The gospel of Nicodemus occupies the following 3 pages.

C.25 The foundation of all Christian doctrine hinges on the truth of the resurrection. Jesus said,

John 11.25-26 "I am the resurrection and the life. He who believes in Me, though he may die, he shall live. And whoever lives and believes in Me shall never die."

1 Joseph says: And why do you wonder that Jesus has risen? But it is wonderful that He has not risen alone, but that He has also raised many others of the dead who have appeared in Jerusalem to many. And if you do not know the others, Symeon at least, who received Jesus, and his two sons whom He has raised up-them at least you know.

For we buried them not long ago; but now their tombs are seen open *and* empty, and they are alive, and dwelling in Arimathaea. They therefore sent men, and they found their tombs open and empty. Joseph says: Let us go to Arimathaea and find them.

2 Then rose up the chief priests Annas and Caiaphas, and Joseph, and Nicodemus, and Gamaliel, and others with them, and went away to Arimathaea, and found those whom Joseph spoke of. They made prayer, therefore, and saluted each other. Then they came with them to Jerusalem, and brought them into the synagogue, and secured the doors, and placed in the midst the old *covenant* of the Jews; and the chief priests said to them: We wish you to swear by the God of Israel and Adonai, and so that you tell the truth, how you have risen, and who has raised you from the dead.

3 The men who had risen having heard this, made upon their faces the sign of the cross, and said to the chief priests: Give us paper and ink and pen. These therefore they brought. And sitting down, they wrote thus:-

Chapter 2

1 O Lord Jesus Christ, the resurrection and the life of the world, grant us grace that we may give an account of Thy resurrection, and Thy miracles which Thou didst in Hades. We then were in Hades, with all who had fallen asleep since the beginning of the world. And at the hour of midnight there rose a light as if of the sun, and shone into these dark *regions;* and we were all lighted up, and saw each other. And straightway our father Abraham was united with the patriarchs and the prophets, and at the same time they were filled with joy, and said to each other: This light is from a great source of light. The prophet Hesaias (Isaiah), who was there present, said: This light is from the Father, and from the Son, and from the Holy Spirit; about whom I prophesied when yet alive, saying, The land of Zabulon, and the land of Nephthalim, the people that sat in darkness, have seen a great light.

2 Then there came into the midst another, an ascetic from the desert; and the patriarchs said to him: Who art thou? And he said: I am John, the last of the prophets, who made the paths of the Son of God straight, and proclaimed to the people repentance for the remission of sins. And the Son of God came to me; and I, seeing Him a long way off, said to the people: Behold the Lamb of God, who taketh away the sin of the world. And with my hand I baptized Him in the river Jordan, and I saw like a dove also the Holy Spirit coming upon Him; and I heard also the voice of God, even the Father, thus saying: This is my beloved Son, in whom I am well pleased. And on this account He sent me also to you, to proclaim how the only begotten Son of God is coming here, that whosoever shall believe in Him shall be saved, and whosoever shall not believe in Him shall be condemned. On this account I say to you all, in order that when you see Him you all may adore Him, that now only is for you the time of repentance for having adored idols in the vain upper world, and for the sins you have committed, and that this is impossible at any other time.

Chapter 3

While John, therefore, was thus teaching those in Hades, the first created and forefather Adam heard, and said to his son Seth: My son, I wish thee to tell the forefathers of the race of men and the prophets where I sent thee, when it fell to my lot to die. And Seth said: Prophets and patriarchs, hear. When my father Adam, the first created, was about to fall once upon a time into death, he sent me to make entreaty to God very close by the gate of paradise, that He would guide me by an angel to the tree of compassion and that I might take oil and anoint my father, and that he might rise up from his sickness: which thing, therefore, I also did. And after the prayer an angel of the Lord came, and said to me: What, Seth, dost thou ask? Dost thou ask oil which raiseth up the sick, or the tree from which this oil flows, on account of the sickness of thy father? This is not to be found now. Go, therefore, and tell thy father, that after the accomplishing of five thousand five hundred years from the creation of the world, thou shall come into the earth the only begotten Son of God, being made man; and He shall anoint him with this oil, and shall raise him up; and shall wash clean, with water and with the Holy Spirit, both him and those out of him, and then shall he be healed of every disease; but now this is impossible.

When the patriarchs and the prophets heard these words, they rejoiced greatly.

Chapter 4

1 And when all were in such joy, came Satan the heir of darkness, and said to Hades: O all-devouring and insatiable, hear my words. There is of the race of the Jews one named Jesus, calling himself the Son of God; and being a man, by our working with them the Jews have crucified him: and now when he is dead, be ready that we may secure him here. For I know that he is a man, and I heard him also saying, My soul is exceeding sorrowful, even unto death. He has also done me many evils when living with mortals in the upper world. For wherever he found my servants, he persecuted them; and whatever men I made crooked, blind, lame, lepers, or any such thing, by a single word he healed them; and many whom I had got ready to be buried, even these through a single word he brought to life again.

2 Hades says: And is this *man* so powerful as to do such things by a single word? or if he be so, canst thou withstand him? It seems to me that, if he be so, no one will be able to withstand him. And if thou sayest that thou didst hear him dreading death, he said this mocking thee, and laughing, wishing to seize thee with the strong hand; and woe, woe to thee, to all eternity! Satan says: O all-devouring and insatiable Hades, art thou so afraid at hearing of our common enemy? I was not afraid of him, but worked in the Jews, and they crucified him, and gave him also to drink gall with vinegar. Make ready, then, in order that you may lay fast hold of him when he comes.

3 Hades answered: Heir of darkness, son of destruction, devil, thou hast just now told me that many whom thou hadst made ready to be buried, be brought to life again by a single word. And if he has delivered others from the tomb, how and with what power shall he be laid hold of by us? For I not long ago swallowed down one dead, Lazarus by name; and not long after, one of the living by a single word dragged him up by force out of my bowels: and I think

that it was he of whom thou speakest. If, therefore, we receive him here, I am afraid lest perchance we be in danger even about the rest. For, lo, all those that I have swallowed from eternity I perceive to be in commotion, and I am pained in my belly. And the snatching away of Lazarus beforehand seems to me to be no good sign: for not like a dead body, but like an eagle, he flew out of me; for so suddenly did the earth throw him out. Wherefore also I adjure even thee, for thy benefit and for mine, not to bring him here; for I think that he is coming here to raise all the dead. And this I tell thee: by the darkness in which we live, if thou bring him here, not one of the dead will be left behind in it to me.

Chapter 5

1 While Satan and Hades were thus speaking to each other, there was a great voice like thunder, saying: Lift up your gates, O ye rulers; and be ye lifted up, ye everlasting gates; and the King of glory shall come in. When Hades heard, he said to Satan: Go forth, if thou art able, and withstand him. Satan therefore went forth to the outside. Then Hades says to his demons: Secure well and strongly the gates of brass and the bars of iron, and attend to my bolts, and stand in order, and see to everything; for if he come in here, woe will seize us.

2 The forefathers having heard this, began all to revile him, saying: O all-devouring and insatiable! open, that the King of glory may come in. David the prophet says: Dost thou not know, O blind, that I when living in the world prophesied this saying: Lift up your gates, O ye rulers? Hesaias said: I, foreseeing this by the Holy Spirit, wrote: The dead shall rise up, and those in their tombs shall be raised, and those in the earth shall rejoice. And where, O death, is thy sting? where, O Hades, is thy victory?

3 There came, then, again a voice saying: Lift up the gates. Hades, hearing the voice the second time, answered as if forsooth he did not know, and says: Who is this King of glory? The angels of the Lord say: The Lord strong and mighty, the Lord mighty in battle. And immediately with these words the brazen gates were shattered, and the iron bars broken, and all the dead who had been bound came out of the prisons, and we with the n And the King of glory came in in the form of a man, and all the dark places of Hades were lighted up.

Chapter 6

1 Immediately Hades cried out: We have been conquered: woe to us! But who art thou, that hast such power and might? and what art thou, who comest here without sin who art seen to be small and yet of great power, lowly and exalted, the slave and the master, the soldier and the king, who hast power over the dead and the living? Thou wast nailed on the cross, and placed in the tomb; and now thou art free, and hast destroyed all our power. Art thou then the Jesus about whom the chief satrap Satan told us, that through cross and death thou art to inherit the whole world?

2 Then the King of glory seized the chief satrap Satan by the head, and delivered him to His angels, and said: With iron chains bind his hands and his feet,

and his neck, and his mouth. Then He delivered him to Hades, and said: Take him, and keep him secure till my second appearing.

Chapter 7

1 And Hades receiving Satan, said to him: Beelzebul, heir of fire and punishment, enemy of the saints, through what necessity didst thou bring about that the King of glory should be crucified, so that he should come here and deprive us *of our power?* Turn and see that not one of the dead has been left in me, but all that thou hast gained through the tree of knowledge, all hast thou lost through the tree of the cross: and all thy joy has been turned into grief; and wishing to put to death the King of glory, thou hast put thyself to death. For, since I have received thee to keep thee safe, by experience shall thou learn how many evils I shall do unto thee. O arch-devil, the beginning of death, root of sin, end of all evil, what evil didst thou find in Jesus, that thou shouldst compass his destruction? how hast thou dared to do such evil? how hast thou busied thyself to bring down such a man into this darkness, through whom thou hast been deprived of all who have died from eternity?

Chapter 8

1 While Hades was thus discoursing to Satan, the King of glory stretched out His right hand, and took hold of our forefather Adam, and raised him. Then turning also to the rest, He said: Come all with me, as many as have died through the tree which he touched: for, behold, I again raise you all up through the tree of the cross. Thereupon He brought them all out, and our forefather Adam seemed to be filled with joy, and said: I thank Thy majesty, O Lord, that Thou hast brought me up out of the lowest Hades. Likewise also all the prophets and the saints said: We thank Thee, O Christ, Saviour of the world, that Thou hast brought our life up out of destruction.

2 And after they had thus spoken, the Saviour blessed Adam with the sign of the cross on his forehead, and did this also to tire patriarchs, and prophets, and martyrs, and forefathers; and He took them, and sprang up out of Hades. And while He was going, the holy fathers accompanying Him sang praises, saying: Blessed is He that cometh in the name of the Lord: Alleluia; to Him be the glory of oil the saints.

Chapter 9

1 And setting out to paradise, He took hold of our forefather Adam by the hand, and delivered him, and all the just, to the archangel Michael. And as they were going into the door of paradise, there met them two old men, to whom the holy fathers said: Who are you, who have not seen death, and have not come down into Hades, but who dwell in paradise in your bodies and your souls? One of them answered, and said: I am Enoch, who was well-pleasing to God, and who was translated hither by Him; and this is Helias the Thesbite; and we are also to live until the end of the world; and then we are to be sent by God to withstand Antichrist, and to be slain by him, and after three days to rise again, and to be snatched up in clouds to meet the Lord.

Chapter 10

1 While they were thus speaking, there came another lowly man, carrying also upon his shoulders a cross, to whom the holy fathers said: Who art thou, who hast the look of a robber; and what is the cross which thou bearest upon thy shoulders? He answered: I, as you say, was a robber and a thief in the world, and for these things the Jews laid hold of me, and delivered me to the death of the cross, along with our Lord Jesus Christ. While, then, He was hanging upon the cross, I, seeing the miracles that were done, believed in Him, and entreated Him, and said, Lord, when Thou shall be King, do not forget me. And immediately He said to me, Amen, amen: to-day, I say unto thee, shall thou be with me in paradise. Therefore I came to paradise carrying my cross; and finding the archangel Michael, I said to him, Our Lord Jesus, who has been crucified, has sent me here; bring me, therefore, to the gate of Eden. And the flaming sword, seeing the sign of the cross, opened to me, and I went in. Then the archangel says to me, Wait a little, for there cometh also the forefather of the race of men, Adam, with the just, that they too may come in. And now, seeing you, I came to meet you.

2 The saints hearing these things, all cried out with a loud voice: Great is our Lord, and great is His strength.

Chapter 11

1 All these things we saw and heard; we, the two brothers, who also have been sent by Michael the archangel, and have been ordered to proclaim the resurrection of the Lord, but first to go away to the Jordan and to be baptized. Thither also we have gone, and have been baptized with the rest of the dead who have risen. Thereafter also we came to Jerusalem, and celebrated the Passover of the Resurrection. But now we are going away, being unable to stay here. And the love of God, even the Father, and the grace of our Lord Jesus Christ, and the communion of the Holy Spirit, be with you all.

2 Having written these things, and secured the rolls, they gave the half to the chief priests, and the half to Joseph and Nicodemus. And they immediately disappeared: to the glory of our Lord Jesus Christ. Amen.

Commentary on the Gospel of Nicodemus by S.N.Strutt - 06/05/2024

C.26 These 11 chapters, I feel, are probably genuine, although a few things need to be more fully explained.

C.27 Is this story according to the Bible in general? It would appear that it is merely adding details to the Bible story of Jesus' resurrection and his descent into Hell for 3 and a half days in order to win many of those in Hell to become saved and to move on with Christ to the higher regions of Heaven or the Heavenly City as mentioned in Revelation 21-22.

C.28 This story is mentioning that all the Patriarchs from Adam to the prophet John were all sitting in darkness near to the Gates of Hell. This could give the wrong impression. When one reads the Gospels, you find that Jesus tells the Story of Lazurus and the rich man. There was Hell and its torments down in Hades. There also was Paradise a heavenly place right next to Hell.

Some sort of wayfaring station for the righteous in the days before Jesus the Messiah had brought Salvation. Those such as Adam all the way to John the Baptist did not go to Hell when they died. They went to Paradise which is as the 'Garden of Eden', and which used to indeed be inside the earth.

C.29 It is stated in the Hebrew book of Jubilees, that when Enoch was translated, that he was taken to the **Garden of Eden.** There he wrote down his 366 books of all that would happen from Pre-Creation until eternity.

C.30 Setting the scene: The Patriarchs were living in Paradise, but they were waiting for the promise of the Messiah coming and specifically waiting for Him to 'bust open' the 'Gates of Hell' in order to release many souls that had been bound for a long time. In fact, in many cases from Pre-flood times. The witness that I get is, that God invited all the Patriarchs to come and 'sit in the darkness' next to the Gates of Hell, so that they could directly witness the triumphant march into Hades of Christ the Messiah with his angels. The Patriarchs had the privilege or in fact the honour to see in person Christ's harrowing of Hell. Or in other words his busting down the Gates of Hell that could not resist Him as Hades, has also stated in this 'Gospel of Nicodemus'.

C.31 How could **Hades,** which is a **place,** actually talk as a person as in this story? It would appear that Hades also has its own spirit. It would appear that Death, Hell and Hades were evil spirits, that were created because of the disobedience of mankind in the very beginning of time such as the Garden of Eden and in the Preflood times. It must have been fascinating for all the Patriarchs to see the fulfilment of all of their prophecies about Christ and the harrowing of Hell. They had the best seats in God's cinema to actually witness this amazing event of Christ busting into Hell and rescuing millions of souls for the Glory of God.

CHAPTER 43

I my children, measured and wrote out every work and every measure and every righteous judgement.

2 As *one* year is more honourable than another, so is *one* man more honourable than another, some for great possessions, some for wisdom of heart, some for particular intellect, some for cunning, one for silence of lip, another for cleanliness, one for strength, another for comeliness, one for youth, another for sharp wit, one for shape of body, another for sensibility, let it be heard everywhere, but there is none better than he who fears God, he shall be more glorious in time to come.

Proverbs 14.26-27 In the fear of the Lord is strong confidence: and his children shall have a place of refuge. The fear of the Lord is a fountain of life, to depart from the snares of death.

CHAPTER 44

> THE Lord with his hands having created man, in the likeness of his own face, the Lord made him small and great.
>
> 2 Whoever reviles the ruler's face, and abhors the Lord's face, has despised the Lord's face, and to who vents anger on any man without injury, the Lord's great anger will cut him down, he who spits on the face of man reproachfully, will be cut down at the Lord's great judgement.

Titus 3.1-3 Put them in mind to be subject to principalities and powers, to obey magistrates, to be ready to every good work. [2] To speak evil of no man, to be no brawlers, but gentle, shewing all meekness unto all men.

[3] For we ourselves also were sometimes foolish, disobedient, deceived, serving divers lusts and pleasures, living in malice and envy, hateful, and hating one another.

Hebrew 13.17 Obey them that have the rule over you and submit yourselves: for they watch for your souls, as they that must give account, that they may do it with joy, and not with grief: for that is unprofitable for you.

> 3 **Blessed is the man who does not direct his heart with malice against any man**, and helps the injured and condemned, and raises the broken down, and shall do charity to the needy, because on the day of the great judgement every weight, every measure and every makeweight *will be* as in the market, that is to say *they are* hung on scales and stand in the market, *and every one* shall learn his own measure, and according to his measure shall take his reward.

Matthew 5.44 But I say unto you, 'Love your enemies, bless them that curse you, do good to them that hate you, and pray for them which despitefully use you, and persecute you'.

Galatians 6.7 Be not deceived; God is not mocked: for whatsoever a man soweth, that shall he also reap.

Matthew 16.27 For the Son of Man shall come in the glory of His Father and the holy angels and then shall he reward every man according to his works.

CHAPTER 45

WHOEVER hastens to make offering before the Lord's face, the Lord for his part will hasten that offering by granting of his work.

2 But whoever increases his lamp before the Lord's face and make not true judgement, the Lord will *not* increase his treasure in the realm of the highest.

3 When the Lord demands bread, or candles, or flesh (*sc.* cattle), or any other sacrifice, then that is nothing; but God demands pure hearts, and with all that *only* tests the heart of man.

Psalm 51.16-17 For You do not desire sacrifice, or else I would give *it;*
You do not delight in burnt offering. The sacrifices of God *are* a broken spirit,
A broken and a contrite heart. These, O God, You will not despise.

CHAPTER 46

> HEAR, my people, and take in the words of my lips.
>
> 2 If anyone bring any gifts to an earthly ruler, and have disloyal thoughts in his heart, and the ruler know this, will he not be angry with him, and not refuse his gifts, and not give him over to judgement?

Jeremiah 17.5 Thus saith the Lord; Cursed be the man that trusts in man, and maketh flesh his arm, and whose heart departs from the Lord.

> 3 Or if one man make himself appear good to another by deceit of tongue, but *have* evil in his heart, then will not *the other* understand the treachery of his heart, and himself be condemned, since his untruth was plain to all?

Psalm 120.3 What shall be given unto thee? or what shall be done unto thee, thou false tongue?

Jeremiah 17.9 The heart is deceitful above all things, and desperately wicked: who can know it?

> 4 And when the Lord shall send a great light, then there will be **judgement for the just and the unjust,** and there no one shall escape notice.

Matthew 5.45 That ye may be the children of your Father which is in heaven: for he maketh his sun to rise on the evil and on the good and send rain on the just and on the unjust.

CHAPTER 47

> AND now, my children, lay thought on your hearts, mark well the words of your father, which are all come to you from the Lord's lips.

Psalms 19:14 - Let the words of my mouth, and the meditation of my heart, be acceptable in thy sight, O LORD, my strength, and my redeemer.

Matthew 12:37 - For by thy words thou shalt be justified, and by thy words thou shalt be condemned.

> 2 Take these books of your father's handwriting and read them.
>
> 3 For the books are many, and in them you will learn all the Lord's works, all that has been from the beginning of creation, and will be till the end of time.

C.1 Imagine that originally Enoch wrote 366 books. Wow! I wonder what he wrote in them? Well, only Enoch in the entire Bible spent so long a time in heaven and the spirt world and came back to write it down, so he had a lot to write.

C.2 In the Apocryphal book of 2nd Esdras it took more than a month to write down 96 books in rewriting the Torah or the Old Testament that had been destroyed in the time of Nebuchadnezzar and the Babylon empire around 589 BC.

C.3 For Enoch to have written down 366 books it would have taken a lot longer than 30 days. I mention this because this 2nd Book of Enoch states that Enoch was told to spend 30 days with his children and then he would be taken up to heaven or raptured.

C.4 In other apocryphal accounts of this same event Enoch was given 1 year to be ready to go permanently to heaven or to be translated to heaven as in the 1st Book of Enoch.

> 4 And if you will observe my handwriting, you will not sin against the Lord; because there is no other except the Lord, neither in heaven, nor in earth, nor in the very lowest places, nor in the one foundation.

Isaiah 45.5 I am the Lord, and there is none else, there is no God beside me: I girded thee, though thou hast not known me.

> 5 The Lord has placed the foundations in the unknown, and has spread forth heavens visible and invisible; he fixed the earth on the waters, and created countless creatures, and who has counted the water and the foundation of the unfixed, or the dust of the earth, or the sand of the

> sea, or the drops of the rain, or the morning dew, or the wind's breathings? Who has filled earth and sea, and the indissoluble winter?

Job 38.4 "Where were you when I laid the foundation of the earth? Tell me, if you have understanding.

Isaiah 48.13 "Surely My hand founded the earth. And My right hand spread out the heavens. When I call to them, they stand together.

Psalm 104.5 He established the earth upon its foundations. So that it will not totter forever and ever.

> 6 I cut the stars out of fire, and decorated heaven, and put it in their midst.

Hebrews 1.7 And of the angels he saith, Who maketh his angels spirits, and his ministers a flame of fire.

Mark 13.25- 27 And the stars of heaven shall fall, and the powers that are in heaven shall be shaken.

[26] And then shall they see the Son of man coming in the clouds with great power and glory.

[27] And then shall he send his angels and shall gather together his elect from the four winds, from the uttermost part of the earth to the uttermost part of heaven.

CHAPTER 48

> THAT the sun go along the seven heavenly circles, which are the, appointment of one hundred and eighty-two thrones, that it go down on a short day, and again one hundred and eighty-two, that it go down on a big day, and he has two thrones on which he rests, revolving hither and thither above the thrones of the months, from the seventeenth day of the month Tsivan it goes down to the month Thevan, from the seventeenth of Thevan it goes up.

C.1 What are the 7 circles of the heavens? They are 7 different obits. Could be the orbits of 7 planets or 7 stars. In mentioning 182 thrones that it goes down on a short day and 182 on a big day! What does this all mean? It is certainly mysterious. Obviously, Enoch could see things behind this physical dimension or the inner workings of both the sun the moon and the planets, stars, and constellations. He could see all of space as though it were close by to him and not far away. How was that even possible? Only by the miracles of God Himself. [Here is an interesting link to Dante's Inferno: 9 Spheres of Heaven (Dante's Paradiso) - History Lists

C.2 See 1st Enoch and the Book of the Luminaries chapters 72-79 or my book Enoch Insights with the same chapters.

C.3 You can also find a strange description about far away objects appearing as though they are all close-up in the apocryphal Books of the Lost Books of Adam and Eve or in my book Eden Insights

Eden Insights Chapter 1.1-2 'On the third day God planted the Garden of Eden in the East of the earth, on the boarder of the world eastward, beyond which towards the sun-rising one finds nothing but water that encompasses the whole world and reached to the borders of heaven.

> 2 And to the north of the Garden of Eden there is a sea of water, clear and pure to the taste, unlike anything else: so that through the clearness thereof one may look into the depths of the earth.'

> 3 And thus it goes close to the earth, then the earth is and makes grow its fruit, and when it goes away, then the earth is sad, and trees and all fruits have no florescence.

C.4 'When it goes away' - this is talking about the sun. In winter the sun is further away from the earth, when it appears for less hours and in the summer, it is closer and is seen for many more hours. We therefore have the 4 seasons of summer, autumn, winter and spring.

C.5 Florescence – def. - the process of flowering:

> 4 All this he measured, with good measurement of hours, and fixed a measure by his wisdom, of the visible and the invisible.
>
> 5 From the **invisible** he made **all things visible**, himself being **invisible**.

C.6 'From the invisible he made all things visible, himself being invisible'. Now that is a big statement:

Romans 1.20 For the invisible things of him from the creation of the world are clearly seen, being understood by the things that are made, even his eternal power and Godhead; so that they are without excuse:

2 Cor 4.18 So we look not at the things which are seen, but at the things which are unseen; for the things which are visible are temporal [just brief and fleeting], but the things which are invisible are everlasting and imperishable.

Hebrews 11.3,27 By faith we understand that time was created by the word of God, so that what is seen was made from things that are invisible. By faith he forsook Egypt, not fearing the wrath of the king: for he endured, as seeing him who is invisible.

> 6 Thus I make known to you, my children, and distribute the books to your children, into all your generations, and amongst the nations who shall have the sense to fear God, let them receive them, and may they come to love them more than any food or earthly sweets, and read them and apply themselves to them.

1 Tim 4.15 Study to show thyself approved unto God a workman that needs not to be ashamed rightly dividing the Word of Truth.

Hebrews 4.12 For the word of God is quick, and powerful, and sharper than any two-edged sword, piercing even to the dividing asunder of soul and spirit, and of the joints and marrow, and is a discerner of the thoughts and intents of the heart.

> 7 And those who understand not the Lord, who fear not God, who accept not, but reject, who do not receive them (*sc.* the books), a terrible judgement awaits these.

Proverbs 14.27 The fear of the Lord is a fountain of life, that one may avoid the snares of death.

Proverbs 8.13 "The fear of the Lord is to hate evil, pride and arrogance and the evil way. And the perverted mouth, I hate.

Psalm 9.17 The wicked shall be turned into hell and all the nations that forget God.

> 8 Blessed is the man who shall bear their yoke and shall drag them along, for he shall be released on the day of the great judgement.

C.7 What yoke is this talking about? Why is Adam and Eve or mankind having to <u>drag</u> their yoke along? I think that that is what it is talking about 'The burden of their life'? God originally gave Adam and Eve the yoke of hard work and having to till the land and to have large families. God wanted man to keep busy lest he get into too much mischief.

C.8 Adam had the yoke of having to work very hard in order to feed his budding family. He had to watch out for rocks, weeds, briars and thorns and not just concern himself with the flowers and crops. Adam had to work hard to cultivate the good and fruitful, and he had to watch out for the thorns and destructive elements such as the weather and other things such as tares that Satan might sow in the ground when he was not looking.

C.9 As has famously been said, 'To take care of a garden the gardener cannot just love flowers, but he has to hate the weeds as well'.

C.10 Adam's yoke was to cultivate the land for food and produce whatever was needed. Eve was told by God that because of her sin, that her conception would be greatly multiplied in her life, and that she would have to bear many children, which she did. I don't think Eve was punished in this exactly this way, for eating an apple, but that it had to do with <u>conception</u> as in the case of her first-born Cain. Who was the father of Cain is the big question?

1 John 3.12 Not as Cain, who was <u>of</u> that <u>wicked one</u>, (Satan) and slew his brother. And wherefore slew he him? Because his own works were <u>evil</u>, and his brother's righteous.

C.11 The tragedy in modern times especially in the Western nations is that many never marry or have children anymore and the population is drastically going down which will result in the end of humanity in the West if something does not change very soon. This is why countries like the USA allow so many illegal immigrants through their borders because they say they need the 'workforce' which should have been provided by the Western nations having families and children. Man going away from God's laws is the reason humanity is going down.

C.12 It is very easy to see that God' commands to Adam and Eve have been severely interfered with by Satan and his devils who push nothing but lies like abortion and ruin the land with their chemicals and chemtrails. The globalists are trying to eliminate mankind altogether and replace them by A.I and machines incrementally by systematically killing mankind off completely with wars, abortion, famine and chemicals which change the food and poison the people, as well as altering the climate and making it dangerous to live on this planet – deliberately of course. Did you know that 60,000,000 babies are aborted every year?

C.13 One day mankind will have to go back to God's laws in order to survive and be able to carry his yoke instead of <u>drag</u> it as mentioned in verse 8 of this chapter.

Mathew 11.30 Jesus: 'My yoke is easy, and my burden is light'..

Luke 14.33 For whosoever he be of you that forsakes not all that he that he cannot be my disciple.

2 Corinthians 5:10 - For we must all appear before the judgment seat of Christ; that everone may receive the things done in his body, according to that he hath done, whether it be good or bad.

1 Cor 6.9-10 Know ye not that the unrighteous shall not inherit the kingdom of God? Be not deceived: neither fornicators, nor idolaters, nor adulterers, nor effeminate, nor abusers of themselves with mankind, Nor thieves, nor covetous, nor drunkards, nor revilers, nor extortioners, shall inherit the kingdom of God.

CHAPTER 49

> I SWEAR to you, my children, but I swear not by any oath, neither by heaven nor by earth, nor by any other creature which God created.

James 5.12 "But above all things, my brethren, swear not, neither by heaven, neither by the earth, neither by any other oath: but let your yea be yea; and *your* nay, nay; lest ye fall into condemnation."

> 2 The Lord said: 'There is no oath in me, nor injustice, but truth.'

John 14.6 I am the Way the Truth and the life. No man cometh unto the Father except by Me.

> 3 If there is no truth in men, let them <u>swear by the words 'yea, yea,' or else, 'nay, nay</u>!

Matthew 5.34-37 But I say unto you, 'Swear not at all; neither by heaven; for it is God's throne:[35] Nor by the earth; for it is his footstool: neither by Jerusalem; for it is the city of the great King.[36] Neither shalt thou swear by thy head, because thou canst not make one hair white or black. [37] But let your communication be, <u>Yea, yea; Nay, nay</u>: for whatsoever is more than these cometh of evil.'

> 4 And I swear to you, yea, yea, that there has been no man in his mother's womb, *but that* already before, even to each one there is a place prepared for the repose of the soul, and a measure fixed how much it is intended that a man be tried in this world.

C.1 Every soul in on probation in this life. Every man will be judged by what he has done, and indeed by what he has said.

Matthew 12.36-37 But I say unto you, 'That every idle word that men shall speak, they shall give account thereof in the day of judgment. For by thy words thou shalt be justified, and by thy words thou shalt be condemned.'

Galatians 6.7 Be not deceived; God is not mocked: for whatsoever a man soweth, that shall he also reap.

> 5 Yea, children, deceive not yourselves, for there has been previously prepared a place for every soul of man.

Luke 12.20-21 But God said unto him, Thou fool, this night thy soul shall be required of thee: then whose shall those things be, which thou hast provided? [21] So is he that lays up treasure for himself, and is not rich toward God.

C.2 There are many verses in this chapter advising against '**swearing**'. Why is that? What was the origin of swearing and why is it so evil? The secret to this is in the 1st Book of Enoch. The following is taken from my book Enoch Insights which is based on 1st Enoch:

C.3 Cursing was started by the Fallen angels and Satan

ENOCH INSIGHTS CHAPTER 5.6 [Here Enoch is addressing directly the Fallen Angels] 'In your days ye shall make your names an eternal execration unto the righteous, and by you shall all who curse curse'. And all the sinners and godless shall imprecate by you. And for you the godless shall be a curse and all the righteous shall rejoice and there shall be forgiveness of sins and every mercy, peace and forbearance. There shall be salvation unto them, a goodly light, and for all you sinners there shall be no salvation, but upon you shall abide a curse.

C.4 What this above verse is stating from the 1st Book of Enoch is that when people today curse, they are letting Fallen angels/devils and demons speak right through them. This is why cursing is not advised, but rather blessing and praise and thanksgiving..

CHAPTER 50

> I HAVE put everyman's work in writing and none born on earth can remain hidden nor his works remain concealed.
>
> 2 I see all things.

Hebrews 4.13 Neither is there any creature that is not manifest in his sight: but all things are naked and opened unto the eyes of him with whom we have to do.

> 3 Now therefore, my children, in patience and meekness spend the number of your days, that you inherit endless life.

Luke 21.19 In your patience possess ye your souls.

Isaiah 30.15 For thus saith the Lord God, the Holy One of Israel; In returning and rest shall ye be saved; in quietness and in confidence shall be your strength: and ye would not.

> 4 Endure for the sake of the Lord every wound, every injury, every evil word and attack.

2 Tim 3.2 "Thou therefore endure hardness, as a good soldier of Jesus Christ."

> 5 If **ill-requitals** befall you, **return *them*** not **either to neighbour** or **enemy**, because the **Lord will return *them* for you and be your avenger** on the day of great judgement, that there be no avenging here among men.

C.1 Requittal: return a favour to (someone):
"to win enough to requite my friends"

> 6 Whoever of you spends gold or silver for his brother's sake, he will receive ample treasure in the world to come.
>
> 7 Injure not widows nor orphans nor strangers, lest God's wrath come upon you.

Matthew 5.42-48 Give to him that asks thee, and from him that would borrow of thee turn not thou away.[43] Ye have heard that it hath been said, Thou shalt love thy neighbour, and hate thine enemy.[44] But I say unto you, Love your enemies, bless them that curse you, do good to them that hate you, and pray for them which despitefully use you, and persecute you;[45] That ye may be the children of your Father which is in heaven: for he maketh his sun to rise on the evil and on the good, and sends rain on the just and on the unjust. [46] For if ye love them which love you, what reward have ye? do not even the publicans the same? [47] And if ye salute your brethren only, what do ye more than others? do not even the publicans so? [48] Be ye therefore perfect, even as your Father which is in heaven is perfect.

CHAPTER 51

> 1 Stretch out your hands to the poor according to your strength.
>
> 2 Hide not your silver in the earth.

C.1 Don't bury your riches in the ground. In the past some people had too many riches to actually carry with them in a practical manner, so they would result to burying their money in different places when no one was looking. Gold, silver and other treasures. The problem with this world is that they value their riches in terms of silver and gold and money, when these are certainly not the true riches, and the ones that will last forever. The rich go down to the bottom of the sea with their silver and gold as in the story of the Titanic. If they had let go of their silver and gold, they might have floated to the surface and lived...

> 3 Help the faithful man in affliction, and affliction will not find you in the time of your trouble.

C.2 Do you know a good person who is heavily afflicted? Then do what you can to help him in his affliction. Of course, one might say in modern times that we have hospitals for doing that job. However, I think that the verse is saying something much deeper. Help others in their affliction and when you yourself suddenly have some troubles, the help will be there for you. Like unto 'what you sow you will reap'. There is a lot more going on in the spirit world which affects us than most people seem to realize.

> 4 And every **grievous** and **cruel yoke** that come upon you **bear all for the sake of the Lord**, and thus you will **find your reward in the day of judgement**.

C.3 Life can throw some cruel yokes your way as life is not meant to be easy all the time. There is a reason for this, which we will only fully understand when we get to eternity.

Matthew 5.41- [41] And whosoever shall compel thee to go a mile, go with him twain.

[42] Give to him that asks thee, and from him that would borrow of thee turn not thou away.

[43] Ye have heard that it hath been said, Thou shalt love thy neighbour, and hate thine enemy.

[44] But I say unto you, Love your enemies, bless them that curse you, do good to them that hate you, and pray for them which despitefully use you, and persecute you;

[45] That ye may be the children of your Father which is in heaven: for he maketh his sun to rise on the evil and on the good, and sends rain on the just and on the unjust.

⁴⁶ For if ye love them which love you, what reward have ye? do not even the publicans the same?

> 5 It is good to go morning, midday, and evening into the **Lord's dwelling**, for the glory of your creator.

Psalm 150.6 Let everything that breathe praise the Lord, praise ye the Lord.

> 6 Because **every breathing** thing **glorifies him**, and every **creature visible** and **invisible returns him praise.**

Psalm 91.1-8 He that dwelleth in the secret place of the most High shall abide under the shadow of the Almighty.² I will say of the Lord, He is my refuge and my fortress: my God; in him will I trust.³ Surely he shall deliver thee from the snare of the fowler, and from the noisome pestilence.⁴ He shall cover thee with his feathers, and under his wings shalt thou trust: his truth shall be thy shield and buckler.⁵ Thou shalt not be afraid for the terror by night; nor for the arrow that flies by day;⁶ Nor for the pestilence that walketh in darkness; nor for the destruction that wastes at noonday.⁷ A thousand shall fall at thy side, and ten thousand at thy right hand; but it shall not come nigh thee.⁸ Only with thine eyes shalt thou behold and see the reward of the wicked.

CHAPTER 52

> BLESSED is the man who opens his lips in praise of God of Sabaoth and praises the Lord with his heart.

Romans 9.29 And as Esaias said before, except the Lord of the Sabaoth had left us a seed, we had been as Sodom and made as Gomorrah.

James 5.4 Behold the hire of the labourers who have reaped down your fields which is of you kept back by fraud, cries: and the cries of them which have reaped are entered into the ears of the Lord of Sabaoth.

C.1 The title "the Lord of Sabaoth" means "the Lord of hosts. It is the title of Jehovah God's military might, His strength to win battles" The Lord is commander of the angelic soldiers as well as the armies of Israel. Sabaoth means "armies" or "hosts". Jehovah Sabaoth can be translated as "The Lord of Armies". This name denotes His universal sovereignty over every army, both spiritual and earthly.

> 2 Cursed every man who opens his lips for the bringing into contempt and **calumny** of his neighbour, because he brings God into contempt.

C.2 Calumny - *definitions*: 1) A misrepresentation intended to harm another's reputation. 2) Speech against God.

Exodus 20.17 "Thou shalt not covet thy neighbour's house, thou shalt not covet thy neighbour's wife, nor his manservant, nor his maidservant, nor his ox, nor his ass, nor any thing that *is* thy neighbour›s."

> 3 Blessed is he who opens his lips blessing and praising God.
>
> 4 Cursed is he before the Lord all the days of his life, who opens his lips to curse and abuse.
>
> 5 Blessed is he who blesses all the Lord's works.
>
> 6 Cursed is he who brings the Lord's creation into contempt.

Romans 1.20 "For the invisible things of him from the creation of the world are clearly seen, being understood by the things that are made, *even* his eternal power and Godhead; so that they are without excuse:"

> 7 Blessed is he who looks down and raises the fallen.

Ecclesiastes 4.10 For if they fall, the one will lift up his fellow: but woe to him that is alone when he falls; for he hath not another to help him up.

> 8 Cursed is he who looks to and is eager for the destruction of what is not his.
>
> 9 Blessed is he who keeps the foundations of his fathers, made firm from the beginning.

Proverbs 22.28 "Remove not the ancient landmark, which thy fathers have set."

> 10 Cursed is he who perverts the decrees of his forefathers.
>
> 11 Blessed is he who implants peace and love.

Matthew 22.39 "And the second *is* like unto it, Thou shalt love thy neighbour as thyself."

> 12 Cursed is he who disturbs those that love their neighbours.
>
> 13 Blessed is he who speaks with humble tongue and heart to all.

Proverbs 6.16-17 These six things doth the **LORD** hate: yea, **seven** are an abomination unto him: "A proud look, a lying tongue, and hands that shed innocent blood,"

> 14 Cursed is he who speaks peace with his tongue, while in his heart there is no peace but a sword.

Psalm 55.21 "*The words* of his mouth were smoother than butter, but war *was* in his heart: his words were softer than oil, yet *were* they drawn swords."

> 15 For all these things will be laid bare in the weighing-scales and in the books, on the day of the great judgement.

Romans 2.16 In the day when God shall judge the secrets of men by Jesus Christ according to my gospel.

CHAPTER 53

> AND now, my children, do not say: 'Our father is standing before God, and is praying for our sins,' for there is there no helper of any man who has sinned.

Romans 14.12 So then every one of us shall give account of himself to God.

> 2 You see how I wrote all works of every man, before his creation, *all* that is done amongst all men for all time, and none can tell or relate my handwriting, because the Lord sees all the imaginings of man, how they are vain, where they lie in the treasure-houses of the heart.

Galatians 6.7 Be not deceived; God is not mocked: for whatsoever a man sows that shall he also reap.

> 3 And now, my children, mark well all the words of your father, that I tell you, lest you regret, saying: 'Why did our father not tell us?'

I Corinthians 6.9-13 Know ye not that the unrighteous shall not inherit the kingdom of God? Be not deceived: neither fornicators, nor idolaters, nor adulterers, nor effeminate, nor abusers of themselves with mankind,[10] Nor thieves, nor covetous, nor drunkards, nor those who revile, nor extortioners, shall inherit the kingdom of God.[11] And such were some of you: but ye are washed, but ye are sanctified, but ye are justified in the name of the Lord Jesus, and by the Spirit of our God.[12] All things are lawful unto me, but all things are not expedient: all things are lawful for me, but I will not be brought under the power of any.[13] Meats for the belly, and the belly for meats: but God shall destroy both it and them. Now the body is not for fornication, but for the Lord; and the Lord for the body.

CHAPTER 54

> AT that time, not understanding this let these books which I have given you be for an inheritance of your peace.

Jeremiah 30.2 "Thus says the Lord, the God of Israel, 'Write all the words which I have spoken to you in a book.

> 2 Hand them to all who want them, and instruct them, that they may see the Lord's very great and marvellous works.

Deuteronomy 31.24 It came about, when Moses finished writing the words of this law in a book until they were complete,

Romans 2.15 In that they show the work of the Law written in their hearts, their conscience bearing witness and their thoughts alternately accusing or else defending them,

THE BOOK OF REMEDIES – given to Moses by one of the angels of the Presence which showed herbs and plants with cures for all diseases.

Comment:1 Hezekiah censored the Book of Remedies, according to the Jewish book The Talmud, which they say probably originally descended from Noah or one of his sons. The book was dictated to Noah by an angel. God told Hezekiah to hide away the Book of Remedies as it was causing people in Israel to misuse its knowledge and power.

Here is some more information concerning the Book of Remedies and why it was banned by Hezekiah, king of Israel around 750 BCE.

The following is in my opinion excellent material: 'Despite the protests of Maimonides, the Talmudic sages may indeed be relating to the pitfalls of medical knowledge.

Elsewhere in rabbinic literature, we find a harsh and unusual statement: "The best of the doctors is destined for Gehenna" **(M. Kiddushin 4:14).**

Jewish scholars have offered different explanations for this unsympathetic verdict, all of them limiting the judgment to a certain class of doctors: doctors who cause death when they could save lives (Rashi, 11th century, France); doctors who act in bad faith (Ri, 12th century, Germany); doctors who act recklessly and callously (Ramban); doctors who pretend to be experts when they are truly ignorant of the profession (Kalonymus ben Kalonymus, 14th century, Provence) or doctors who act when there are others who have greater expertise than them (Rabbi Simon Duran, 14th-15th centuries, Majorca-Algiers).

One commentator, himself a recognized physician, appended this adage to doctors who perform internal operations, perhaps reflecting the state of medical knowledge in his day (Rabbi Isaac Lampronti, 17th-18th centuries, Italy).

We might offer another possible understanding of this unforgiving declaration.

The best of doctors may be inclined to credit their own acumen for their medical achievements. Such foolishness, say the sages, leads one from the path of God.

The faculties with which we are endowed and the opportunities that befall us, should not be seen as the strength of our own hands.

Rather, it behoves us to remember God and His role behind the scenes as the playmaker and facilitator (Deuteronomy 8:17-18).

An oft-recounted parable tells of a person drowning at sea. As he struggles in the water gasping for breath he fervently prays to God for salvation. Seemingly out of nowhere a boat sidles up to him and throws a buoy in his direction. The man refuses the assistance preferred: "I am waiting for God to save me!" he calls, and continues to gallantly tread water, praying for redemption through God's mighty hand. A helicopter miraculously flies by and offers the drowning man a rope-ladder to climb out of the clutches of the ocean. Once again, the help tendered is rebuffed: "God will save me!" he shouts and continues to valiantly keep afloat, passionately beseeching the Almighty to save him. As his strength wanes and his demise approaches, the man lets out one last heartfelt prayer, and a piece of driftwood slides within reach. Instead of clutching it, the man pushes it aside, thinking: "Surely, God will not forsake me." Alas, the waters finally overtake him, and the man appears in Heaven before God: "Why did You not heed my heartfelt prayers? Where were You in my time of need?" he complains. In a booming voice God responds: "Who do you think sent the boat, the helicopter and the piece of driftwood!?" Seeking medical advice is not folly. The challenge is to recognize that professional medical assistance attained is truly a gift from God. As such, the doctor is a messenger of God, charged with the eminent task of saving lives. But it is not the doctor who heals, nor is it the medicine or ointment; God is the true healer'. (Source: Ref: https://www.jpost.com/Jewish-World/Judaism/ World-of-the-Sages-Books-of-Remedies])

CHAPTER 55

> *Here Enoch shows his sons, telling them with tears: 'My children, the hour has approached for me to go upon to heaven; behold, the angels are standing before me.'*
>
> MY children, behold, the day of my term and the time have approached.
>
> 2 For the angels who shall go with me are standing before me and urge me to my departure from you; they are standing here on earth, awaiting what has been told them.
>
> 3 For to-morrow I shall go up on to heaven, to the uppermost **Jerusalem** to my eternal inheritance.

C.1 It is interesting to note that Enoch mentions New Jerusalem as is mentioned in Revelation 21-22. The town of physical Jerusalem was a town which king David conquered and made the capital of Israel around 3000 years ago or about 2000 years after the death of King David. It is clear from the definition before of Jerusalem that the city could not have been called Jerusalem until it was given that name by King David of old.

C.2 The word Jerusalem means in Hebrew 'Pointing the way to Peace' - The place name Jerusalem (pronounced *yerushalaim* in Hebrew) is a combination of two words. The first is *yeru* meaning "flow". This word has several applications such as the flowing of water in a river, the throwing of something as being flowed out of the hand or as the flowing of a finger in the sense of pointing out the way one should go. This last use is the use in the name *yerushalaim*. The *shalayim* is from the word *shalam* meaning complete and whole (the word Shalom is also derived from *shalam*, while it is usually translated as peace it more means to be complete or whole). When these two words are put together they mean something like "pointing the way to completeness".: Definition of Hebrew Names: Jerusalem | AHRC (ancient-hebrew.org)

C.3 It is just outstanding to see how God revealed to Enoch more than 5000 years ago that a 'City of Peace' would arise in the Promised land called Jerusalem and that it would be symbolic of the eternal Heavenly City called New Jerusalem in the Book of Revelation 21-22.

> 4 Therefore I bid you do before the Lord's face all *his* good pleasure.

Proverbs 7.2 "Keep my commandments, and live; and my law as the apple of thine eye."

CHAPTER 56

METHOSALAM (METHUSELAH) having answered his father Enoch, said: 'What is agreeable to thy eyes, father, that I may make before thy face, that thou mayst bless our dwellings, and thy sons, and that thy people may be made glorious through thee, and then *that* thou mayst depart thus, as the Lord said?

2 Enoch answered to his son Methosalam *and* said: ‹Hear, child, from the time when the Lord anointed me with the ointment of his glory, *there has been no food* in me, and my soul remembers not earthly enjoyment, neither do I want anything earthly!

Job 23.12 "Neither have I gone back from the commandment of his lips; I have esteemed the words of his mouth more than my necessary *food*."

Matthew 4.4 But he answered and said, It is written, 'Man shall not live by bread alone, but by every word that proceeds out of the mouth of God'.

CHAPTER 57

MY child Methosalam (Methuselah), summon all thy brethren and our household and the elders of the people, that I may talk to them and depart, as is planned for me.'

2 And Methosalam. made haste, and summoned his brethren, Regim, Riman, Uchan, Chermion, Gaidad, and all the elders of the people before the face of his father Enoch; and he blessed them, *and* said to them:

C.1 These names are the Syriac translation of the Old Hebrew names.

CHAPTER 58

> LISTEN to me, my children, to-day.
>
> 2 In those days when the Lord came down on to earth for Adam's sake, and visited all his creatures, which he created himself, after all these he created Adam, and the Lord called all the beasts of the earth, all the reptiles, and all the birds that soar in the air, and brought them all before the face of our father Adam.

Genesis 1.1 In the beginning God created the heaven and the earth.

John 1.1-3 In the beginning was the Word, and the Word was with God, and the Word was God. The same was in the beginning with God. All things were made by him; and without him was not anything made that was made.

> 3 And Adam gave the names to all things living on earth.

Genesis 2.20 "And Adam gave names to all cattle, and to the fowl of the air, and to every beast of the field.

> 4 And the Lord appointed him ruler over all and subjected to him all things under his hands, and made them dumb and made them dull that they be commanded of man, and be in subjection and obedience to him.

Genesis 1.26 And God said, 'Let us make man in our image, after our likeness: and let them have dominion over the fish of the sea, and over the fowl of the air, and over the cattle, and over all the earth, and over every creeping thing that creeps upon the earth.'

> 5 Thus also the Lord created every man lord over all his possessions.
>
> 6 The Lord will not judge a single soul of beast for man's sake but adjudges the souls of men to their beasts in this world; for men have a special place.

C.1 It states in the Book of Jasher that man had a special place on the earth and that he was 'endowed with speech'.

Jasher 1.2 And God formed man out of the ground, and he blew on his nostrils the breathe of life, and man became a living soul 'endowed with speech'.

C.2 However, in the Book of Jubilees it also states: 'God closed the mouths of the animals' which must have meant that in the beginning of Creation and whilst Adam and Eve were in the Garden of Eden the animals could talk with Adam and Eve, as evidenced by the serpent talking to Eve.

Jubilees 3.28 'And on that day was closed the mouth of all beasts and of cattle, and of birds, and of whatever walks and whatever moves, so that they could no longer speak. For they had all spoken one with another with one lip and one tongue.

C.3 God is stating that He holds man accountable as to how he treats his beasts and will be judged accordingly.

> 7 And as every soul of man is according to number, similarly beasts will not perish, nor all **souls of beasts which the Lord created, till the great judgement, and they will accuse man, if he feed them ill.**

C.4 There are two stories that I know of where God opened the mouth of an animal to let it momentarily speak to man. In the Bible - the story of Balaam's ass that spoke with Balaam. There is another story mentioned in the Book of Jasher in chapter 43, where a captured wolf reassures Jacob that he did not destroy and devour Jacob's son Joseph Numbers:

Numbers 22.28 And the Lord opened the mouth of the ass, and she said unto Balaam, 'What have I done unto thee, that thou hast smitten me these three times'?

Jasher 43.43 And the Lord opened the mouth of the beast (wolf) in order to comfort Jacob with these words, and it answered Jacob and spoke these words unto him.

CHAPTER 59

> **WHOEVER defiles the soul of beasts, defiles his own soul.**

C.1 A good question to ask is how can you destroy both the soul and body of a beast?

Proverbs 12.10 "A righteous *man* regards the life of his beast: but the tender mercies of the wicked *are* cruel."

> 2 For man brings clean animals to make sacrifice for sin, that he may have cure of his soul.
>
> 3 And if they bring for sacrifice clean animals, and birds, man has cure, he cures his soul.

C.2 Why is the sacrifice of animals even mentioned in the time of Enoch, as we understand from the Bible, that blood sacrifices of animals did not start until after the Great Flood in Noah's time, or at least man did not eat the sacrifice. Before the Great Flood man only ate vegetables and fruits. Actually, the first animal sacrifice recorded in the Bible was made by Abel in Pre-flood times, sacrificing a lamb on the altar to God. The difference is that mankind was only eating fruits and vegetables in Pre-Flood times, and they did not start to eat meat until after the Great Flood. However, apparently, according to the Book of Enoch and the Bible, there were animal blood sacrifices before the Great Flood as in the case of Abel. So, this Book of Enoch 2 got this point right!

> 4 All is given you for food, bind it by the four feet, that is to make good the cure, he cures his soul.
>
> 5 But whoever kills beast without wounds, kills his own soul, and defiles his own flesh.

Proverbs 17.13 "Whoso rewards evil for good, evil shall not depart from his house."

> 6 And he who does any beast any injury whatsoever, in secret, it is evil practice, and he defiles his own soul.

C.3 I would imagine that God is warning people through Enoch not to have anything to do with bestiality, the very thing that many of the perverse leaders of this world are into, and which is pushed by demons, devils and evil spirits.
EVIL SPIRITS - THEIR ORIGIN.
Genesis Chapter 6
Genesis 6.1-5 And it came to pass, when men began to multiply on the face

of the earth, and daughters were born unto them, 2 That the sons of God saw the daughters of men that they were fair; and they took them wives of all which they chose. 3 And the Lord said, My spirit shall not always strive with man, for that he also is flesh: yet his days shall be an hundred and twenty years. 4 There were giants in the earth in those days; and also after that, when the sons of God came in unto the daughters of men, and they bare children to them, the same became mighty men which were of old, men of renown. 5 And God saw that the wickedness of man was great in the earth, and that every imagination of the thoughts of his heart was only evil continually.

Enoch chapter 15 1-12 And He answered me, and said to me with His voice: "Hear! Do not be afraid, Enoch, you righteous man, and scribe of righteousness. Come here and hear my voice. 2 And go say to the Watchers of Heaven, who sent you to petition on their behalf: You ought to petition on behalf of men, not men on behalf of you. 3 Why have you left the High, Holy and Eternal Heaven, and lain with women, and become unclean with the daughters of men, and taken wives for yourselves, and done as the sons of the earth, and begotten giant sons? 4 And you were spiritual, Holy, living an eternal life, but you became unclean upon the women, and begot children through the blood of flesh, and lusted after the blood of men, and produced flesh and blood, as they do, who die and are destroyed. 5 And for this reason I give men wives; so that they might sow seed in them, and so that children might be born by them, so that deeds might be done on the Earth. 6 But you, formerly, were spiritual, living an eternal, immortal life, for all the generations of the world. 7 For this reason I did not arrange wives for you; because the dwelling of the spiritual ones is in Heaven. 8 And now, the giants who were born from body and flesh will be called Evil Spirits on the Earth, and on the Earth will be their dwelling. 9 And evil spirits came out from their flesh, because from above they were created, from the Holy Watchers was their origin and first foundation. Evil spirits they will be on Earth and 'Spirits of the Evil Ones' they will be called. 10 And the dwelling of the Spirits of Heaven is Heaven, but the dwelling of the spirits of the Earth, who were born on the Earth, is Earth. 11 And the spirits of the giants do wrong, are corrupt, attack, fight, break on the Earth, and cause sorrow. And they eat no food, do not thirst, and are not observed. 12 And these spirits will rise against the sons of men, and against the women, because they came out of them during the days of slaughter and destruction.

Luke 10:17 "And the seventy returned again with joy, saying, Lord, even the devils are subject unto us through thy name."

Revelation 12:12 Therefore rejoice, ye heavens, and ye that dwell in them. Woe to the inhabitants of the earth and of the sea! For the devil is come down unto you, having great *wrath, because he knows that he hath but a short time."

*Great Wrath: Wrath is defined as anger, fury, rage, also, not to be confused with divine chastisement.

1 Peter 5:8 Peter warns us that: "your adversary (opponent, enemy, foe, opposer) the devil, as a roaring lion, walketh about, seeking whom he may devour". What have we, mankind, done to incur such hatred and anger from Satan.

C.4 Is it only just irrational insanity of wanting to destroy God's creation, "except those days should be shortened, there should no flesh be saved" or is there an underlying reason behind this hatred?

CHAPTER 60

> HE who works the killing of a man's soul, kills his own soul, and kills his own body, and there is no cure for him for all time.

C.1 What is this verse possibly talking about? This to me sounds just like the merchants who try the souls of the nations. The kind of people who show no mercy and kindness to others, but work them as slaves, and abuse them, like the poor of the world. They are the demonic. Of course, all who are of this description are going to hell and the lake of fire eventually. Those who simply do not yield to God's Spirit of love and kindness and mercy and forgiveness, but are in constant rebellion against Holy Spirit Mother and against Christ Her Son.

> 2 He who puts a man in any snare, shall stick in it himself, and there is no cure for him for all time.

Ecclesiastes 27.26 "Whoso digs a pit shall fall therein: and he that sets a trap shall be taken therein."

> 3 He who puts a man in any vessel, his retribution will not be wanting at the great judgement for all time.
>
> 4 He who works crookedly or speaks evil against any soul, will not make justice for himself for all time.

James 4.11 "Speak not evil one of another, brethren. He that speaks evil of *his* brother, and judges his brother, speaks evil of the law, and judges the law: but if thou judge the law, thou art not a doer of the law, but a judge."

SATAN THE DECEIVER – the one who started the spiritual darkness.

C.2 In Chapters 25-26 of this book it is shown that in Pre-Creation God the Father originally created both the light and the potential for the darkness and made an entity in charge of the darkness.

He also created His Son Jesus to be in charge of the light and all the higher realms of the spirit world.

God knew in His great wisdom that darkness would be created. Not just physical darkness as a contrast to the physical light but also spiritual darkness as a contrast to the light.

C.3 The spiritual darkness started with Satan and the Fallen angels in the 'Great Rebellion' in Pre-Creation times as Satan announced:

Isaiah 14:14 I will ascend above the heights of the clouds; I will be like the Most High.

Revelation 12.9 And the great dragon was cast out, that old serpent, called the Devil, and Satan, which **deceives** the whole world: he was cast out into the earth, and his angels were cast out with him."

C.4 Evil and darkness was brought into the physical world by the sins of Adam and Eve

C.5 Later in time it was the sons and daughters of Cain which brought great evil and darkness to the planet

C.6 The fallen angels came after that and really totally corrupted the earth and went in to the daughters of Cain and fathered evil Giants. Sirens of female demons came into existence through disobedience and the daughters of Cain co-habiting with the Fallen angels. All this brought a great deal of spiritual darkness or absence of the light and truth.

C.7 In the book of Exodus, chapter 20, verse 4, we find an unusual verse: "Thou shalt not make unto thee any graven image, or any likeness of anything that is in heaven above, or that is in the earth beneath, or that is in the water under the earth." A graven image is: "an image of wood, stone, or metal shaped with a sharp cutting instrument as distinguished from one cast in a mold".

Philippians 2.4 "At the name of Jesus every knee should bow, of things in heaven, and things in earth, and things under the earth". Why did God warn the Israelites not to make an image to anything in the "water under the earth" and what is it that has knees, whose habitation is "under the earth".

C.8 These are questions we hope to answer as we continue on in our discussion. Before we do though, we want to present a few more scriptures to help bolster our premise.

Ezekiel 26:20 "When I shall bring thee down with them that descend into the pit, with the people of old time, and shall set thee in the low parts of the earth, in places desolate of old, with them that go down to the pit, that thou be not inhabited; and I shall set glory in the land of the living.

Ezekiel 31:14 To the end that none of all the trees by the waters exalt themselves for their height, neither shoot up their top among the thick boughs, neither their trees stand up in their height, all that drink water: for they are all delivered unto death, to the nether parts of the earth, in the midst of the children of men, with them that go down to the pit.

1Peter 3:19 By which also he (Jesus) went and preached unto the spirits in prison.

1Peter 4:6 For this cause was the gospel preached also to them that are dead, that they might be judged according to men in the flesh, but live according to God in the spirit.

Revelation 5:13 And every creature which is in heaven, and on the earth, and under the earth, and such as are in the sea, and all that are in them, heard I saying, Blessing, and honour, and glory, and power, be unto him that sitteth upon the throne, and unto the Lamb for ever and ever.

Revelation 9:11 And they had a king over them, which is the angel of the bottomless pit, whose name in the Hebrew tongue is Abaddon, but in the Greek tongue hath his name Apollyon."

Revelation 11:7 And when they shall have finished their testimony, the beast that ascendeth out of the bottomless pit shall make war against them, and shall overcome them, and kill them.

C.9 Are there "beings" of some type living below the surface of the earth on which we live. If the Bible is to be believed this would certainly appear to be the case. The Book of 1 Peter even says that Jesus preached (told them His plan of salvation) to the spirits in prison.

1 Peter 3.19-20 By which also he went and preached unto the spirits in prison; Which sometime were disobedient, when once the longsuffering of God waited in the days of Noah, while the ark was a preparing, wherein few, that is, eight souls were saved by water.

C.10 Incidentally, if there was no possibility of salvation why would Jesus make the effort to preach to them? Another point to bring out is Genesis, chapter 3, verses 1-4:

Genesis, chapter 3, verses 1-4: "Now the serpent was more subtil than any beast of the field which the LORD God had made. And he said unto the woman, Yea, hath God said, Ye shall not eat of every tree of the garden? And the woman said unto the serpent, 'We may eat of the fruit of the trees of the garden: But of the fruit of the tree which is in the midst of the garden, God hath said, Ye shall not eat of it, neither shall ye touch it, lest ye die.' And the serpent said unto the woman, Ye shall not surely die".

C.11 These verses do not represent an allegory, but rather an actual conversation that took place between a human being, Eve, and a serpent. Jesus does not refer to the story of the Creation of Adam and Eve as an allegory but as an actual historical event.

Matthew 19:4 "And he answered and said unto them, Have ye not read, that he which made them at the beginning made them male and female.

Mark 10:6 But from the beginning of the creation God made them male and female.

C.12 Also in Luke, chapter 23, verses 23-38, Jesus' lineage is traced back to Adam. Now to give you some idea of how thinking has changed, especially in western culture, we wanted to share some quotes from Martin Luther concerning negative spiritual entities and demons.

C.13 Martin Luther 1483 - 1546 changed the course of Western civilization by initiating the Protestant Reformation. As a priest and theology professor, he confronted indulgence salesmen with his 95 Theses in 1517. Luther strongly disputed their claim that freedom from God's punishment of sin could be purchased with money. His refusal to retract all of his writings at the demand of Pope Leo X in 1520 and the Holy Roman Emperor Charles V at the Diet of Worms meeting in 1521 resulted in his excommunication by the pope and condemnation as an outlaw by the emperor.

C.14 Luther taught that salvation is a free gift of God and received only by grace through faith in Jesus as redeemer from sin, not from good works. His theology challenged the authority of the pope of the Roman Catholic Church by teaching that the Bible is the only source of divinely revealed knowledge. His translation of the Bible into the language of the people (instead of Latin) made it more accessible, causing a tremendous impact on the church and on German culture. It fostered the development of a standard version of the German language, added several principles to the art of translation, and influenced the translation of the King James Bible. His hymns inspired the development of singing in churches. His marriage to Katharina Von Bora set a model for the practice of clerical marriage, allowing Protestant priests to marry.

C.15 Martin Luther speaking about demons around 1530 AD: "A large number of deaf, crippled and blind people are afflicted solely through the malice of the demon. And one must in no wise doubt that plagues, fevers and every sort of evil come from him. As for the demented, I hold it certain that all beings deprived of reason are thus afflicted only by the Devil.

C.16 At Poltersberg, there is a lake similarly cursed. If you throw a stone into it, a dreadful storm immediately arises, and the whole neighboring district quakes to its centre. 'Tis the devils kept prisoner there. Demons live in many lands, but particularly in Prussia.

"How often have not the demons called 'Nix,' drawn women and girls into the water, and there had commerce with them, with fearful consequences. I myself saw and touched at Dessay, a child of this sort, which had no human parents, but had proceeded from the Devil. He was twelve years old, and, in outward form, exactly resembled ordinary children. In Switzerland, on a high mountain, not far from Lucerne, there is a lake they call Pilate's Pond, which the Devil has fixed upon as one of the chief residences of his evil spirits....

Many demons are in woods, in waters, in wildernesses, and in dark poolly places ready to hurt...people. Our bodies are always exposed to Satan. The maladies I suffer are not natural, but Devil's spells.

Snakes and monkeys are subjected to the demon more than other animals. Satan lives in them and possesses them. He uses them to deceive men and to injure them."

"Some [demons] are also in the thick black clouds, which cause hail, lightning and thunder, and poison the air, the pastures and grounds.

The best way to get rid of the Devil, if you cannot kill it with the words of Holy Scripture, is to rail at and mock him. Music, too, is very good; music is hateful to him, and drives him far away.

The Devil can so completely assume the human form, when he wants to deceive us, that we may well lie with what seems to be a woman, of real flesh and blood, and yet all the while 'tis only the Devil in the shape of a woman.

'Tis the same with women, who may think that a man is in bed with them, yet 'tis only the Devil; and...the result of this connection is oftentimes an imp of darkness, half mortal, half devil.... The Devil...clutched hold of the miserable young man...and flew off with him through the ceiling, since which time nothing has been heard of [him].

The Devil fears the word of God, He can't bite it; it breaks his teeth. "The Devil, it is true, is not exactly a doctor who has taken degrees, but he is very learned, very expert for all that.

He has not been carrying on his business during thousands of years for nothing.... The winds are nothing else but good or bad spirits.

Hark! how the Devil is puffing and blowing.... ...two devils rose from the water, and flew off through the air, crying, 'Oh, oh, oh!' and turning one over another, in sportive mockery....

We need not invite the Devil to our table; he is too ready to come without being asked. The air all about us is filled with demons....

When I was a child there were many witches, and they bewitched both cattle and men, especially children."

CHAPTER 61

> AND now, my children, keep your hearts from every injustice, which the Lord hates. Just as a man asks (*sc.* something) for his own soul from God, so let him do to every living soul, because I know all things, how in the great time (*sc.* to come) are many mansions prepared for men, good for the good, and bad for the bad, without number many.

Jn 14.2 In My Father's house are many mansions, behold I go to prepare a place for you that where I am there may you be also.

> 2 Blessed are those who enter the good houses, for in the bad (*sc.* houses) there is no peace nor return (*sc.* from them).

C.1 You don't want to go to the houses of the wicked down in Hell, so be kind to others in this life. The wicked will have no peace no matter where they are as they constantly reject God and His Heavenly Holy Spirit as well as Jesus. Make sure that you are personally saved by Jesus Christ and thus you are not going to the 'houses of the dead' or to Hell. Get your mansion in Heaven by receiving Jesus Christ as your personal saviour. See the prayer for salvation at the end of this book in case you have not received Jesus yet.

> 3 Hear, my children, small and great! When man puts a good thought in his heart, brings gifts from his labours before the Lord's face and his hands made them not, then the Lord will turn away his face from the labour of his hand, and he (sc. man) cannot find the labour of his hands.
>
> 4 And if his hands made it, but his heart murmur, and his heart cease not making murmur incessantly, he has not any advantage.

Philippians 2.14-16 Do all things without murmurings and disputes: [15] That ye may be blameless and harmless, the sons of God, without rebuke, in the midst of a crooked and perverse nation, among whom ye shine as lights in the world; [16] Holding forth the word of life; that I may rejoice in the day of Christ, that I have not run in vain, neither laboured in vain.

CHAPTER 62

> BLESSED is the man who in his patience brings his gifts with faith before the Lord's face, because he will find forgiveness of sins.

James 1.4-8 But let patience have *her* perfect work, that you may be perfect and complete, lacking nothing. ⁵ If any of you lack wisdom, let him ask of God, who gives to all liberally and without reproach, and it will be given to him. ⁶ But let him ask in faith, with no doubting, for he who doubts is like a wave of the sea driven and tossed by the wind. ⁷ For let not that man suppose that he will receive anything from the Lord; ⁸ *he is* a double-minded man, unstable in all his ways.

> 2 But if he take back his words before the time, there is no repentance for him; and if the time pass and he do not of his own will what is promised, there is no repentance after death.
>
> 3 Because every work which man does before the time, is all deceit before men, and sin before God.

James 3.13 Who is a wise man and endued with knowledge among you? Let him shew out of a good conversation his works with meekness of wisdom.

CHAPTER 63

> WHEN man clothes the naked and fills the hungry, he will find reward from God.

Matthew 5.42 Give to him that asks thee, and from him that would borrow of thee turn not thou away.

> 2 But if his heart murmur, he commits a double evil: ruin of himself and of that which he gives; and for him there will be no finding of reward on account of that.

Philippians 2.14-15 Do all things without murmurings and dispute: that ye may be blameless and harmless, the sons of God, without rebuke, in the midst of a crooked and perverse nation, among whom ye shine as lights in the world.

> 3 And if his own heart is filled with his food and his own flesh (*sc.* clothed) with his clothing he commits contempt, and forfeit all his endurance of poverty, and will not find reward of his good deeds.
>
> 4 Every proud and magniloquent man is hateful to the Lord, and every false speech, clothed in untruth; it will be cut with the blade of the sword of death, and thrown into the fire, and shall burn for all time.'

Proverbs 22.22-23 [22] Rob not the poor, because he is poor: neither oppress the afflicted in the gate: [23] For the Lord will plead their cause and spoil the soul of those that spoiled them.

CHAPTER 64

WHEN Enoch had spoken these words to his sons, all people far and near heard how the Lord was calling Enoch. They took counsel together:

2 'Let us go and kiss Enoch' and two thousand men came together and came to the place Achuzan where Enoch was, and his sons.

C.1 original Hebrew the word for 'property' is 'Achuzah' {אחוזה} and it is derived from the Hebrew root A-CH-Z {א-ח-ז} which means 'to hold' or 'holdings.' This Hebrew word – 'Achuzah' – has a more deeper layered **meaning** than simply 'property.'

3 And the elders of the people, the whole assembly, came and bowed down and began to kiss Enoch and said to him:

4 'Our father Enoch, be thou blessed of the Lord, the eternal ruler, and now bless thy sons and all the people, that we may be glorified to-day before thy face.

5 For thou shalt be glorified before the Lord's face for all time, since the Lord chose thee, rather than all men on earth, and designated thee **writer** of all his creation, visible and invisible, and redeemer of the sins of man, and helper of thy household.'

CHAPTER 65

AND Enoch answered all his people saying: 'Hear, my children, before that all creatures were created, the Lord created the visible and invisible things.

Romans 1.20 For the invisible things of God are clearly seen being understood by the things which are made even His eternal Godhead so that they are without excuse.

2 And as much time as there was and went past, understand that after that he created man in the likeness of his own form, and put into him eyes to see, and ears to hear, and heart to reflect, and intellect wherewith to deliberate.

3 And the Lord saw all man's works, and created all his creatures, and divided time, from time he fixed the years, and from the years he appointed the months, and from the months he appointed the days, and of days he appointed seven.

4 And in those he appointed the hours, measured them out exactly, that man might reflect on time and count years, months, and hours, *their* alternation, beginning, and end, and that he might count his own life, from the beginning until death, and reflect on his sin and write his work bad and good; because no work is hidden before the Lord, that every man might know his works and never transgress all his commandments, and keep my handwriting from generation to generation.

5 When all creation visible and invisible, as the Lord created it, shall end, then every man goes to the great judgement, and then all time shall perish, and the years, and thenceforward there will be neither months nor days nor hours, they will be stuck together and will not be counted.

6 There will be one aeon, and all the righteous who shall escape the Lord's great judgement, shall be collected in the great aeon, for the righteous the great aeon will begin, and they will live eternally, and then too there will be amongst them neither labour, nor sickness, nor humiliation, nor anxiety, nor need, nor violence, nor night, nor darkness, but. great light.

C.1 This is a key verse and tells us a lot mentioning how the righteous will escape God's Great Judgment at the end of the Millennium. A new Age or aeon will begin for all of the righteous. A wonderful aeon where the righteous will no longer encounter: *' labour, nor sickness, nor humiliation, nor anxiety, nor need, nor violence, nor night, nor darkness, but. great light.'*

> 7 And they shall have a great indestructible wall, and a paradise bright and incorruptible, for all corruptible things shall pass away, and there will be eternal life.

C.2 THIS CHAPTER 65: AEON OF ETERNITY. = SUMMARY OF THIS BOOK.

In Chapters **25** We Saw The Pre-Creation Time of The Creation Of Light And Chapter **26** The Creation Of Darkness. Now in Chapter **65** We See The 'End of All Things'. In this chapter 65, we see the end of the epoch or aeon of time and the beginning of Eternity, where there is no more evil or spiritual darkness. All of God's Creation becomes creative and productive without interference by sickness or death or Hell or pain or torture, as all the former things have come to an abrupt end.

C.3 The righteous shall reign with Christ for 1000 years during the Golden Age of the Millennium and then shall come the Great Judgement of all. All the evil spirits and the wicked and ungodly and unrepentant have been thrown into the Lake of Fire after the Great White Throne Judgment which happens right after the 1000 year Golden Reign of the Millennium with Christ and His saints ruling the earth. After that Eternity of the New Heaven and the New Earth wherein there is no more time.

Revelation 10.6-7 There should **be time no longer**: But in the days of the voice of the seventh angel, when he shall begin to sound, the mystery of God should be finished, as he hath declared to his servants the prophets.

Revelation 20.1-4,7-14.

20.1 And I saw an angel come down from heaven, having the key of the bottomless pit and a great chain in his hand.

² And he laid hold on the dragon, that old serpent, which is the Devil, and Satan, and bound him a thousand years,

³ And cast him into the bottomless pit, and shut him up, and set a seal upon him, that he should deceive the nations no more, till the thousand years should be fulfilled: and after that he must be loosed a little season.

⁴ And I saw thrones, and they sat upon them, and judgment was given unto them: and I saw the souls of them that were beheaded for the witness of Jesus, and for the word of God, and which had not worshipped the beast, neither his image, neither had received his mark upon their foreheads, or in their hands; and they lived and reigned with Christ a thousand years.

7 And when the thousand years are expired, Satan shall be loosed out of his prison,

8 And shall go out to deceive the nations which are in the four quarters of the earth, Gog and Magog, to gather them together to battle: the number of whom *is* as the sand of the sea.

9 And they went up on the breadth of the earth, and compassed the camp of the saints about, and the beloved city: and fire came down from God out of heaven and devoured them.

10 And the devil that deceived them was cast into the lake of fire and brimstone, where the beast and the false prophet *are*, and shall be tormented day and night for ever and ever.

11 And I saw a great white throne, and him that sat on it, from whose face the earth and the heaven fled away; and there was found no place for them.

12 And I saw the dead small and great, stand before God; and the books were opened; and another was opened, which is the book of life: and the dead were judged out of those things which were written in the books according to their works.

13 And the sea gave up the dead which were in it; and death and hell delivered up the dead which were in them: and they were judged every man according to their works.

14 And death and hell were cast into the lake of fire. This is the second death. 15 And whosoever was not found written in the Book of Life was cast into the Lake of Fire.

CHAPTER 66

AND now, my children, keep your souls from all injustice, such as the Lord hates.

2 Walk before his face with terror and trembling and serve him alone.

Proverbs 14.26 In the fear of the Lord is strong confidence and His children shall have a place of refuge.

3 Bow down to the true God, not to dumb idols, but bow down to his picture, and bring all just offerings before the Lord's face. The Lord hates what is unjust.

4 For the Lord sees all things; when man takes thought in his heart, then he counsels the intellects, and every thought is always before the Lord, who made firm the earth and put all creatures on it.

5 If you **look to heaven**, the Lord is there; if you **take thought of the sea's deep** and all the under-earth, the Lord is there.

C.1 In the book of Exodus, chapter 20, verse 4, we find an unusual verse: "Thou shalt not make unto thee any graven image, or any likeness of anything that is in heaven above, or that is in the earth beneath, or that is in the water under the earth."

C.2 This last verse seems to be referring to a **HOLLOW EARTH** where inside the earth we have the underworld which is full of activity.

6 For the Lord created all things. **Bow not down to things made by man**, leaving the Lord of all creation, because no work can remain hidden before the Lord's face.

7 Walk, my children, in longsuffering, in meekness, honesty, in provocation, in grief, in faith and in truth, in *reliance on* promises, in illness, in abuse, in wounds, in temptation, in nakedness, in privation, loving one another, till you go out from this age of ills, that you become **inheritors of endless time**.

8 Blessed are the just who shall escape the great judgement, for they **shall shine forth more than the sun sevenfold**, for in this world the **seventh part is taken off from all**, light, darkness, food, enjoy-

> ment, sorrow, paradise, torture, fire, frost, and other things; he put all down in writing, that you might read and understand.'

C.3 THE HOLLOW EARTH
'PARADISE' & HELL

Is it just possible that 1) 'The Original Garden of Eden', was located inside the earth. 2) Then, <u>after the Flood,</u> mankind came to live on the outer surface of the earth?

There is evidence that not only are there cities inside the earth, but that also there are the remains of ancient cities, built long before the Great Flood.

C.4 In the book, '**Journey to Gragau**' by **Alan Trenholm**[*1], Alan states that he went on a spirit trip down through the crust of the earth whilst riding a horse. He travelled widely inside the earth and visited both Paradise and Hell.

Whist riding the horse down into Hell, through the many strata of the earth's crust, just before entering the Inner Earth, he states that he felt a clammy hand reach out and grab his leg, which was presumably one of the inmates of Hell itself.

C.5 His spirit guide explained to Alan that the "clammy hand" that he felt, was belonging to one of the "rock people". When Alan asked his very first question; "*Who are the rock people*? The explanation given is what *gives it all away* concerning *when man moved from the INNER EARTH to the OUTER EARTH!* She explained that the "rock people" were spirits of the people from before the Flood, who were buried in the rubble of their former cities, and in imprisonment in the strata of the earth, because they didn't honour God. Instead, they honoured themselves, and their cities, often built with the price of human blood and sacrifice. The incident mentioned about a being that grabbed Alan's leg, happened *just before he entered the inner surface of the earth*, howbeit, in the *lower dimension* of Hell. The important point here that it shows that "being" was *buried in the rubble of cities on the inside of the earth and not the outside.*

C.6 From this we can indeed deduce that as the <u>first cities of man were built on the inner surface of the physical earth</u>, that it is more than likely that *mankind first came onto the outer surface of the earth where we live today after the Flood at Noah's time.* This is just one example concerning cities inside the earth, and the rubble of ancient cities.

[See the dramatic, amazing and insightful book, [*1] "Journey to Gragau" by Alan Trenholm. Alan's "spirit trip" down to Hell, which he claims was 100% real: '**Journey to Gragau**' - www.amazon.com]

C.7 This could also explain why much of the book of Enoch, & the topography of the earth as described by Enoch sounds like, that when he was actually describing the earth, most of the time like he was actually talking about the INNER EARTH, because that is where he lived before the Great Flood.

C.8 Remember that in the book of 1st Enoch, Enoch has talked about dinosaurs and dragons, and large creatures and both sea and land monsters. He also talks a length about the land of a 'thousand mountains', often volcanic in nature, and something that simply does not exist today; at least not on the outer surface of the planet, as we now know it today. He has also described trees as being exceedingly high and unlike the trees in our modern world. He also went to the ends of the earth and saw the Northern Polar Entrance.

C.9 Enoch stated that the seas only occupied one seventh of the earth's surface. Sounds like a very different world being described by Enoch. Today the outer surface of the earth, where we live is 80% seas. Only 8% of the planet is inhabitable today! The rest is seas, ice, deserts and jungles. What a contrast that to the original Creation which God made.

C.10 I believe that Enoch also visited the *uninhabited outer surface of the earth where we live today*. We know from Enoch's book, that he also visited both the higher dimensions of Heaven itself, as well as the lower dimensions of both Hell and the Lake of fire.

C.11 To learn a lot more about these fascinating topics, I highly recommend the above-mentioned book by Alan Trenholm, about Hell, the Lake of fire, demons and Fallen Angels, as it gives an *amazing amount of insightful information about the lower worlds and the future of our planet.*

C.12 Let's compare conditions on the earth before the Flood and after the Flood

CONDITIONS BEFORE & AFTER THE FLOOD

Before the Flood	After the Flood
People lived up to almost 1000 years	Noah 350 more years after Flood and total age of 950 years
	Shem 500 years after the Flood total 600 years
	Son of Shem ARPHAXAD 438 years
	90 YEARS LATER ARPHAXAD'S great-grandson Peleg lived only 209 years
	Another 90 YEARS LATER Peleg's great grandson Nahor only lived to be....148 years
	(Noah was still alive when Nahor 8 generations after Noah, had already died!)
	Isaac 180
	Jacob 147
	Joseph 110
	(There were 13 generations from Noah to Joseph and a total of 640 years)
	Less than 800 years later in 2000 BCE, King David stated that a man's life was 70 years

C.13 Something was very different about the surface of the earth and the heavens above the earth, after the FLOOD. God had cursed man at the time of the FLOOD, and stated that a man's life would be 120 years only.

Why did men live to be almost 1000 years old before the Flood and less and less after the flood and their ages dwindled down from 950 to only 70 years in only 1600 years.

I propose that <u>before the flood mankind lived inside a very protected earth</u>. After the Flood mankind now lived on the outer surface of the earth, that was no longer protected as greatly as before the Flood. <u>The earth lost its protective shield of water about the earth</u>. We started to feel the influence of cosmic rays, which reduced the length of people's lives.

C.14 I believe that not only is the earth Hollow, but also the moon, and the sun and the stars, as hollow objects are much easier to cause to spin. Solid objects are not. Because of centrifugal forces, when one puts clothes in a washing machine, all the clothes that occupied the centre of the machine, once put in the centrifuge, all material is flung to the sides of the machine. The same is true of the earth and all other astral bodies.

My theory is that the entire universe down to the earth, within earth, & Hell &Tartarus below that, consists of globes and circular orbits.

1) The Earth is the centre of the universe

2) The Earth is hollow

3) All astral bodies are hollow

4) The sun and the moon rotate around the earth and not the earth around the sun.

5) The universe is not oval or ovuloid but is actually global in shape, with the earth at the very centre of it.

6) Before the Flood, the Earth was protected by a layer of water around 5-15 metres thick, 100 miles above the earth's surface all away around the earth. (Apparently 100 miles up in the atmosphere, is where both gravitational and centrifugal forces which are in opposite direction to each other, cancel each other out.) This caused the earth to act like a green-house and was the reason why the vegetation grew to be so big.

7) The protection above the earth, also acted like a "pressurized hyperbaric oxygen chamber", and thus large creatures like dinosaurs, which today scientists can't understand how they could have been breathing with such small lungs. Well there's your answer: the earth had a much higher oxygen content than today and it was also pressurized, thus making it much easier to breath for the dinosaur.

EZE.31:16 I made the nations to shake at the sound of his fall, when I cast him down to hell with them that descend into the pit: and all the trees of Eden, the choice and best of Lebanon, all that drink water, shall be comforted in the <u>nether parts of the earth</u>.

C.15 (See 2nd Book 'EZRA *insights*' by the same author for a lot more about the Hollow Earth or the 'Womb of the Earth' as God Himself calls the inside of our planet in II EZDRAS.)

1ST ENOCH CH22.1-2 And thence I went to another place, and he showed me in the west another great and high mountain of hard rock; and there was in it *four hollow places*, deep and wide and very smooth. How smooth are the hollow places and deep and dark to look at.

2 Then Raphael answered, one of the holy angels who was with me, and said unto me, "These *hollow places* have been created for this very purpose, that the *spirits of the souls of the dead should assemble therein*, yea that *all the souls of the children of men should assemble here.*

3 "And these places have been made to receive them till the day of their judgement, and till their period appointed, till the great judgement (comes) upon them."

C.16 The Great White Throne Judgment comes at the End of the 1000 Year Millenium

Revelation 20.12-14 And I saw the dead, small and great, stand before God; and the books were opened: and another book was opened, which is the book of life: and the dead were judged out of those things which were written in the books, according to their works.

13 And the sea gave up the dead which were in it; and death and hell delivered up the dead which were in them: and they were judged every man according to their works.

14 And death and hell were cast into the lake of fire. This is the second death.

C.17: These hollow places must be very large indeed if they can contain all the souls of men who have ever lived.

BIBLE VERSES ABOUT THE HOLLOW EARTH

PHI.2:10 That at the name of Jesus every knee should bow, of things in heaven, and things in earth, and things under the earth

EPH.4:9 (Now that he ascended, what is it but that he also descended first into the lower parts of the earth?

EXO.20:4 Thou shalt not make unto thee any graven image, or any likeness of anything that is in heaven above, or that is in the earth beneath, or that is in the water under the earth.

GEN.1:6 And God said, 'Let there be a firmament in the midst of the waters, and let it **divide** the **waters** from the **waters**.'

ISA.40:22 It is he that sits upon the circle of the earth, and the inhabitants thereof are as grasshoppers; that stretches out the heavens as a curtain, and spreads them out as a tent to dwell in:

AMO.9:2 Though they dig into hell, thence shall mine hand take them; though they climb up to heaven, thence will I bring them down:

PHI.2:10 That at the name of Jesus every knee should bow, of things in heaven, and things in earth, and things under the earth;

MY OWN THEORY ABOUT THE ORIGINAL CREATION

My own idea, (which needs yet to be proven), is that not only was there a layer of water above the atmosphere, as other scientists have speculated, but that also above the INNER EARTH, around 50-100 miles above the surface of the INNER EARTH there was also an INNER canopy of water for the same reason, which made the inner earth also like a greenhouse.

The outer waters above the earth acted like a changeable lens, and the inner earth waters acted like a perfect internal mirror. There were portals in the earth or better said dimensional gates, which allowed light to get through the surface of the earth in selected places around the world in perfect order. At least 12 portals that we know of. Unfortunately, since the Flood, those portals no longer work the way they used to in Pre-Flood times, and in modern times they have become dangerous areas known as the 12 Bermuda triangles around the world, where ships and planes and even high altitude satellites get caught in the dimensional voids or areas between dimensions, which we call Bermuda triangles. ***See Chapter 2 From my first book, "OUT OF THE BOTTOMLESS PIT" about the Bermuda Triangles. Five in the northern hemisphere and 5 in the southern Hemisphere. The two so-called Poles of the Earth, would have also conceivably been light sources to the INNER EARTH as they are today in modern times. A total of 12 PORTALS.

I propose that God's original creation was far more fantastic and beautiful than He is given credit for.

What if Adam and Eve were indeed placed in the Garden of Eden inside the earth. They might have been able to see the inner sun, but what about all the beautiful Cosmos of stars, not to the mention the Sun and the Moon, which normally one could only see from the outer surface of the earth?

God would certainly have created the earth in such a way, that His first children Adam and Eve could clearly have see His magnificent creation of the Sun, the Moon and the stars!

Obviously if that 1st assumption is correct, then God must have arranged the planet in such a way that Adam and Eve could still easily see the beautiful stars and the sun and Moon and planets, but how was that even possible?

The bible tells us that God is the Father of Lights, and I put it to you that the earth was in the beginning both like a projector with moveable lenses, and a mirror and original light sources.

What was seen of the universe by Adam and Eve on the INNER EARTH in the Garden of Eden was a perfect internal REFLECTION.

The waters above the earth acted as a giant moveable lens, letting in the light. The inner waters above the inner earth acted as a perfect mirror.

There are invisible portals (today known as Bermuda Triangles) which sometimes, act as dimensional gate-ways, which before the flood allowed the light to travel through the very surface of the earth. Today 10 of the Bermuda Triangles (Gate-ways) are at around 30 degrees Latitude, in 5 points equidistant in the Northern Hemisphere, and 5 points equidistant in the southern Hemisphere. Strangely enough in modern times these Bermuda Triangles are mostly listed as to the immediate right of a land mass. I propose that as

Enoch mentioned in his book, that there used to be a lot less water in the seas of our planet. Originally, all the "light portals" or "Bermuda Triangles" today, would have, for convenience been on the land area, and not in the sea.

The light then focused on the waters above the inner earth surface, which was like a perfect mirror, which reflected all the light of the cosmos and the sun and moon and stars back down onto the surface of the inner earth.

When it comes to LIGHT, water itself has amazing qualities and has been known to sometimes act as a lens, and sometimes act as a mirror, and at other times as a magnifying glass. Whether acting as a lens or a mirror would depend on different factors, but primarily on the temperature of the waters.

Amazingly enough I have just found some evidence to support my theory of the INNER WATERS & OUTER WATERS. The inner waters acting more like a perfect mirror in order to reflect the light perfectly onto the surface of inner earth. The light would have come through the portals (Bermuda Triangles).

Today I was reading a very famous book called, 'Flying Saucers From The Earth's Interior (1960) by Raymond W Bernard. He was talking about many different explorers & scientists who have descended through the North Pole (Northern Aperture), and have tried different experiments to show that the earth is in fact Hollow. One of the amazing things that the scientists and explorers mention is that in going through the hole at the north and on their way onto the under surface of inner earth, at some point the sky acts very odd and appears as a mirror in the sky, which he stated that no one, at that time, understood the cause of this phenomenon. Although scientists suspected ice-crystals. Well when I read this, I was completely blown away, as one would say, because my theory above, is that there used to be a layer of water above the outer surface of the earth, which acted more like a lens and sometimes like a magnifying glass, and another layer of water above the INNER EARTH, which because of the uniform temperature, somehow acted more like a perfect internal mirror, allowing for total internal reflection.

The fact that scientific observers have found one area of the sky where this mirror effect is still evident, and formed by water in the form of ice-crystals is very encouraging. Apparently, this connecting northern aperture which directly connects our outer world with the inner world, is the only remaining location on the entire planet, where the mirror waters in the sky are yet still working!

The Inner Earth today has a uniform temperature of around 73 degrees F by all reports. I also think that God being the amazing and incredible creator that He is, that He created the outer-earth waters above the earth, as a giant changeable lens.

When night time came, the stars and in fact the whole universe would have been seen as being much closer to the earth

At night time, somehow the waters above the earth, acted as a giant magnifying glass.

If the above theory is correct, then at different times of the year, Adam and Eve could have clearly seen the 12 Astrological Star arrangements in the sky from Aries to Taurus, as though they were all very close-up.

It must have been absolutely both spectacular and astoundingly beautiful, and breath-taking.

The curse of the Bermuda Triangles wouldn't even exist today, if man hadn't been so rebellious, destructive, violent and perverse, in the first place, which resulted in the judgement of the Flood, and also unfortunately, caused the destruction of the giant projector of the earth, mentioned above.

All we apparently have left of that original light projector, is the defective "Light Portals" (Bermuda Triangles)

CHAPTER 67

WHEN Enoch had talked to the people, the Lord sent out darkness on to the earth, and there was darkness, and it covered those men standing with Enoch, and they **took Enoch up on to the highest heaven,** where the Lord is; and he received him and placed him before his face, and the darkness went off from the earth, and light came again.

2 **And the people saw and understood not how Enoch had been taken,** and glorified God, and **found a roll in which was traced 'the invisible God'**; and all went to their homes.

CHAPTER 68

> ENOCH was born on the sixth day of the **month Tsivan**, and lived three hundred and sixty-five years.

C.1 Tsivan (Hebrew: Sivan; from Akkadian : simānu, meaning "Season; time") is May through June, at the end of spring, on the Gregorian calendar. Sivan is the third month of the Hebrew calendar. It begins around the third week of May towards the end of the spring season.

> 2 He was taken up to heaven on the first day of the month Tsivan and remained in heaven sixty days.
>
> 3 He wrote all these signs of all creation, which the Lord created, and wrote three hundred and sixty-six books, and handed them over to his sons and remained on earth thirty days and was again taken up to heaven on the sixth day of the month Tsivan, on the very day and hour when he was born.
>
> 4 As every man's nature in this life is dark, so are also his conception, birth, and departure from this life.
>
> 5 At what hour he was conceived, at that hour he was born, and at that hour too he died.
>
> 6 Methosalam and his brethren, all the sons of Enoch, made haste, and erected an altar at the place called **Achuzan**, whence and where Enoch had been taken up to heaven.
>
> 7 And they took sacrificial oxen and summoned all people and sacrificed the sacrifice before the Lord's face.
>
> 8 All people, the elders of the people and the whole assembly came to the feast and brought gifts to the sons of Enoch.
>
> 9 And they made a great feast, rejoicing and making merry three days, praising God, who had given them such a sign through Enoch, who had found favour with him, and that they should hand it on to their sons from generation to generation, from age to age.
>
> 10 Amen.

APPENDIX I Background History of the Book of Enoch

What other evidences for Enoch's authenticity (as a sacred text) are there?

Why isn't it in the Bible today?

Since it's English translation in the 1800's from texts found in Ethiopia in 1768, The Book of Enoch (known today as 1st Enoch) has made quite a stir in academic circles. 1 Enoch has been authenticated as existing and in wide use before the church age (most scholars now date it at 200 BC). Multiple copies were discovered in 1948 in the Dead Sea Scrolls. This of course has caused many to wonder why it is not included in modern Bibles.

1st Enoch Chapter 6 relates the story of the Fallen angels in great detail. It lists the names of 18 "prefect" angels - of 200 - who committed this sin. According to the text, these angels also taught mankind the "making of swords and knives, shields and breastplates (metallurgy); ... magical medicine, dividing of roots (medicinal and hallucinogenic use); incantations, astrology, the seeing of the stars, the course of the moon, as well as the deception of man."

By Noah's time, "The earth also was corrupt (wasting - KJV notation) before God, and the earth was filled with violence... all flesh had corrupted his way upon the earth." Gen 6:10-11. Afraid of the consequences, these angels appeal to Enoch to intercede with God on their behalf; God instead uses Enoch to deliver a message of judgment against them. Aside from the "taking of wives," God states that he would not forgive them for teaching mankind magical arts and warlike ways.

The increasing acceptance and popularization of this important book among theologians helps cast light on the extra-terrestrial hypothesis (ETH) in general.

Enoch is an ancient writing, which states that angels & not true space aliens, as stated by many UFO cults, and popular modern authors Erich Von Daniken & Zachariah Sitchin visited ancient Earth and polluted mankind's DNA. While this case can easily be made solely from the canonized Bible.

Enoch is yet another witness against these bad interpretations of Earth's pre-deluvian era (i.e., before the flood of Genesis 6). The fact that they also gave mankind technology which supposedly "advanced our race" (but which we actually used to destroy each other, and to incur God's judgment), lends itself to a more sinister understanding of today's UFO phenomenon

Genesis 6 / Book of Enoch	Today / Any episode of the X-Files
Supernatural Beings identified as angels	Supernatural Beings identified as ET's
Took as wives "any whom they chose"	Abduction Phenomenon
Hybrid Race of Nephilim	Missing Fetuses, Hybrids, Cloning
Introduced Destructive Technology: Wepons of warfare/pschorophic drugs Bombers, etc / Occult /Astology and Sorcery	Hitler's Foo Fighters / Roswell Crash / "Back-engineering" of Stealth
	New Age Doctrines
Weapons of Warfare / Psychotropic Drugs / Astrology & Sorcery	
Worshipped as Gods (Annanuki) / old, men of renown…"	Nephilim hybrids were "heroes of Zechariah Sitchin / UFO Cults / Immunity for Abduction Crimes /
Gen 6:4 - the factual basis for "Space Brothers"	"Spirit Guides, Ascended/Masters and/or
Greco-Roman deities	
"And the Lord said, "I will destroy man whom I have created from the face of the earth ..but Noah found grace in his sight. Genesis 6.7-8	"As it was in the days of Noah, so shall it be at the coming of the Son of Man Matthew 24:37

(Editor: See my 1st book, **'OUT OF THE BOTTOMLESS PIT'** at www. amazon.co.uk
for much more information concerning the topic of Aliens, Alien Abductions and many Paranormal coverups.)

THE *SERPENT* DIETY RACE IS REAL?
http://www.ancientpages.com/2017/10/24/mysterious-nagas-serpent-people-live-secret-underground-cities/

FLYING MACHINES IN ANCIENT INDIA:
http://www.ancientpages.com/2014/05/27/vimanas-flying-machines-soaring-through-ancient-sky-of-india/

DRAGONS http://www.ancientpages.com/2016/11/02/dragons-dragon-kings-ancient-mythology/

APPENDIX II What other evidences for Enoch's authenticity (as a sacred text) are there? Why isn't the Book of Enoch in the Bible today? One reason given by churches: Jesus said that angels can't have sex, proving this book's falsehood… The idea that Jesus said that angels cannot have sex is a very common objection to The Book of Enoch, and the angelic understanding of Genesis 6 in general. However, it is also a very common misinterpretation of what he actually said. (Matt 22:30)

MAT.22:30 For in the resurrection they neither marry, nor are given in marriage, but are as the angels of God in heaven

This verse is not saying that people can't have sex in heaven. The opposite is true, where love and sex are a much more complete experience in the spirit world, according to those who have spoken from beyond, of which there are many examples written. (See the book 'Journey to Gragau' about a trip to hell and also about the nature of both angels and spirit helpers.)

Beyond that misunderstanding, there is no doubt today that The Book of Enoch was one of the most widely accepted and revered books of Jewish culture and doctrine in the century leading up to Jesus' birth. It is usually noted first that New Testament author Jude directly quotes from 1 Enoch - "Behold he comes with ten thousand of his saints to execute judgment ..." (1 Enoch 2, Jude 14-15). Additionally, "the citations of Enoch by the Testaments of the Twelve Patriarchs... show that at the close of the second century B.C., and during the first century B.C., this book was regarded in certain circles as inspired" (1). Aside from Jude, Peter and Paul's affirmations of the angelic/ hybrid interpretation, recognition of 1 Enoch "... is given amply in the Epistle of Barnabus, and in the third century by Clement and Irenaeus" (1). The Catholic Church's Origen - known as "the father of theology" - affirmed both the Book of Enoch and the fact that angels could and did co-habitate with the daughters of men. He even warned against possible angelic and/or Nephilim infiltration of the church itself. Oddly, while thousands of his writings are still considered by them as "sacred," this very issue got him labelled as a heretic when the faulty Sons of Seth "doctrine" was conceived! (2) Additionally, the Coptic Orthodox Churches of Egypt (estimated approximately 50-100 A.D.) still include Enoch as canonized text in the Ethiopic Old Testament (2). This fact alone should carry great weight for Western Christians when honestly studying the "case" for Enoch. Given their 1900+ year history, the fact that they were never "ruled" by Rome's theology, and that they currently number over 10 million - this is a VERY significant portion of The Body of Christ that has historically esteemed 1 Enoch as inspired doctrine. Some today (who do not seem to believe in the inspiration of scripture) claim that most major themes of the New Testament were in fact "borrowed" from 1 Enoch. "It appears that Christianity later adopted some of its ideas and philosophies from this book, including the Final Judgment, the concept of demons, the Resurrection, and the coming of a Messiah and Messianic Kingdom" (3).

No doubt, these themes are major parts of 1 Enoch, and appear there as complete theologies a full 200 years before any other NT writings. Christian author Stephen Quayle writes, "Several centuries before and after the appearance of Jesus in Jerusalem, this book had become well known to the Jewish community, having a profound impact upon Jewish thought.

The Book of Enoch shows the GEO-CENTRIC universe or the earth as the centre of the universe and not the modern HELIO-CENTRIC with the sun as the centre of our 'so called' solar system, and also appears to have instilled the idea that the coming Messiah would be someone who had pre-existed as God (4)."

Translator RH Charles also stated that "the influence of 1 Enoch on the New Testament has been greater than all of the other apocryphal and pseudepigraphic books put together" (3).

The conclusions are somewhat inescapable given Enoch's dating and wide acceptance between 200 B.C. and 200 A.D. - either Christian authors, and especially the Nicene Council, did plagiarize their theology directly from Enoch, or the original version of Enoch was also inspired. James H Charlesworth, director of Dead Sea Studies at Yale University, says in The Old Testament Pseudeipgrapha & The New Testament (Trinity Press International), "I have no doubt that the Enoch groups deemed the Book of Enoch as fully inspired as any biblical book. I am also convinced that the group of Jews behind the Temple Scroll, which is surely pre-Qumranic, would have judged it to be quintessential Torah -- that is, equal to, and perhaps better than, Deuteronomy....Then we should perceive the Pseudeipgrapha as they were apparently judged to be: God's revelation to humans (2 & 5)." But perhaps the most telling argument for 1 Enoch's "inspiration" may well be that the Jewish understanding of the term "Son of Man" as a Messianic title comes - not truly from our Old Testament canon - but from the Book of Enoch!

APPENDIX III - SON OF MAN: 1 Enoch Chapters 46,68,70

Ever wonder why Jesus refers to himself in the gospels as the "Son of Man" rather than the Son of God? (2) Of over 100 uses of the phrase "son of man" in the OT, it refers almost always to "normal" men (93 times specifically of Ezekiel, and certainly not as Messiah!), but is used only one time in the entire OT, in one of Daniel's heavenly visions, to refer to divinity. Despite the Old Testament's frequent lack of divine application of the phrase, 1 Enoch records several trips to heaven, using the title "Son of Man" unceasingly to refer to the pre-incarnate Christ. Of particular Messianic significance, Enoch describes the following scene (2): The angels "glorify with all their power of praise; and He sustains them in all that act of thanksgiving while they laud, glorify and exalt the name of the Lord of Spirits forever and ever... Great was their joy. They blessed, glorified and exalted because the name of the Son of Man was revealed to them (1 Enoch 68:35-38)." Both His disciples, and especially the Sanhedrin knew what Jesus was claiming - 84 times in the gospels! - when referring to Himself as the "Son of Man." This claim was considered an obvious blasphemy to the Pharisees & Sadducees, but it is eternal life to all who confess that Jesus of Nazareth was, and is, the Son of Man, The Messiah, God in the flesh, The Holy One of Israel, God's Christ - the Lord of All to whom every knee shall bow (Philippians 2:8-10). Using "normal rules" of scriptural interpretation, we are never to draw firm doctrine from only one passage of scripture. Right? Daniel's single use of "Son of Man" (in a "night vision" at that - Dan 7:13), would not be sufficient to claim that the phrase is indeed Messianic, especially given the other 107 times it is not used in that way. 1 Enoch is the missing "second witness" needed (according to all other rules of interpretation) to understand the phrase's double meaning as an enduring Messianic title. It has been argued ever since Enoch's first English translation, that by using this title so familiar to the Jews, Jesus was actually affirming the truth of this book, that the prophet was taken on many trips to heaven before his "final" translation, and that he was the one whom Enoch saw there - the pre-existent Son of Man, whom Enoch prophesied would judge the souls of all men. Interestingly, Daniel is ALSO the only OT use of the term "watcher" to ever refer to angels (Daniel 4:13, 17, 23 KJV). Strong's Concordance defines a watcher as a "guardian angel". "The distinguishing character of the Watcher (opposed to other angels in the canon) appears to be that it spends much time among men, overseeing what they are doing. It is also interesting to note that both times one of these angels appeared to Daniel, he took pains to note that it was "an holy one," suggesting that some Watchers are not aligned with God while others are ." Found nowhere else in the OT canon but the book of Daniel, "watcher" is patently Enoch's term for these

angels. Likewise, Daniel alone used Enoch's term "Son of Man" to refer to the pre-incarnate Christ, adding further intrigue to the case for 1 Enoch's inspiration, and an overall understanding of its doctrinal acceptance among both Old and New Testament writers.

What we lose out on today by not examining 1 Enoch - even if only for its historical significance - is that it is actually more splendid than any other book in our canon in its exultation of Christ as King! It also gives clear, stern and oft-repeated warnings to the unsaved of swift destruction at the 'Coming of The Lord', but is also full of amazing promises of future glory for the elect! We are of course wise to stay clear of dangerous heresy, but... ask yourself if the below sounds like false doctrine? Keep in mind, this was written at least 200 years before Christ walked the earth, and perhaps before Noah's birth: Then shall the kings, the princes, and all who possess the earth, glorify Him who has dominion over all things, Him who was concealed; for from eternity the Son of Man was concealed, whom the Most High preserved in the presence of His power and revealed to the elect.

He shall sow the congregation of the saints, and of the elect; and all the elect shall stand before Him in that day. All the kings, the princes, the exalted, and those who rule over the earth shall fall down on their faces before Him and shall worship Him. They shall fix their hopes on this Son of Man... Then the sword of the Lord of Spirits shall be drunk from them (the lost); but the saints and the elect shall be safe in that day; nor the face of the sinners and the ungodly shall they thence-forth behold. The Lord of Spirits shall remain over them; And with this Son of Man shall they dwell, eat, lie down, and rise up for ever and ever...

Enoch 61:10-13

APPENDIX IV: WHY ARE THE BOOKS OF ENOCH NOT IN THE BIBLE?

Uncertain, as well as multiple authorship, and several slightly varying texts are among the main reasons cited for Enoch not "making it" into the generally recognized canon. In truth, the spiritual agenda(s) of the early Roman Church is most likely the ultimate reason however, and we will examine this agenda here as well. Let's begin with the first two though, before moving to the more incredulous, but quite valid "conspiracy theories." "The Book of Enoch, like the book of Daniel, was originally written in Aramaic, and partly in Hebrew (1)." While there may have been Hebrew translations during the centuries B.C. (which early church leaders may or may not have had access to), today only the Ethiopic manuscripts exist, as well as some incomplete Greek and Latin translations, plus one Aramaic fragment from the Dead Sea Scrolls. By the time of Jesus' birth, "average" Jews were reading mainly the Greek Septuagint translation of their own Torah (completed 200 B.C.), as a result of their years of foreign captivity and then-current Roman occupation. To coin the vernacular, they had been assimilated. So, unless an authentic Aramaic version appears miraculously today, there will never be any completely indisputable way to argue for a modern "canonization" of 1 Enoch, as the originals are lost, probably forever. The honest problem facing the infant Roman Church of 390 A.D., when first assembling today's Bible, was that the existing copies of 1 Enoch varied, albeit in minor ways. "Unlike the (rest of the) Bible which was carefully copied and checked for errors by Jewish and Christian scribes throughout its history, The Book of Enoch is available in a number of ancient manuscripts that differ slightly from one another... and many errors have crept in... There is no way of knowing which versions are (exactly faithful to) the original and which are the errors. While this doesn't change its stories in any substantial manner, it does make it impossible to anchor beliefs or arguments on any given section... (4)." Another less important but quite "legitimate" issue is that 1 Enoch is actually a collection of at least four different "books," possibly written by various authors over many centuries, and possibly not by the true Enoch of Genesis 5. The Artisan Publishers' introduction to The Book of Enoch says "there can be no shadow of doubt" that there is a diversity of authorship and perhaps even time periods represented across the span of 1 Enoch, but that there is also "nonetheless, uniformity." They attribute this to the very possible idea that as God raised up prophets (after Malachi...?), they published under the safety of a revered pseudonym, to avoid persecution and possible death at the hands of the religious powers-that-were, who wanted no "fresh words" from God(1). This could well be the case but would make the book(s) of Enoch no less inspired of God if true. However, only the NT Book of Hebrews (written centuries closer to the Bible's assembly, with multiple matching manuscripts) has been accepted as canon with such uncertain authorship - without even a good solid guess agreed upon, that is. Since "the real" Enoch of Genesis 5 was transported to heaven - permanently- it would be no stretch to imagine that it was also a normal experience during his lifetime. After all, the Bible says he walked with God for 300 years! (Genesis5:22) The first 36 chapters (detailing the watchers' fall) are sometimes only reluctantly attributed to Enoch (given their pre-diluvian history), but there are varying theories regarding the rest of the book(s). For much of the 1800's, it was argued that the remaining chapters were actually the work of an early Christian scribe, but these claims were decisively put to rest with the discovery of the Dead Sea Scrolls, as were JT Milik's claims that chapters 37-71 were Christian. Charlesworth says "The consensus communis is unparalleled in almost any other area of research; no specialist now argues that I *Enoch 37-71 is (written by a first-century) Christian and (that it) post-dates the first century... (2) and (5)." With this in mind, we must again face up to the very real dilemma of stating that that either the entire New Testament was "drawn" in a natural, secular way from 1 Enoch - with no supernatural inspiration – or that 1 Enoch and The New Testament are both from God. It is also considered that possibly a single author assembled older prophets' inspired works around 200 B.C. and simply added Enoch's name to them all, to ensure widespread acceptance - "Hardly a practice that inspires confidence in the text (4)." But in reality, it is no secret academically that certain canonized OT books, as well as Mark's gospel, may have been originally written by another - or even multiple - inspired author(s) and later were also assembled under the inspiration of God by a single author, who put either his own, or the original author's name, to the work. For example, most agree that Moses actually wrote Job's story from other existing texts (or that he knew him personally), before he even wrote Genesis. Most of the Major Prophets and historical books contain clear breaks in the time period and were finally assembled many years later - as the author "was carried along by the Holy Spirit (1 Peter 2:21)." Christians need to get over the idea that "inspiration" means the writer went into some mystical trance, while God "possessed them" and wrote the Bible. Inspiration simply means they were obedient to God's leading and wrote what He said OR supernaturally revealed to them, or even that he guided their research, helping them discern truth from error, for the purpose of writing "an orderly account (Luke 1:3)." Here, Luke states that his gospel was an extended research project! In that vein, I.D.E. Thomas has recently suggested one other possibility perhaps not considered in academic circles before the 1986 publication of The Omega Conspiracy. "Thomas suggests that the compiler may have written his book from texts originally written by Enoch himself. In such a case it would make perfect sense for the compiler to attach Enoch's name to the book for which he had provided the material (4) and (6)." Even with all of this said, there is still no "clean" explanation for Enoch's 1000-year disappearance from even popular literature though. Despite the above reasons for not canonizing the book, it is painfully apparent that the church did in fact supress The Book of Enoch. Only in studying both the goals and motives - positive and negative - of the Roman Church do the truest reason for Enoch's "fall from grace" become apparent.

APPENDIX V: WHY WERE THE BOOKS OF ENOCH NOT CANONISED?
Officially speaking, there are "good enough" reasons to have disqualified Enoch from canonization. But only assuming you wanted to in the first place ... With all of the evidence in, we have to own the fact that 1 Enoch was not

merely "rejected for canonization." It was buried. Flat out suppressed. It was quite intentionally lost to history, with all copies destroyed or left to rot 10 stories deep under the Vatican. Enoch was not merely "left out of the Bible." It was dropped like a bad habit. Enoch was suppressed and labelled as heresy specifically to *hide the truth of the fallen angels' past, present and future activity on earth*, according to Origen. [Adamantius Origen, was Greek (A.D. 184-254), was born in Alexandria, Egypt, and was one of the most famous "church fathers, & was also a prolific writer.]

APPENDIX VI: THE 'TRANSLATION' OF ENOCH – (From my book 'Enoch Insights' Book 1 - based on 1st Book of Enoch)

The problem that we face today, is that normally most people are supposedly in most cases, too scared, to even contemplate communicating with the "Dead". In fact to most modern religions, it is simply taboo, based on Old Testament laws of Moses, where you could be "stoned to death" for communicating with the dead. I believe that God in His great wisdom and foresight, realised that future communication with those who have passed on, might became problematic in the future for most human beings, which is completely understandable. So, God choose Enoch, to be a *type of intercessor between Himself and mankind*. The fact that *Enoch hadn't actually "died"*, would have given reassurance to both Methuselah and Noah, that it was actually perfectly OK, for them to communicate directly with Enoch even after his "translation to heaven", as he had not "died" but was translated to another higher plane, but still had a physical improved supernatural body, such as Jesus had after His Resurrection.

Powers and Ability to move fast, of those who have passed on to the positive spirit world:

The day is coming when nobody will move rapidly except us. (Those who have been saved through Jesus Christ)

One of these days soon we will be trading in our old, worn-out, fleshly, earthy body for an entirely new Heavenly model! We'll be able to fly through the air and up through the clouds and all the way to the moon and the stars, and we'll fly with not just the speed of light, which is not fast enough to get around through such a big Universe! But our new spiritual bodies will move with the speed of thought! All you'll have to do is think yourself someplace and you'll be there! No time wasted, no cars, no stinky fumes, no flat tires, no accidents and you're there!

The eternal flesh of the future, the supernatural, miraculous, resurrected, transformed, fleshly bodies of the future are going to be like the angels of God! We will look like we do now, only better! Just as Jesus did after His resurrection.

He could eat and drink and they could feel Him and touch Him as well as see Him, and yet He was in a miraculous supernatural body, His new resurrected body" (Lk.24:36-43). He said we were going to have bodies like His! (1Jn.3:2; 1Cor.15:42-58). He could appear or disappear, He could walk right through walls or locked doors, and He could fly with the speed of thought!

Whissssst! - And you're there!

With the above thoughts in mind, I don't think it was so difficult for Enoch to communicate with both Methuselah and Noah from the positive spirit world or in his particular case the Garden of Eden, which is sort of in-between world half physical and half spiritual.

APPENDIX VII - THE COMPARISON BETWEEN THE K.J.V of the BIBLE AND THE SEPTUAGINT VERSIONS AND ORIGINAL LANGUAGE

The Bible agrees with the Septuagint LXX except for the ages of the Patriarchs Arphaxad down to Nahor, where the Septuagint has added 100 years to the age of each of the Patriarchs. Why did this happen you may ask? I covered this at length in my book 'Jasher Insights'

Book of Jubilees The only complete version of Jubilees is in Ethiopian, although large fragments in Greek, Latin and Syriac are also known. It is believed that it was originally written in Hebrew.

About the Book of Jubilees: If at times one gets the impression that you are reading a first draft of Genesis, you are in good company. R.H. Charles, the translator, a distinguished academic Biblical scholar, concluded that Jubilees was a version of the Pentateuch, written in Hebrew, parts of which later became incorporated into the earliest Greek version of the Jewish Bible, the Septuagint. (Source: http:// www.sacred-texts.com/bib/jub/index.htm

C.1 In general, I personally prefer to read the Septuagint version of the Old Testament than the K.J.V. as it tends to have more details. However.

C.2 There is one area, where the Septuagint and the K.J.V of the Bible seriously disagree, which has become a point of contention with some.

C.3 Below I first put the Bible Longevity Chart as shown in the KJV of the Bible and in the following page a chart showing what it would look like going by the Septuagint version of the Bible.

C.4 The K J Version of the Old Testament in the Bible commissioned by King James I of England, (who came to the throne in 1601) was put together in 1611 and involved 70 Old Testament experts working on it.

C.5 The Septuagint or LXX for short, version of the Old Testament was also put together by 70 Jewish Old Testament scholars in around 275 B.C. So, you might ask: 'What is the difference between them?' That is a very good question. In general, I would state that the Septuagint is a much more original Old Testament account. The K.J.V was seriously influenced by a Jewish Masoretic sect in 100 AD who tried to alter and rewrite the Septuagint which resulted in the Masoretic Old Testament text from which the King James Bible O.T came into being.

C.6 Although in general I believe the Septuagint to in general being a more accurate account of the ancient Hebrew Old Testament, there is one area of the Septuagint that doesn't seem to add up - literally: Something doesn't seem right with the Septuagint Longevity Chart and the question is why? Did someone tamper with the timeline and if they did, what was the reason? Both the Bible and the Apocryphal books of both Jasher and Jubilees agree on the Longevity Timelines. Even the Septuagint agrees with these three other books in the timeline from Adam to Shem.

C.7 Where the problem arises in the Septuagint is the ages of Shem's son Arphaxad and resultant descendants until Terah the father of Abraham. The Septuagint adds 100 years to each of 8 descendants coming after Shem. (See the chart below.) This would result in the age of the earth no longer being around 6000 years as recording in the Bible and other Apocryphal books but more like 6800 years old. If the Septuagint longevity chart were correct it would mean that many of the stories as given in the Jewish Apocryphal book of Jasher & Jubilees would have to be incorrect. Why? Because according to both the Bible and the Apocryphal books of Jasher and Jubilees Noah and Shem were still alive in Abraham's time, even though Abraham was in fact the 10th generation after Noah as a direct descendent.

C.8 So, was the Longevity Time Chart correct? Well since there is a general agreement between both the KJV of the Bible and both the Apocryphal books of Jasher and Jubilees, the preponderance of scripture would state that the Bible's Longevity Chart is in fact the correct one.

C.9 Another consideration is the following: When King James of English commissioned 70 experts to put the modern K.J.V. Bible together, those experts were not under any sort of pressure to comply with certain agendas. The king simply wanted a good version of both the New and Old Testaments to be combined and made available for all English-speaking peoples.

C.10 However, when the Septuagint was put together in around 300 BC it was put together by 70 Jewish Old Testament scholars who were living in Egypt at the time as slaves to the Grecian Empire, which was ruled in the Sleucian south part of a 4 part empire by a Pharaoh who was de-facto a stooge of the Grecian empire. The Egyptian Empire.

C.11 Egypt was powerful around 2000BC - 1500 BC and was wrecked by God Himself in the Judgments of the '10 Plagues' at the time of Moses in around 1520 BC.

C.12 Look at today. The Egyptians claim that their ancestors were the makers of the amazing Pyramids and other structures such as the Sphinx. However closer investigation shows that in fact these amazing structures were built further back in time and before the Great Flood.

C.13 I propose that Pharaoh, one of the main sponsors of the Septuagint made a simple stipulation to the 70 enslaved Jewish Old Testament scholars. He wanted the writings in the Septuagint to put the time of the Great Flood further back in time, so that Pharoah could continue to state that the Pyramids were made after the Great Flood and not before. So, he had the scholars simply add 800 years to the Longevity chart by altering the date at which each first children was born to Shem and then Arphaxad and then Salah, Eber, Peleg, Reu, Serug, Nahor & Terah. They simply added 100 years to each one of them, which is very odd, and it looks odd on the time-chart for several reasons.

C.14 Here is some interesting info about the Egyptians: The scholars of the present day who write about Egypt are in gross error. They accept so many things concerning the Egyptians as history, science, and learning, which nevertheless have no other foundation than astrology and false visions.

They esteem the Egyptians more ancient than they really are, because in those early times they appear to have possessed such knowledge of abstruse and hidden things. But I saw that, even at the coming of Semiramis to Memphis, these people, in their pride had designedly confused their calendar.

Their ambition was to take precedence of all nations in point of time. With this end in view, they drew up a number of complicated calendars and royal genealogical tables. By this and frequent changes in their computations, order and true chronology were lost. That this confusion might be firmly established, they perpetuated every error by inscriptions and the erection of great buildings.- SOURCE: http://alternativegenhist.blogspot.com/2010/12/dating-of-flood-and-creation-of-adam.html

C.15 Consider the following: Just before the Great Flood, God said that He would destroy all of mankind except for Noah and family. He also stated that from now one Mankind would live for only 120 years. Therefore, the Septuagint versions that Arphaxad waited until he was 135 years old before having his firstborn child doesn't seem right, when God had just stated that man would start to live progressively shorter in years and eventually it would narrow down to only 120 years old. It was stated in this Book of Jubilees in Abraham's time. Abraham himself still lived to be 175, but it was stated even in his time than soon man would only live to be 120 then 75 years of age and finally only 70. This is exactly what has happened since Abraham's time. King David who lived 1000 years after Abraham only lived to be 70 years of age.

C.16 Since the time of King David 3000 years ago, which was half of the World's History of approximately 6000 Years to date, the length of a man's life has generally stayed around 70 Years on average.

C.17 The exception to that, has been in different Dark Ages & the Industrial Age, when millions of people's lives were cut short by plague and by pollution causing the disease called consumption (T.B.), which also killed so many people during the coal mining age of the 19th century. In fact, just 150 years ago, many people lived very short lives, such as 35 years, due to the heavy industrialization in the world.

MORE ON THE SEPTUAGINT

There are at least forty-five instances where Jesus quotes scripture from the Old Testament. What is interesting to note is that Jesus as well as the apostles when quoting from the Old Testament were not quoting from a Hebrew manuscript but from a Greek manuscript which was known as the Septuagint, also sometimes called the LXX, or the AB, Apostles Bible.

As is pointed out below almost all translations of the Old Testament in the early days of Christianity were translated from the Septuagint and not Hebrew manuscripts. The question arises as to what is the Septuagint and where did it come from? The following is a very condensed version of a much longer article. If you would like to read the entire article use this link: http://www.ecclesia.org/truth/septuagint.html The Septuagint (LXX)

History of the Septuagint Here is a little background on the Septuagint. This is from the Preface and Introduction to the Septuagint itself written by Sir Lancelot C.L. Brenton in 1851: "The Septuagint (from the Latin septuaginta, meaning "seventy," and frequently referred to by the roman numerals LXX) is the Greek translation of the Old Testament.

The name derives from the tradition that it was made by seventy (or seventy-two) Jewish scholars at Alexandria, Egypt during the reign of Ptolemy Philadelphus (285-247 B.C.)." "The earliest version of the Old Testament Scriptures which is extinct, or of which we possess any certain knowledge, is the translation executed at Alexandria in the third century before the Christian era."

"The Septuagint version having been current for about three centuries before the time when the books of the New Testament were written, it is not surprising that the Apostles should have used it more often than not in making citations from the Old Testament.

They used it as an honestly made version in pretty general use at the time when they wrote. They did not on every occasion give an authoritative translation of each passage de nova [which means anew], but they used what was already familiar to the ears of converted Hellenists, when it was sufficiently accurate to suit the matter in hand.

In fact, they used it as did their contemporary Jewish writers, Philo and Josephus. "The veneration with which the Jews had treated this version [the Septuagint] (as is shown in the case of Philo and Josephus) [because Philo and Josephus quoted the Septuagint], gave place to a very contrary feeling when they [the Jews] found how it could be used against them in argument: hence they decreed the version, and sought to deprive it of all authority.

Previous to this, it was the Word of God as they were concerned. But as soon as the early church started using it against them, they tried to discredit the Septuagint. As the Gentile Christians were generally unacquainted with Hebrew, they were unable to meet the Jews on the ground which they now took; and as the Gentile Christians…fully embraced…its authority and inspiration." The Jews upheld the Septuagint very strongly for the first 300 years as the Word of God, but when the Christians took a hold of it, then the Jews rejected it.

Then the Jews started rewriting the Septuagint in the 2nd and 3rd centuries to suit their purposes.

The following is from the introduction of the book called "Grammar of the Septuagint Greek" by Connie Bearer and Stock, written in 1905: "We are familiar with the constant appeal made by the writers of the New Testament to quote scripture, an appeal couched in such words as "it is written" or "as the scripture saith." In the great majority of cases, the scripture thus appealed to is undoubtedly the Septuagint. Seldom, if ever, is it the Hebrew original. We have seen how, even before the Christian era, the Septuagint had acquired for itself the position of an inspired book. Some four centuries after that era, Augustine remarks that the Greek speaking Christians, for the most part, did not even know that there was any other Word of God than the Septuagint."

When other nations became converted to Christianity and wanted the scriptures in their own languages, it was almost always the Septuagint which formed the basis of the translation. This was so in the case of the early Latin version, which was in use before the Vulgate, and it was so also in the case of the translations made in Coptic, Ethiopic, Armenian, Georgian, Gothic, and other languages.

The only exception to the rule is the first Syriac version, which was made direct from the Hebrew. This Syriac version, when translated into English, lines up harmoniously with the Septuagint when translated into English.

The reason the Septuagint came about is because in Alexandria, Alexander the Great had come through and conquered many of those nations, and Greek became the predominant language. So, they took the original Law, and translated it into Greek for those Jews that no longer spoke Hebrew, and also to convert many of the Greeks over to Judaism.

They translated the original into the Greek at approximately 285 BC. Basically, you see many of the quotes from the New Testament and they're direct quotes from the Septuagint, you don't find the same terminology in the original Hebrew. Hebrew text which has come down to us as the present Masoretic text. "...the writers of the New Testament seem often to differ from those of the Old, because they appear uniformly to quote from some copy of the Septuagint version; and most of their quotations agree verbally, and often even literally, with one or other of the copies of that version which subsist to the present day."

Almost every Bible in existence uses the Masoretic Hebrew (and not the Septuagint) for its Old Testament translation. What is alleged to be Hebrew today, or is spoken as Hebrew, is the Masoretic Hebrew.

Nobody really knows what the original Hebrew sounded like, or how it was pronounced. The following quote is from Wikipedia concerning Isaiah 7:14 and shows the difference between the Masoretic Hebrew text and the Septuagint. This is just one of many differences. Read the entire article here: https://en.wikipedia.org/wiki/Septuagint

"In the Early Christian Church, the presumption that the Septuagint was translated by Jews before the era of Christ, and that the Septuagint at certain places gives itself more to a christological interpretation than 2nd-century Hebrew texts was taken as evidence that "Jews" had changed the Hebrew text in a way that made them less christological.

For example, Irenaeus concerning Isaiah 7:14: The Septuagint clearly writes of a virgin (Greek παρθένος) that shall conceive. While the Hebrew text was, according to Irenaeus, at that time interpreted by Theodotion and Aquila (both proselytes of the Jewish faith) as a young woman that shall conceive.

According to Irenaeus, the Ebionites used this to claim that Joseph was the (biological) father of Jesus. From Irenaeus' point of view that was pure heresy, facilitated by (late) anti-Christian alterations of the scripture in

Hebrew, as evident by the older, pre-Christian, Septuagint."

APPENDIX VIII: - Prisca Sapientia (Ancient Wisdom)

Enoch Chapter 82.5 And the account thereof is accurate and the recorded reckoning thereof exact; for the luminaries, and months and festivals, and years and days had Uriel shown and revealed to me to whom the Lord of the whole creation of the world hath subjected the host of heaven; and he had power over night and day in the heaven to the light to give light to men. The sun, moon and stars, and all the powers to the heaven which

revolve in the circular chariots.

The ancient "sacred year" consisted of 360 days, the numbering of which was a common practice among the ancients, according to the historian Immanuel Velikovshy:

When the year changed According to Error Flynns' Book, 'Temple at the centre of Time' there used to be 360 Days in the year. This fact is borne out by the Egyptians, Babylonians, Assyrians, Persians, the Chinese. The Chinese later added 5 more days to make 365, but why?

from 360 to 365, the Chinese added five and one-quarter days to their year. Plutarch wrote that in the time of Romulus, the Roman year was made up of 360 days only, and various Latin authors say the ancient month was thirty days in length.

Ancient absolute constants in mathematics, were revealed unto Moses by God Himself

Here is some amazing information about ABSOLUTE CONSTANTS in MATHS:

1x2=2

1x2x3=6

1x2x3x4=24

1x2x3x4x5=120

1x2x3x4x5x6=720

1x2x3x4x5x6x7=5,040= (7 x 360) x 2 or (14 x 360)

These feats are accomplished through simple arithmetic using the base number 2,540 and variations of 7 and 360.

The moon's diameter is determined by subtracting the number of degrees in a circle, 360, from 2520, equalling 2160 miles

The average distance between the surface of the earth and the moon is found by multiplying 77.77 times pi seven times

77.77x π x π x π x π x π x π x π = 234,888 statute miles

The point being that many calculations concerning the distance, the weight, the diameter, the circumference of the planets and moon, sun and stars, can be made using the constants of 7, π & 360 in particular. How is that even possible? Co-incidence? I don't think so! It looks like that it is God's Absolute

Maths of Creation. David Flynn has done an excellent job in the discovering the ancient wisdom or Prisca Sapientia:-

(See Errol Flynn's book, 'At the centre of Time' Available on Amazon.com)

APPENDIX IX: TIME CHARTS
Years After |↓←(Around 4000 BCE)

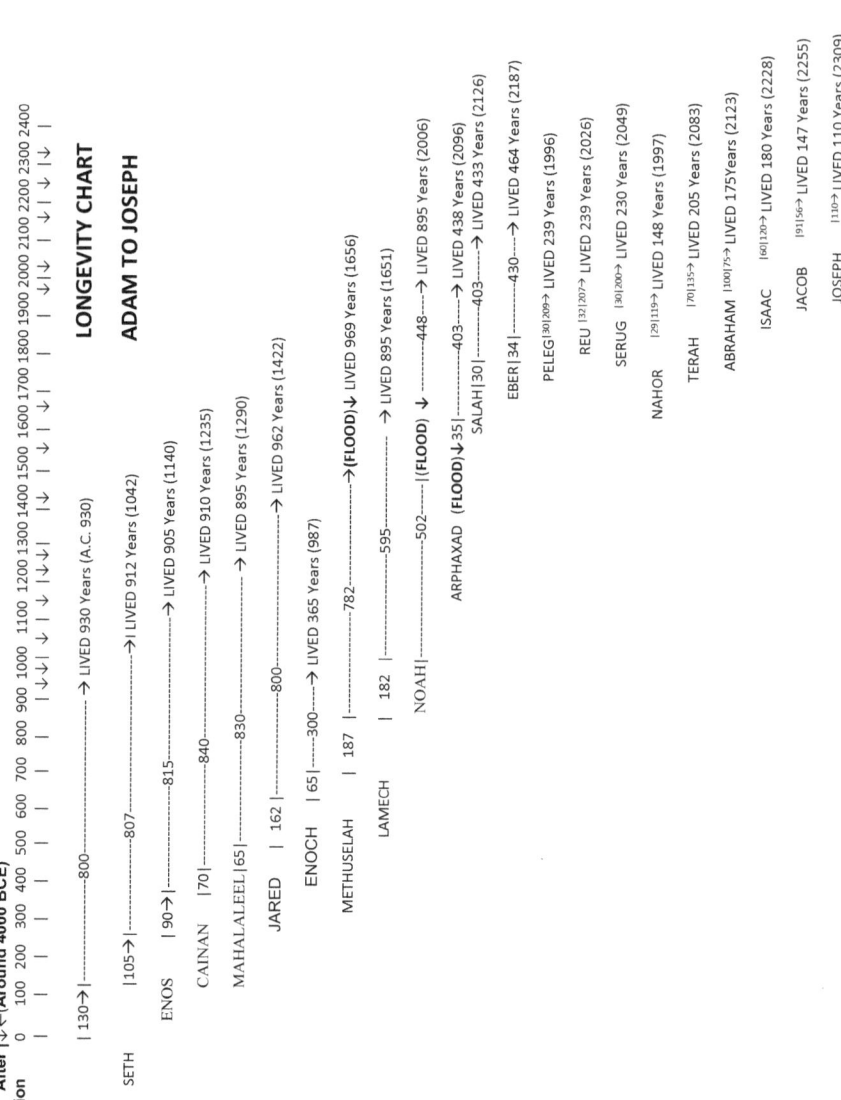

Years After | ↓ ← (**Around 4000 BCE**)
Creation 2300 2400 2500 2600 2700 2800 2900 3000 3100 3200 3300 3400 3500 3600 3700 3800 3900 4000→ CONTINUING (NOT TO SCALE)
A.C. | | | | | | | | | | | | | | | | | |......   6000
                                                                                                                                              |
JOSEPH | 110 |→ LIVED 110 Years (2309)

KING DAVID LIVED | 70 |→ LIVED 70 Years (3000)

JESUS CHRIST |33 |→   LIVED 33 Years (4030)

MODERN MAN→ 70 Years(2017

OBS. Since the time of King David 3000 years ago, which was actually half of the World's History of approximately 6000 Years to date, the length of a man's life has generally stayed around **70 Years on average**.

The exception to that, has been in different DARK AGES & THE INDUSTRIAL AGE, when millions of people's lives were cut short by plague and by pollution causing the disease called *consumption* (T.B.), which also killed so many people during the coal mining age of the 19th century. In fact just 150 years ago, many people lived very short lives, such as 35 years, due to the heavy industrialization in the world.

248

OBS. Since the time of King David 3000 years ago, which was actually half of the World's History of approximately 6000 Years to date, the length of a man's life has generally stayed around **70 Years on average**.

The exception to that, has been in different DARK AGES & THE INDUSTRIAL AGE, when millions of people's lives were cut short by plague and by pollution causing the disease called *consumption (T.B.)*, which also killed so many people during the coal mining age of the 19th century. In fact just 150 years ago, many people lived very short lives, such as 35 years, due to the heavy industrialization in the world.

7000 YEARS OF WORLD HISTORY

"IN THE TENTH WEEK, IN THE SEVENTH PART"

One week here = 700 years

One day=100 years

```
Years After |↓←(Around 4000 BCE)
Creation    2300 2400 2500 2600 2700 2800 2900 3000 3100 3200 3300 3400 3500 3600 3700 3800 3900 4000→ CONTINUING (NOT TO SCALE)
A.C.         |    |    |    |    |    |    |    |    |    |    |    |    |    |    |    |    |    .....
JOSEPH  | 110 |→ LIVED 110 Years (2309)
```

DATE	NOTABLE EVENT
1st WEEK: YEAR	0 CREATION
1st WEEK: YEAR the 7th from Adam.)	700, ENOCH (born in 622; 7th part of the first WEEK. Enoch was also
2nd WEEK: YEAR	1400 NOAH
3rd WEEK: YEAR	2100 ABRAHAM
4th WEEK: YEAR	2800 KING DAVID
5th WEEK: YEAR	3500 CAPTIVITY IN BABYLON
6th WEEK: YEAR ROME	4200 THE EARLY CHURCH ESTABLISHED & RECOGNIZED BY
7th WEEK: YEAR	4900 THE CRUCADES IN THE HOLY LAND
8th WEEK: YEAR	5600 THE KING JAMES BIBLE (1601AD)
9th WEEK: YEAR	2300 MILLENIUM
10th WEEK: YEAR NEW EARTH	3000 GREAT WHITE THRONE JUDGEMENT & NEW HEAVEN AND

DATE			NOTABLE EVENT	QUOTE FROM ENOCH	COMMENTS

1st WEEK: YEAR   0   CREATION

700   ENOCH (born in 622; 7th part of the first WEEK. Enoch was also the 7th from Adam.)

(Enoch 93.2) "I was born the seventh in the first week, while judgement and righteousness still endured"

2nd WEEK: YEAR   1400   NOAH "second week great wickedness" "<u>first end</u>. And in it <u>a man shall be saved</u>"

3rd WEEK: YEAR   2100   ABRAHAM "third week" "plant of righteous judgement" "his posterity" "<u>the plant of righteousness" (JESUS)</u> MOSES (2500) "visions of the holy and righteous shall be seen, and a law for all generations"

4th WEEK: YEAR   2800   KING DAVID "fourth week" "fifth week, at it close*, the house of glory and dominion shall be built forever;(KING SOLOMON) (3100)

5th WEEK: YEAR   3500   CAPTIVITY IN BABYLON "in the sixth week" "shall be blinded",(-time between the testaments 400 BCE until the time of CHRIST in 30 BCE.) <u>"a man shall ascend"</u> (Jesus) "At its close, the house of dominion shall be burnt with fire, and the whole race of the chosen shall be dispersed." (70 AD under the Romans)

6th WEEK: YEAR   4200   THE EARLY CHURCH ESTABLISHED & RECOGNIZED BY ROME "seventh week" "apostate generation arise" (THE DARK AGES of False Religions)

7th WEEK: YEAR   4900   THE CRUCADES IN THE HOLY LAND

8th WEEK: YEAR   5600   THE KING JAMES BIBLE (1601AD) <u>eighth week,</u> sword shall be given to it, that a righteous judgement may be executed to the oppressors, and sinners shall be delivered it to the hands of the righteous. And at its close, they shall acquire houses through their righteousness, and a house shall be built for the Great King in glory for evermore.

"at its close shall be elected the elect righteous one the eternal plant of righteousness., to receive sevenfold instruction concerning all His creation." (The KING JAMES BIBLE?) "ninth week", the righteous judgement shall be revealed to the whole world. All the works of the godless shall vanish from all the earth, and the world shall be written down for destruction. (2024?) or later? 2ND COMING OF CHRIST & THE WRATH OF GOD

9th WEEK: YEAR   2300   MILLENIUM

10th WEEK: YEAR   3000   GREAT WHITE THRONE JUDGEMENT & NEW HEAVEN AND NEW EARTH "tenth week in the seventh part, there shall be the great eternal judgement, in the which He will execute vengeance amongst the angels. And the first heaven shall depart and pass away, and a new heaven shall appear, and all the powers of the heaven shall give sevenfold light." (Enoch 92.9)

APPENDIX X: ABOUT THE AUTHOR: MY PERSONAL TESTIMONY. - HOW I GOT SAVED.

My background

I was brought up in a middle-class family, which actually had its roots in the Aristocracy.

My father was a Wing Commander in the RAF, a spitfire pilot during the 2nd World War who was decorated by the queen and received an O.B.E medal of honour for his invention of the very first Flight Simulator, which enabled pilots to train on the ground for the first-time using electronics just after the 2nd World War. Because he was in the military at the time of his amazing invention the military took all of the credit. If he had been a civilian at the time of his invention, he would have been a billionaire for sure as his invention is used by all countries today. His two brothers were killed in action during the 2nd world war. As a result of all this, he became an atheist.

My mother took care of our large family of 6 brothers and sisters. As my father was in the military as a pilot, we lived abroad in several places when I was young, including Cyprus and Aden in Greece.

After being to boarding schools, and studying for some years at university, while living in Northern England, I decided to travel around with the aim to do something different and to meet other young people, which was common place in those days (1971).

I then travelled over to Scandinavia during my university vacations. I hitch-hiked all around Scandinavia. I was invited to stay with some friendly Norwegian families. I worked my way as a job chainsaw cutting-down trees and travelled some.

While being in Norway, and working there sawing down trees, I fell in-love with the beautiful nature, including one of the many beautiful women there.

(Later I ended up marrying one of them)

I finally left university in the UK to go and see this beautiful girl in Norway. However, it was not to be, and instead I had my heart broken. I then started studying at another university in Oslo. Well, it sounds funny, today, but back then I felt very frustrated, as I had just lost my job, and now my girlfriend.

So, on the day she said goodbye, I decided to turn to alcohol, for relief, and while taking a train home to my apartment, I started to review my life so far, until that time, (19 years old), and decided that life itself was just too confusing, and almost pointless.

Before moving to Norway, I had another very big setback. My family had been very involved in serving in the military. My father had been a decorated spitfire pilot Wing Commander in the Second World War, and later on a jet pilot. My uncles had served in the military as officers and both were killed in action.

My dream when I was 18 was to also become a fighter pilot. Well, I managed to pass all of the academic exams to become a pilot in the military down at Biggin Hill in England, but then strangely the doctors found something unusual about my heart.

This condition has not at all hindered me while on the ground, but apparently, it would have caused a "black-out" for me while flying at high altitudes in a fighter plane. I know now that God intervened so that I would not become a pilot, as He had other plans, and wanted me to become a missionary.

So, after having quit university, my life seemingly having fallen apart, everything else seemed in vain. I got into a very bad mood, which is not normal for me, and for some strange reason, I decided it was time to jump off the train!

I know it sounds very funny and even totally unimaginably silly today! However, at that time, I thought well I am an atheist, but before I do anything stupid, I had better challenge God to do something, if He was there at all.

So, I called out and said, "If there is a God up there then show yourself right now, or I am going to throw myself on the train tracks".

I was dead serious. (excuse the pun)

What happened next was truly remarkable!

I suddenly "out of the blue" felt a strong comforting and reassuring feeling about me, and I heard a distinct voice speaking in my head saying, "You're not *really* going to throw yourself off of the train are you?"

I retorted, well of course not! I asked who was speaking to me, and the voice told me it was Jesus, who was speaking to me. I asked him what I was supposed to do with my life, as I found life so confusing, and very difficult to understand how to live my life. I told Him that Love was very complicated! He told me to get myself a Bible and to start studying the New Testament.

Jesus also told me that he had entered my soul when I had desperately called out to Him, and that I had gotten "born again" and that was why I could feel the reassurance of His loving and comforting spirit about me. (John 15.26)

In fact so strong was this very comforting reassurance, that I had suddenly totally lost my severe depression and sadness. Instead, I was totally both happy and felt free in spirit. (2 Corinthians 5.17)

It was as if I had been a chained eagle before, that had now been totally set free. It was so wonderful. I could fly in spirit! At that moment, I knew that God and Jesus and His Holy spirit were in fact real.

That was such a wonderful realization and experience of Salvation. I suppose you could say that it was similar to a small child who has gotten hurt by falling over and skinning his knee.

He runs home to his mother who picks him up and comforts him. She gives him so much un-conditional love. So much so that he forgets about the pain.

So was it for me! The voice said to me, "Ok she has left you, but are there not many other fish in the sea?"

I answered, Yes, of course, you are completely right, and I stopped being sad about my former girlfriend from that moment onwards. I went back to my apartment and eventually started studying the Bible.

I came upon this beautiful verse in Revelations Chapter 3 verse 20.

"Behold, I stand at the door and knock, if any man hear My voice and open the door, I will come into him and sup with him and he with Me.

When I read that verse for the very first time, it dawned on me that that must have been what happened to me on the train. I had actually gotten Saved.

While I was on the train, the voice also told me that God wanted me to spend my whole life telling others about Jesus, and that he is real! To tell others that anyone can get saved if they just get desperate enough, to want to know the truth. Jesus said, "I am the way, the truth and the life, and no man cometh unto the Father but by Me." (John 14.6)

I have spent the 50 odd years since then witnessing to people in different countries, from many different backgrounds. I don't say to people "Come to church", but come to Jesus, as He will take care of you.

All you need to do is to receive Him into your heart, ask him to forgive your sins, and He will readily give you Eternal life no matter who you are. If Jesus could save me, who was a lost atheist, He can also save you! (2 Corinthians 5.17)

Eternal Life does not depend on how good you are, but just on Jesus, and His wonderful sacrifice on the cross for all of humanity.

It is important to realize that we are all sinners in need of a Saviour. (Romans 3.23) Getting saved is permanent. Once in Forever in! John 3.36. He who believes on the son, has everlasting life. (Ephesians 2.8-9)

As my testimony clearly proves, you do not have to go to church to get saved.

Salvation is freely available for all. There is no Jew or Gentile, or any other race discrimination when it comes to getting saved. All are one in Christ Jesus.

Since Jesus came to me personally, when I was practically an atheist before, and took the time to get me saved, I have come to realize that God does not want to put people into a religious box of some kind. He wants everyone to know Him personally through prayer and through diligently studying His Word the Bible. He wants us to show His love to others everywhere, especially by offering them hope of the same personal Salvation that we have been granted by his grace.

Of course I *do think it advisable to seek out fellowship with other like-minded Christians*, especially to strengthen your Faith whilst still a new Christian.

"Neglect not the assembling together of yourselves together as the manner of some is".

However, sometimes it is not possible to congregate with other Christians in large numbers, and that is when the verse "where two or three are gathered together in My name there am I in the midst of you" verse comes in very useful. (Matthew 18.20)

It really is wonderful to know Jesus and that He keeps us safe from all real Harm. He does not necessarily take away all of our problems, but He does carry us through them. No matter what they are. He surrounds us with His Angels and encourages us and comforts us through His Word.

I really think it essential to be a good scribe of God's Word. (2 Timothy 2.15: "Study to show yourself approved unto men, a workman that needs not to be ashamed, rightly dividing the Word of Truth.")

The Joy of being a real "Born again Christian" is in being truly close to Jesus and His Holy Spirit as well as telling others, about how very wonderful He is.

He is real, and can live in our hearts and desires to live in your heart also. It is really so simple to get saved. Just reach out and tell Him that you really want Him to come into your life right now.

Ask Him to forgive all of your sins, and give you eternal life. It is also wise to ask Him to fill you with His Holy Spirit.

The Holy Spirit will help you to love others and to read God's Word; and will also be great Comforter to you during your life. (John 14.26)

When I was a brand new Christian, living by myself in my apartment, as I studied the Bible I started to grow spiritually. I became concerned about others and wanted to tell others about Jesus.

Then it was that I met the worst drug addict in our town. In fact he was a drug-pusher.

I witnessed to him and asked him to pray and ask Jesus to both save him and to deliver him from drug addiction. He did. He got saved. As a result he was a tremendous witness to those with whom he was associated. That made me very happy to see his life change so drastically.

One morning, I was smoking a cigarette, (I didn't know any better in those days), when clear as a bell I heard Jesus' voice saying in my heart "You put more trust in that cigarette, than you do in Me."

I was shocked. "What do you mean Lord, I asked?" he answered me, "Well, every time you have a problem, or are lonely, or stressed, you immediately pull out a cigarette, instead of coming to Me. Come to Me and I will help you with every detail of your life"

Up until then I had been smoking 25 cigarettes/day. After Jesus spoke to me clearly about this matter, amazingly I was able to quit smoking that very same day, without any withdrawal symptoms. Jesus really is so wonderful if we pray and ask Him to take over completely in our lives. He loves to help us and especially loves our communications with Him, where we make a big effort to include Him in everything we do. Then our life becomes so much fuller. Scripture tells us that we are all part of the Bride of Christ. That is a very intimate relationship, being so close to Christ. He really does love each one of us very much, and we just need to ask him to draw us ever closer to Him.

There is absolutely nothing that He can't do.

"For with Me Nothing shall be impossible"- (Gospel of Luke 1.17)

I distinctly remember another morning, I woke up speaking in tongues, and I didn't know what on earth I was saying. A Christian friend explained to me later about the "Gifts of the spirit" as mentioned in 1 Corinthians 12.10 & Romans 12.6.

On another occasion I heard the Lord clearly saying to me,

"Ask Me for anything you desire, and I will perform it!" I thought for a few minutes, and decided that I had lost my beautiful girlfriend, and that I would very much like to have a new beautiful girlfriend.

I was living in a very small room, and wanted to have a bigger apartment. I also asked to have a lot more money. I was a pianist and so I asked for Jesus to help me to find a rock band to join. I also liked young people so I asked for a job working with the youth. I was 19 at the time.

Stunningly, within one year, Jesus had supplied everything I had asked for, including I became the leader of a Youth Club, of 150 teenagers. I also ran a disco at a nightclub. I was invited to play in a rock group. I was still studying at university as well. I then inherited some money.

God also gave me a beautiful new girlfriend who became my fiancée.

All happened within one year and I knew it was a miracle!

However, that was but the beginning of the story....

One morning I woke up sad and crying, because it suddenly dawned on me how selfish I had been. I had been asking for things only for me!

So, I said to Jesus, "You have supplied all that I asked for just one year ago, but what do you want from me? In other words what can I do to make you happy and not just me?

Wow! I soon found out that God had completely other plans for my life, than me just living for myself and money, and simply doing any old job that I fancied.

One night soon thereafter, I had a dream that my apartment was just like a doll's house. That is the old-fashioned type, with the front wall of the house hinged onto the front of the house. All of a sudden all of my records and stereo and possessions flew out of the doll's house, as the sides of the doll's house with windows in it opened outwards."

To cut a very long story short I have been a missionary, volunteer and Teacher and writer and educator for the past 50 years, since the above personal testimony and have worked in many countries.

I, together with my wife and family, have tried to help others to the best of our ability. We have been involved in prison ministries, helping children in need, and most recently helping the Philippine disaster, and now the Ukraine.

There is always a need somewhere. It is just a matter of looking around, and getting to work to help others, in whatever way each of us can, as Jesus himself told us.

"Thou shall love the Lord thy God with all of thy heart, soul and mind; & love your neighbour as yourself."

SALVATION
HOW TO GET SAVED?
Finally, **I challenge you, that if you have not already prayed to receive Jesus into your heart**, so that **you can have eternal life**, & be guaranteed an eternal place in Heaven, then please do so immediately, to keep you safe from what is soon coming upon the earth!

If we confess our sins, God will save us from our sins and mistakes.

1 John 1:9 If we confess our sins, He is faithful and just to forgive us our sins and to cleanse us from all unrighteousness.

Jesus stated in **Revelations 3.20** "Behold, I stand at the door and knock, if any man hear my voice, and open the door, I will come in to him and live with him and him with me".

"**He who believes on the Son of God has eternal life.**" John 3.36. **That means right now**!

Once saved, you are eternally saved, and here is a **very simple prayer** to help you to get saved:-

"*Dear Jesus,*

Please come into my heart, forgive me all of my sins, give me eternal life, and fill me with your Holy Spirit. Please help me to love others and to read the Word of God in Jesus name, Amen.

Once you've prayed that little prayer sincerely, then you are guaranteed a wonderful future in Heaven for eternity with your creator, and loved ones. "**For God is Love**" (1 John 4.16)

As I mentioned earlier in this book, your Salvation does not depend on you going to church, and your good works. **Titus 3.5** states "**Not by works of righteousness which we have done, but according to His mercy he saved us**".

Your salvation only depends on receiving Christ as your saviour, not on church or religion!

(If I could get saved having been an atheist and an evolutionist whilst at university, then anyone can get saved! Just challenge God to prove He exists, & ask Him into your heart! He will show up in your life & teach you the truth!) **(John 14.6)**

"He that comes unto Me I will in no wise cast out"- Jesus

Jesus explained that unless you become as a child you won't even understand the Kingdom Of Heaven. (**John 3.3**)

www.ingramcontent.com/pod-product-compliance
Lightning Source LLC
Chambersburg PA
CBHW060948230426
43665CB00015B/2105